Multinational enterprises and social policy

An ILO publication
on multinational enterprises

Multinational enterprises and social policy

56694

International Labour Office   Geneva

ISBN 92-2-101003-1

Studies and Reports, New Series, No. 79

First published 1973
Second impression 1973

PRINTED BY IMPRIMERIE DU COURRIER, GENEVA (SWITZERLAND)

CONTENTS

Contents

PREFACE

This volume is the first fruits of an attempt by the ILO to provide a forum within which the varied interests affected by the relationship between multinational enterprises and social policy can come to terms with each other by rational inquiry, dispassionate discussion and responsible negotiation. We have attempted to approach the whole matter in a spirit which I defined at the 1972 Session of the International Labour Conference in the following terms:

For some, the multinational corporations are an invaluable dynamic force and instrument for the wider distribution of capital, technology and employment; for others, they are monsters which our present institutions, national and international, cannot adequately control, a law unto themselves which no reasonable concept of the public interest or social policy can accept. The debate between these views is as sharp within nations as among nations. It is particularly sharp in the homeland of so many of the multinational corporations, the United States of America. Our role in the matter is not to espouse either of these conflicting views or any variant of them, but to provide an impartial meeting-place where they can evolve pragmatically common-sense solutions for specific problems of an essentially international nature directly within the competence of the ILO. It is in this spirit that we have convened for October of this year a tripartite meeting on the relationship between multinational corporations and social policy to advise us on the desirability and possible scope of ILO action. Our success in the matter will depend on two conditions, the care with which we limit ILO action, but emphatically not the range of vision with which we decide upon such action, to matters clearly within our own responsibility, and the willingness of all concerned to recognise that there are acute problems of immediate urgency and to work out rationally the agreed positive solutions in the absence of which these problems are liable to precipitate arbitrary action in many countries with wholly unpredictable consequences. The task is so complex and controversial that we must approach it, in our tradition, most cautiously but it may well be among the most important tasks which we have ever undertaken.

As the first stage in such an approach the Governing Body convened a Meeting on the Relationship between Multinational Corporations and Social Policy which met in Geneva from 26 October to 4 November 1972. The Meeting was composed of experts drawn from government, employers' and workers' circles. The International Labour Office prepared as the basis of its work an objective analysis of the problems which the development of multinational enterprises has posed or may pose for social policy and of the divergences of views which exist on the subject. The Meeting unanimously reached conclusions concerning the manner in which the ILO should continue to deal with the matter and these have been approved by the Governing Body. The conclusions provide for a programme of studies which holds great promise as a basis for possible action by the ILO.

In pursuance of these conclusions governments have been invited to improve the statistics required for the proposed programme of studies; and employers and workers and their organisations have been invited to provide the data necessary for such statistics and studies; and the report and conclusions have been communicated to the United Nations, UNCTAD, OECD and other bodies, in order that they may be taken into account by these bodies in their own work.

The ILO's Draft Programme and Budget for the 1974–75 biennium approved by the Governing Body in March 1973 provides for a series of studies of such questions as: the employment implications of the activities of multinational enterprises, with a view to determining to what extent such enterprises take account of the availability of workers in deciding in which countries to locate their production and to what extent they adjust technology to the local employment situation; the contribution of multinational enterprises to human resources development in developing countries, their relationship with national training services and the effects of their policies on the personal development of employees of subsidiary companies in the developing world; arrangements for, and problems of, collective bargaining in multinational enterprises and their subsidiaries; special problems in specific industries, beginning with the policies and practices of multinational enterprises in the metal trades in respect of such matters as wages, hours of work and paid vacations, particularly with a view to comparing the situation in such companies with that in other companies in the same country; and the usefulness of international principles and guidelines for multinational enterprises. All of these studies will be factual and objective. It is proposed to publish them in due course after they have been considered by the Governing Body of the International Labour Office.

The present volume, consisting of the working paper submitted to the 1972 Meeting and the report and conclusions adopted by that Meeting, is being published now in response to wishes expressed in the Governing Body, to provide a point of departure for this further work.

20 March 1973.   WILFRED JENKS.

THE RELATIONSHIP
BETWEEN
MULTINATIONAL ENTERPRISES
AND SOCIAL POLICY

A working paper prepared by the
International Labour Office

1. THE NATURE AND SIGNIFICANCE OF MULTINATIONAL ENTERPRISES

There is no agreed definition of the multinational enterprise. [1] Some find its determining characteristic in the organisation of its activities, that is the extent to which its operations in different countries are actually co-ordinated by a corporate centre, or the degree of "global outlook" to be found in the enterprise's decision making. Others use as criteria the number and type of its subsidiaries, the number of countries in which these subsidiaries operate, and the proportion of foreign sales, assets and employment in the enterprise's total sales, assets and employment. Still others look to the nationality mix of its management or to its ownership characteristics. [2]

For the present report, it may suffice to assume that the essential nature of the multinational enterprise lies in the fact that its managerial headquarters are located in one country (referred to, for convenience, as "the home country") while the enterprise carries out operations in a number of other countries as well ("host countries"). The degree of centralised control will vary among enterprises according to such factors as the types of economic activity in which they are engaged, the policies and practices of their managements,

---

[1] The title of the Meeting, as determined by the Governing Body of the International Labour Office, was "Meeting on the Relationship between Multinational Corporations and Social Policy". Accordingly, when this working paper was prepared for the Meeting, the word "corporations" was usually employed. However, during the Meeting it became evident that "enterprises" was a more suitable term. In this revised version of the working paper, therefore, "corporations" has been replaced by "enterprises" in the chapter titles and in the headings within each chapter. Where "corporations" occurs in the text, it should be understood as having the same meaning as "enterprises".

[2] Even the designation "multinational" is not accepted by all. Other terms in use include "international enterprise" and "transnational corporation". Some authors have sought to ascribe technical significance to their choice of terminology. Such nuances of meaning may serve to differentiate among multinational firms for particular analytical objectives, but until a standard terminology is more widely accepted, they will not directly aid in examining the economic and social consequences of multinationals. This report will use the various terms interchangeably.

the particular issues on which central decisions are required, and national regulations. For one authority on the subject of multinational enterprises, presenting an over-all view of the outcome of the research undertaken by the Harvard Multinational Enterprise Project, one way of providing a definition is through "induction and inference". He notes that they are invariably large in size, that they operate in a substantial number of countries, that they have access to a common pool of human and financial resources, and that they control their widespread activities rather than serving merely as exporters or licensers of technology.[1]

This approach permits a review of the characteristics and activities of multinational firms without the straitjacket of a rigorous definition. It leads to an understanding of the elements which such firms have in common, even while drawing attention to their diversity.[2]

MEASURES OF SIZE AND GROWTH

Aggregate figures are impressive. Of the 100 largest economic units in the world, 50 are nation States and 50 are multinational companies.[3] For the major United States, European and Japanese multinational enterprises (estimated to number approximately 300) sales have been growing by about 10 per cent a year, while real gross national product over the world has, on average, been increasing at only about half that rate.[4]

The growth of multinational firms[5] can be seen in a number of ways. In the case, for example, of the 187 US multinationals that have been the subject of intensive study, the number of their foreign manufacturing sub-

---

[1] Raymond Vernon: *Sovereignty at bay: The multinational spread of US enterprises* (London, Longman, 1971), p. 4.

[2] Much of the analysis in this chapter relates to the operation of United States-controlled multinationals, largely because data about such firms are readily available and because far more multinational enterprises are based in the United States than in any other country.

[3] Norman Macrae: "The future of international business", in *The Economist* (London), 22 Jan. 1972, p. xxi.

[4] Ibid.

[5] Again, because of the lack of a definition, the number of enterprises considered to qualify as multinational varies widely. One authority estimates that there are between 75 and 85 US companies that qualify, a similar number of continental European companies and between 35 and 68 British companies (see Sidney E. Rolfe and Walter Damm (eds.): *The multinational corporation in the world economy: Direct investment in perspective*, Praeger special studies in international economics and development (New York, Praeger, 1970), p. 17). At the other extreme, the Union of International Associations, in its 13th (1970–71) edition of the *Yearbook of international organizations* (Brussels), lists 680 enterprises in the multinational category (see pp. 1029 and 1035-1046).

Table 1. Number of foreign manufacturing subsidiaries of 187 United States-controlled multinational enterprises, by area, in selected years, 1901–67

Area	1901	1913	1929	1950	1959	1967
Canada	6	30	137	225	330	443
Europe (incl. the United Kingdom)	37	72	226	363	677	1 438
Latin America	3	10	56	259	572	950
Other	1	4	48	141	312	815
All areas	47	116	467	988	1 891	3 646

Source: J. W. Vaupel and J. P. Curhan: *The making of multinational enterprise* (Boston, Harvard Business School, 1969), Ch. 3, as shown in Raymond Vernon: *Sovereignty at bay: The multinational spread of US enterprises* (London, Longman, 1971), p. 62.

sidiaries is seen from table 1 to have practically doubled between 1950 and 1959, and then almost doubled again by 1967.[1] In Europe the rate of growth of such subsidiaries in the second period was even greater.

If the total US direct investment [2] in foreign countries is taken as the measure, the figures given in table 2 demonstrate a similar growth. Between 1960 and 1970 the total value of US investment abroad more than doubled, while the value of such investment in Europe almost quadrupled. Analysis of its distribution shows that in 1970 US direct investment in industrialised countries amounted to US$53,100 million, or 68 per cent of the total, while US$21,400 million, or 27.4 per cent of the total, was located in developing countries.[3]

In spite of the huge investments of US capital in European countries, there was in 1970 an approximately equal long-term investment by European countries in the United States, as table 3 shows. The nature of the investment differed markedly, with US investments predominantly in plant and equipment and European holdings concentrated in stocks and bonds. Even so, European direct investment of over US$9,500 million indicates the cross-national character of direct investments.

[1] A major study of multinational firms made at Harvard University concentrated its analysis on the operations of 187 US firms. These were selected from among the 500 largest US industrial firms listed by the magazine *Fortune* (Chicago) in 1963 and 1964, on the basis of having manufacturing subsidiaries in six or more countries (see Vernon, op. cit., p. 11).

[2] "Direct investment" includes assets used for sales and distribution purposes, inventory, and so on, as well as investments in all economic sectors, but excludes portfolio investments; while it is therefore more inclusive than a measure related solely to the productive facilities of multinational firms in manufacturing and extractive industries, it nevertheless provides an indication of the growth of the phenomenon under review and is often used in the literature as a proxy measure for investment by multinational firms.

[3] US Department of Commerce: *The multinational corporation*, Vol. I: *Studies on US foreign investment* (Washington, DC, 1972), p. 13.

Table 2. Book value of United States direct investment abroad in selected years, 1950–70
(Millions of US$)

Area	1950	1960	1965	1970 [1]
Africa	287	925	1 918	3 476
Asia	1 001	2 291	3 569	5 613
Canada	3 579	11 198	15 318	22 801
Western Europe	1 733	6 681	13 985	24 471
of which: EEC	(637)	(2 644)	(6 304)	(11 695)
Latin America [2]	4 576	9 271	10 886	14 683
Rest of world	612	2 412	3 798	7 048
All areas [3]	11 788	32 778	49 474	78 090

[1] Provisional figures. [2] Listed as "Latin America and other Western Hemisphere" in the source. [3] Owing to rounding, the totals given in the table may not correspond to the sum of the figures shown in each column.

Source: *Survey of Current Business* (Washington, DC, US Department of Commerce), Aug. 1963, pp. 18-19, Sep. 1967, p. 42, Oct. 1970, p. 31, and Oct. 1971, p. 32.

Table 3. Long-term private assets, 1970
(Millions of US$)

Type of assets	US assets in Europe	European assets in United States
Direct investments	24 471	9 515
Bonds	535	5 214
Corporate stocks	2 563	12 615
Bank claims and other	2 020	4 285
All assets	29 589	31 629

Source: *Survey of Current Business*, Oct. 1971, p. 21.

The cross-national character of direct investments is limited almost entirely to North America and Western Europe so far as the outward flow of investments is concerned. The Organisation for Economic Co-operation and Development (OECD) estimated total private direct investments in the Western world at about US$89,600 million at the end of 1966, of which the United States accounted for slightly more than 60 per cent, Canada for 4 per cent, Japan for slightly less than 1 per cent and Western Europe for about one-third, of which over 50 per cent was held by the United Kingdom.[1]

Another measure of the growth of multinational business is annual capital spending. Between 1965 and 1971 the annual expenditures of US foreign

[1] OECD figures quoted in Rainer Hellmann: *The challenge to US dominance of the international corporation*, translated by Peter Ruof (New York, Dunellen, 1970), p. 4. This book was originally published in German under the title *Weltunternehmen nur amerikanisch?* (Baden-Baden, Nomos Verlagsgesellschaft).

Table 4. Estimates of plant and equipment expenditures by foreign affiliates of
United States corporations in selected years, 1965–71
(Millions of US$)

Affiliates in	1965	1967	1969	1971 [1]
Canada	1 847	2 233	2 331	2 956
Latin America [2]	1 073	1 282	1 857	1 725
Western Europe	2 640	3 631	3 738	5 356
of which: EEC	(1 418)	(2 123)	(2 064)	(3 150)
Japan [3]	..	336	457	704
Rest of world	1 880	1 787	2 405	3 459
All affiliates [4]	7 440	9 268	10 787	14 200

.. = Not available.

[1] Figures estimated on the basis of investment plans reported to the US Department of Commerce in 1971.
Actual investments can deviate from the plans by up to 25 per cent, according to the business climate. [2] Listed
as "Latin America and other Western Hemisphere" in the source. In manufacturing, Argentina, Brazil and
Mexico together account for between 72 and 78 per cent of expenditures, while in petroleum Venezuela accounts
for between 62 and 66 per cent. [3] Manufacturing and petroleum only. [4] Owing to rounding, the totals given in
the table may not correspond to the sum of the figures shown in each column.

Source: *Survey of Current Business*, Mar. 1970, pp. 23-24, and Mar. 1972, pp. 31-32.

subsidiaries almost doubled, while in Japan and Europe, and especially the
the European Economic Community (EEC) countries, they rose even faster.
Table 4 illustrates the world-wide spread of such spending.

Canadian annual direct investment abroad also rose during the 1960s,
with a 50 per cent increase reported from 1961 to 1965 (from Can.$80 million
to 125 million). A particularly interesting aspect of this investment growth
is the increase in that period of almost 200 per cent in the annual investment
outflow to the United States (from Can.$25 million to 70 million).[1]

As shown in table 5, direct investments from the United Kingdom also
followed an upward trend in the 1960s, although at a slower rate than investments from Canada and the United States and with variations between regions
and time periods.

Measures of the size and growth of direct investment abroad from countries
other than the United States are sparse, and often sources within the same
country issue contradictory sets of figures. Table 6 shows, however, that the
rapid growth of direct investment was not limited to the United States, the
United Kingdom and Canada. In the first half of the 1960s France more than
tripled its annual direct investments abroad, while those of the Federal

---

[1] Dominion Bureau of Statistics figures quoted in Jack N. Behrman: *Some patterns in
the rise of the multinational enterprise*, Research paper No. 8 (Chapel Hill, University of
North Carolina, Graduate School of Business Administration, 1969), p. 134. It should be
noted that a substantial part of total Canadian investment abroad (perhaps 40 per cent)
was owned by US residents because of US ownership of Canadian firms undertaking the
investment (see Behrman, op. cit., p. 56).

Table 5. United Kingdom net direct investments abroad [1] in selected years, 1960–66
(Millions of US$)

Area	1960	1962	1964	1966
North America	124.6	51.5	97.4	171.1
Western Europe [2]	71.1	134.7	116.5	172.2
of which: EEC	(60.2)	(81.8)	(102.8)	(141.4)
Latin America [3]	40.9	38.9	50.7	31.4
Overseas Sterling area	477.7	342.4	450.8	332.6
Rest of world	15.7	17.6	21.0	65.5
All areas	730.0	585.1	736.4	772.8

[1] Excluding oil and, for 1960 and 1962, insurance. [2] Comprises members of the European Free Trade Association and the European Economic Community only. [3] Listed as "South and Central America" in the source.

Source: European Free Trade Association: *EFTA foreign investment: Changes in the pattern of EFTA foreign direct investment* (Geneva, Mar. 1969), p. 32.

Table 6. Direct investment outflows from France, the Federal Republic of Germany and the Netherlands in selected years, 1960–65
(Millions of US$)

Country	1960	1962	1964	1965
France	54.4	49.4	132.0	189.0
Federal Republic of Germany	61.8	81.3	233.0	299.0
Netherlands	94.0	106.4	145.0	124.0

Source: Jack N. Behrman: *Some patterns in the rise of the multinational enterprise*, Research paper No. 18 (Chapel Hill, University of North Carolina, Graduate School of Business Administration, 1969), pp. 136, 137 and 139.

Republic of Germany increased nearly five times and those of the Netherlands by more than 30 per cent.

Between 1962 and 1965 net direct investment from Denmark and Sweden almost doubled, rising from US$8 million to 15.3 million in the case of Denmark and from US$57.1 million to 103.4 million in the case of Sweden. It was estimated that between 1960 and 1965 Switzerland almost exactly doubled its net direct investment in countries of the European Free Trade Association (EFTA) alone, increasing them from US$28.4 million to 56.7 million.[1]

One author, however, feels that possibly an even more important measure of the growth of multinational corporations is their cash flow position, as many, if not a majority, of the world's major multinational corporations finance their world-wide expansion out of retained earnings, which in turn

---

[1] European Free Trade Association: *EFTA foreign investment: Changes in the pattern of EFTA foreign direct investment* (Geneva, Mar. 1969), pp. 5 and 26.

are based on a practice of cash flow maximisation. To support this view he refers to estimates, made by the Commission on Industrial Policy of the European Economic Community, of the proportion of self-financing, out of retained earnings, in gross capital formation. According to the author, this proportion is approximately 100 per cent in the United States, the United Kingdom and the Netherlands, 70 to 80 per cent in the Federal Republic of Germany, France and Belgium, and 60 to 70 per cent in Italy and Japan.[1]

CONCENTRATION BY AREA AND INDUSTRY

Area concentration

Foreign investment has tended to be concentrated in certain areas, although the degree of concentration has shifted over time, especially in the past two decades. Table 7 shows the changing geographical distribution of US direct investments abroad from 1950 to 1970. Most striking have been the shift from Latin America, which accounted for over one-third of US direct investments abroad in 1950 but less than one-fifth in 1970, and the corresponding increase in US direct investments in Western Europe, where they more than doubled, and particularly in the countries of the EEC, where they almost trebled. If the distribution between developing and developed countries is considered, the shift is even more marked. As shown in table 8, in 1950 the two groups of countries shared US foreign investments almost equally, but by 1970 the developed market economies had increased their share to more than two-thirds.

Information on the geographical distribution of foreign investment by countries other than the United States is not readily available, although what information is at hand for the most part parallels the trend shown above. In the United Kingdom, for example, the book value of its net assets (excluding petroleum) in developing countries grew from around £1,431 million in 1965 to £1,668 million in 1968. However, the developing countries' share of the United Kingdom's total assets abroad fell from 37 per cent in 1960 to 30 per cent in 1968.[2] This tends to be confirmed by an independent study, which showed that the book value of the assets owned by a sample of British multi-

---

[1] Charles Levinson: *Capital, inflation and the multinationals* (London, George Allen and Unwin, 1971), pp. 152-167.

[2] UNCTAD, Secretariat: *Restrictive business practices*, United Nations Conference on Trade and Development, Third Session, Santiago, Chile, April 1972 (Geneva, doc. TD/122/Supp. 1, 7 Jan. 1972; mimeographed), p. 19.

Table 7. Percentage distribution of United States direct investments abroad, by area, in selected years, 1950–70

Area	1950	1960	1965	1970
Africa	2.4	2.8	3.9	4.4
Asia	8.5	7.0	7.2	7.2
Canada	30.4	34.2	31.0	29.2
Western Europe	14.7	20.4	28.3	31.3
of which: EEC	(5.4)	(8.1)	(12.7)	(15.0)
Latin America	38.8	28.3	22.0	18.8
Rest of world	4.3	7.3	7.7	9.0

Source: Calculated on the basis of figures given in table 2.

Table 8. Percentage distribution of United States direct investments abroad as between developed and developing countries in selected years, 1950-70

	1950	1955	1960	1965	1970
Developed market economies	48.3	54.0	60.6	65.2	68.0
Developing countries	48.7	42.9	35.1	30.8	27.5
International, unallocated	3.0	3.1	4.3	4.0	4.5

Source: *Survey of Current Business*, Aug. 1957, p. 24, Aug. 1959, p. 30, Aug. 1963, pp. 18-19, Sep. 1967, p. 42, Oct. 1970, p. 31, and Oct. 1971, p. 32.

national firms in the developed countries considered in the study grew between 1955 and 1964 by almost 49 per cent, while their assets in the developing countries considered only grew by 41 per cent.[1] While the cumulative flow of investments from the Federal Republic of Germany to developing countries was increasing between 1961 and 1970 in absolute terms (from DM 1,364 million to DM 5,108 million)[2], it was proportionately less than that going to industrialised countries. For instance, at the end of 1964, of a total of DM 7,205 million in direct investments abroad, 67.2 per cent, or DM 4,843.4 million, was invested in industrialised countries, 68 per cent of this sum being invested in European industrialised countries.[3]

Two notable exceptions to the tendency of foreign investments to gravitate to industrialised countries were the initiation of the National Frontier Programme (PRONAF) by the Government of Mexico in 1965 and the increasing

---

[1] W. B. Reddaway et al.: *Effects of UK direct investment overseas. An interim report*, University of Cambridge, Department of Applied Economics, Occasional papers, No. 12 (Cambridge University Press, 1967), pp. 193-194.

[2] UNCTAD: *Restrictive business practices*, op. cit., p. 18.

[3] *Monthly Report* (Frankfurt am Main, Deutsche Bundesbank), Dec. 1965, p. 26.

tendency of electrical/electronics firms to establish subsidiaries in certain parts of Asia (primarily Hong Kong, Singapore and the Republic of Korea). Under the PRONAF the Government of Mexico established an industrial zone bordering on the United States and undertook to provide the infrastructure for industrial estates containing all the services necessary to facilitate industrial development. The Government waived import duties on raw materials and parts imported from abroad as well as duties on the final product, provided that it was exported and that all raw materials and parts left the national territory. Mexican manufacturers selling products into the zone were granted rebates on freight charges and refunds on sales tax. The programme has been successful, with 33 plants in operation by mid-April 1967 [1]; by mid-1972 their number had increased tenfold, to about 330, of which 280 were reported to be wholly US-owned.[2]

The late 1960s saw a sharp rise in the establishment of subsidiaries of European, US and Japanese firms in South-East Asia, mainly in the field of electrical/electronic equipment and instruments. Not only have these establishments multiplied at a rapid rate [3], but an increasing portion of their production is brought back to the home country for further processing and/or sale. This latter development represents a significant change from the previous pattern of goods manufactured abroad being sold in the country of production or in other foreign markets.[4]

Up to now the possibilities for foreign investors in the centrally planned economies have been very restricted. In agreements with the Eastern European countries, foreign private companies are generally limited to selling specialised equipment to a counterpart government corporation and providing the management and technical services needed to launch the venture. These are often termed "turnkey operations". It was recently reported that all Eastern

---

[1] For a more detailed description of this programme see "Economic developments in the Mexican border areas", in *Labor Developments Abroad* (Washington, DC, US Department of Labor), June 1967, pp. -18.

[2] *Quarterly Economic Review: Mexico* (London, Economist Intelligence Unit), 1972, No. 2, p. 9.

[3] In 1968, 25 or more US electronics firms were located in Hong Kong and two of the top three US producers of integrated circuits operated plants in Singapore. See ILO: *General report*, Report I, Metal Trades Committee, Ninth Session, Geneva, 1971, p. 158.

[4] Under tariff schedules 806.30 and 807.00 of the United States, articles repaired, altered, processed, or otherwise changed in condition abroad and articles assembled abroad with components produced in the United States can re-enter the United States with duty charged only on the value added. See US Tariff Commission: *Economic factors affecting the use of items 807.00 and 806.30 of the Tariff Schedules of the United States*, Report to the President on Investigation No. 332-61 under section 332 of the Tariff Act of 1930 (Washington, DC, TC Publication No. 339, Sep. 1970). These schedules may in part explain the increase in US subsidiaries both in South-East Asia and under the PRONAF, although they do not explain the establishment of Western European subsidiaries in South-East Asia.

European countries made some such "industrial co-operation" arrangements during the 1960s, Romania apparently having 19 in effect during 1969.[1]

Yugoslavia has gone further along the road towards joint ventures with multinational corporations than any of the other Eastern European countries. During 1967 the Yugoslav Foreign Investment Law was amended to permit joint ventures by Yugoslav and foreign companies, with the result that one European firm set up a motor vehicle plant and a Canadian firm authorised its British subsidiary to embark on the production of diesel engines for locally made trucks and tractors. It is interesting to note that these companies have both agreed to accept payment in the form of goods produced in the Yugoslav plants concerned.[2] Thus the country benefits inasmuch as new production capacity is added to its economy through multinational corporate investment without affecting national hard currency reserves.

Encouraged by the experience gained, the Government of Yugoslavia in 1972 further revised its foreign investment regulations to permit foreign firms to acquire equal or majority participation in joint ventures with the Government. This allows considerably more freedom to the multinational firm's operations.

There are also instances of undertakings in Eastern European countries making investments abroad. However, data on such investments are not readily available, except in the case of some sales and maintenance facilities.

Industry concentration

Airlines and steamship companies operate multinationally, of course, as do some banks, insurance firms and commercial establishments. Most discussions of multinational firms tend to put all or some of these groups to one side, however, and to focus on the manufacturing and extractive industries. For most analytical purposes this focus proves desirable and even essential; on the other hand, any consideration of the effect of foreign firms on a country's economic development, for example, would be incomplete without reference to the role of multinational banks.

Some shifts had already occurred in the industrial sectors in which multinational firms were prominent prior to the 1950s and 1960s. While multinational firms were increasing in importance in mining and manufacturing, their prominence in developing countries in such sectors as electric power generation, telephone operating systems, sugar growing and refining and the

---

[1] Neil H. Jacoby: "The multinational corporation", in *Center Magazine* (Santa Barbara (California)), May 1970, pp. 46-47.

[2] J. W. Sundelson: "US automotive investments abroad", in C. P. Kindleberger (ed.): *The international corporation* (Cambridge (Massachusetts), MIT Press, 1970), p. 251.

Table 9. Percentage distribution of United States direct investments abroad, by major industrial sector, in selected years, 1955–70

Industrial sector	1955	1960	1965	1970
Mining and smelting	11.4	9.4	7.9	7.8
Petroleum	30.3	33.9	30.9	27.9
Manufacturing	32.9	34.7	39.1	41.3
Other industries	25.4	22.0	22.0	23.0

Source: *Survey of Current Business*, Aug. 1957, p. 24, Aug. 1963, pp. 18-19, Sep. 1967, p. 42, Oct. 1970, p. 31 and Oct. 1971, p. 32.

life insurance business was declining. There are now some indications that traditional oil and mining concessions are becoming more difficult to arrange and that multinationals will increasingly supply "intangible" resources of a managerial, administrative and technical nature, while their proportion of "owned" assets diminishes. The pace of this trend is unclear.[1] However, as table 9 shows, during the 1955–70 period there was a definite increase in US direct investment abroad in the manufacturing industries and a corresponding decrease in mining and smelting and in petroleum.

To try and break down the broad category of "manufacturing" into its constituent industries with any degree of precision is almost impossible on a world-wide basis. Only a few countries regularly publish such information, and the literature on multinational operations is most often filled with substitute data to show trends rather than actual foreign direct investment information by line of industry, or else it falls back on individual examples. However, the information available, including the examples given in this section of this chapter, seems to point to a tendency for foreign investments to gravitate to industries showing one or more of the following characteristics: (1) a high initial capital outlay, (2) a rapid growth rate, (3) a high level of technology, (4) a rapid rate of replacement in the technologies used, and (5) a high degree of concentration in the home country.

Data for the United States show that plant and equipment expenditures by foreign manufacturing affiliates of US corporations rose from US$3,884 million to 6,751 million between 1965 and 1971. Chemicals, machinery and transportation equipment accounted for 67 per cent of such expenditures in 1965 and 65 per cent in 1971. In machinery, expenditures more than doubled, increasing from US$882 million to 2,053 million, while in chemicals they increased

---

[1] For somewhat divergent views of these developments, including the question of the inter-relationship between national powers of expropriation and the changing character of multinational firms, see Peter P. Gabriel's review of *Sovereignty at bay,* by Raymond Vernon (op. cit.), and Professor Vernon's reply, in *Fortune,* Jan. 1972, pp. 119-120.

by 52 per cent (from US$861 million to 1,310 million) and in transportation equipment by slightly less than 15 per cent (from US$873 million to 1,000 million).[1]

In 1964 the largest share of direct investments from the Federal Republic of Germany was in steel construction, mechanical engineering and vehicle- and ship-building, which accounted for DM 1,272 million. Electrical engineering, precision instruments, sports goods, toys, jewellery and hardware production came next, with DM 1,176 million, and were followed by chemicals, plastics, rubber and asbestos processing, with DM 1,101 million. In 1961 chemicals had been first, with DM 716 million, iron and non-ferrous metal production, foundry and steel moulding second, with DM 629 million, and electrical engineering third, with DM 617 million.[2]

Some of the same industries figured prominently during the 1960s as regards foreign-owned capital operating in the Federal Republic of Germany. In 1965 petroleum processing was first, with DM 2,229 million, while steel construction, mechanical engineering and vehicle-building were second, with DM 2,083 million, and the chemical industry third, with DM 1,522 million. By 1970 steel construction, mechanical engineering and vehicle-building were first, with DM 3,178 million, chemicals were second, with DM 2,877 million, and petroleum processing third, with DM 2,837 million. Electrical engineering was fourth in both years, with DM 1,436 million in 1965 and DM 2,559 million in 1970. In both 1965 and 1970 these four industries together accounted for 53 per cent of all foreign-owned capital in the Federal Republic of Germany.[3]

In some countries substantial sectors of the economy are controlled by foreign capital. In Canada, for example, it was reported that in 1963 approximately 60 per cent of the total investment in industrial enterprises was held by foreign owners—48 per cent being held in the United States and 12 per cent elsewhere.[4] In the automotive, rubber, electrical products and petroleum industries US ownership was reported to be 91, 81, 62 and 54 per

---

[1] *Survey of Current Business* (Washington, DC, US Department of Commerce), Mar. 1969, p. 15, and Sep. 1971, p. 29.

[2] *Monthly Report* (Deutsche Bundesbank), Dec. 1965, p. 27.

[3] Ibid., May 1969, p. 27, and Jan. 1972, p. 33.

[4] In 1964 total direct foreign investment in Canada was Can.$15,889 million, of which the United Kingdom's share was 13 per cent and the US share was 78 per cent (see Isaiah A. Litvak and Christopher J. Maule (eds.): *Foreign investment: The experience of host countries*, Praeger special studies in international economics and development (New York, Praeger, 1970), p. 81). By the end of 1968 total direct foreign investments had reached Can.$22,534 million; the United Kingdom's share had fallen to 10.3 per cent, while the US share had increased to 82.1 per cent (figures given in a study published by the Dominion Bureau of Statistics on foreign direct investments, quoted in *Neue Zürcher Zeitung*, 13 June 1972, midday edition, No. 271, p. 11, col. 4).

cent respectively.[1] In addition to the four industries showing high levels of foreign ownership in Canada, multinational firms are especially to be found in machinery and other metal product manufacturing, food processing and chemical production, as well as in some mining operations. When the 187 major US multinational firms that were studied under the Harvard Multi-national Enterprise Project are grouped by industry, three-quarters (143) are found to be in the industries named above.[2] In Australia, for example, in the early 1960s, the then Federal Minister for Works, Senator Gorton, estimated that the foreign-owned share of industry was 95 per cent in motor vehicles, 55 per cent in motor parts and accessories, 83 per cent in telecommunications, 97 per cent in pharmaceutical and toilet preparations, 80 per cent in soap and detergents and 95 per cent in petroleum refining and distribution.[3]

Foreign direct investment in Japan is of relatively recent origin, and foreign enterprises account for only a small proportion of the total turnover of industry as a whole. However, their share in certain sectors of industry is considerable. The following figures show the percentage share of foreign enterprises in the turnover of industry in 1969 [4]:

Industry as a whole	2.8
Food products	0.8
Chemicals	4.6
Pharmaceutical products	7.7
Petroleum	58.3
Rubber articles	20.3
Non-ferrous metals	6.1
General metal trades	6.0
Electrical construction	3.3

In 1963, it has been reported that 13.9 per cent of the total capital stock of 4,045.9 million kroner in Norway was foreign-owned. However, certain

---

[1] Dominion Bureau of Statistics figures quoted in Behrman, op. cit., p. 68. The extensive foreign ownership (particularly US) of Canadian industry has been the topic of numerous studies and of political controversy. In May 972, the Government "announced . . . long-awaited plans to tighten controls over business takeovers by foreign investments". In Australia, on the other hand, although 35 per cent of company income in 1970–71 was payable abroad (as compared to 20 per cent in 1948–49), the Government saw "no economic threat in the increasing foreign ownership of the nation's companies". It conceded, however, that "concern for the nation's identity or defence might be reasons for government intervention". See *International Herald Tribune* (Paris), 4 and 7 May 1972.

[2] Vernon, op. cit., pp. 14-15.

[3] Donald T. Brash: *American investment in Australian industry* (Canberra, Australian National University Press, 1966), p. 33.

[4] "Les capitaux étrangers au Japon", in *Japon-Economie* (Paris, Office franco-japonais), 1971, No. 34, reproduced in *Problèmes économiques* (Paris, La Documentation française), 3 May 1972, p. 22.

manufacturing sectors showed higher rates of foreign ownership than the over-all percentage, for example: 48.1 per cent of a total of 90.8 million kroner of capital stock in the electro-technique industry, 27.9 per cent of a total 503.8 million kroner in the chemical and oil industries, 21.7 per cent of a total of 668.5 million kroner in basic metals and 15.3 per cent of a total of 182.5 million kroner in the food, beverage and tobacco industries.[1]

These figures do not provide an entirely balanced picture, since multinational firms sometimes hold a dominant position—even in highly industrialised host countries—with respect to certain products within a broad industry classification. The manufacture of computers and the production of semi-conductors and transistors are examples of such concentration in Europe generally, and foreign affiliates are recently reported to have controlled 100 and 80 per cent of the ball-bearing industry in Italy and France respectively and at least 75 and 95 per cent of carbon black production in the United Kingdom and France respectively. The following are further examples of manufacturing industries in France which, in 1964, were largely owned by foreign companies: synthetic rubber and margarine, each 90 per cent; agricultural equipment, 70 per cent; telecommunication equipment, 65 per cent; elevators, 60 per cent; electric lamps, office equipment and materials, tyres, and plumbing equipment, each 50 per cent.[2]

* * *

The information provided in this chapter on concentration by area and lines of industry is illustrative of the data available at present. The examples are not necessarily representative of world-wide trends, and there is an obvious need to have access to more precise and comprehensive information before a generalised theory can be formulated on why multinational corporations tend to concentrate in certain areas and industries.

ORGANISATIONAL VARIATIONS

Just as there are variations in the significance of multinational firms among countries and between industries, so there are substantial differences in the types of parent-affiliate relationship. Company policy appears to be

---

[1] Litvak and Maule, op. cit., p. 170.
[2] Ibid., p. 115.

the determining factor in these arrangements, to the extent that national legislation permits, since firms in the same industry exhibit different corporate structures.

The wholly-owned subsidiary is perhaps the most prevalent parent-affiliate relationship, although majority-owned subsidiaries are also widespread. While the parent firm might normally prefer to retain full ownership and control of a newly established subsidiary, such factors as legal restrictions, government pressure, technological considerations, risk sharing and business relationships often result in the establishment of joint ventures with host country nationals or other foreign firms. When the affiliate is acquired through the takeover of an operating unit, effective control may well be exercised through less than 100 per cent stock ownership.

Under pressure from a number of developing countries, multinational firms are often required to undertake operations together with nationals of the host country concerned, and examples are to be found of parent firms holding 50 per cent or 49 per cent of the equity in such subsidiaries. Furthermore, joint ventures of two (and even more) multinational firms are becoming commoner, particularly in such fields as oil prospecting and processing, chemicals and automobiles; companies which are competing vigorously in some product markets combine efforts in jointly owned firms in other countries or activities.[1]

Given this variety of parent-affiliate relationships, it is not surprising that the degree of centralised control varies among firms and among issues within a single firm.

Professor Behrman emphasises the nature of the parent-affiliate relationship when he writes: "What distinguishes the multinational enterprise from its predecessors is the centralisation of policy and the integration of key operations among the affiliates." [2] He suggests that a multinational outlook develops when approximately 25 per cent of a firm's income or sales comes from foreign operations. By this yardstick, he finds nearly 200 US firms to be potential multinational enterprises, but he notes that not all firms meeting this criterion are necessarily multinational in his meaning of the term. Very rapid growth by subsidiaries often permits them to become so independent "that the parent never has the opportunity to form a multinational enterprise". He finds this condition exists particularly in the foreign subsidiaries of European multi-

---

[1] A research project at the Centre for European Industrial Studies at Bath University of Technology (United Kingdom) is concentrating on "multinationally owned" companies, such as Royal Dutch-Shell, Unilever, Agfa-Gevaert and Dunlop-Pirelli. See Michael Whitehead: "The multinationally owned company: A case study", in John H. Dunning (ed.): *The multinational enterprise* (London, George Allen and Unwin, 1971), pp. 307-335.

[2] Behrman, op. cit., p. xiii.

national firms, where there are instances of home country sales as low as 20 per cent of the firm's total sales, and he suggests, in addition, that US subsidiaries of European firms tend to achieve a position of independence such that the parent firm becomes a sort of "international holding company" as it seeks to learn from the subsidiary and to pass the knowledge to its other units.[1] In the case of developing host countries, he finds that manufacturing affiliates tend to be less integrated with the other affiliates of the same multinational enterprise than are the European affiliates, say, with their US parents, and that even marketing activities tend to be less integrated and less centralised when in the less developed countries.[2]

MULTINATIONAL FIRMS, NATIONAL ECONOMIES AND INTERNATIONAL TRADE

The tremendous expansion of international trade in the past quarter of a century has provided an unparalleled growth opportunity for multinational firms, and their activities have, in turn, stimulated trade expansion. Some aspects of this inter-relationship can be observed in terms of capital movements, technology transfers, market developments and national economic policies.[3]

Capital movements

In theory, foreign investments involve a capital flow from countries with more adequate resources to those with less adequate resources. While this explanation may hold for current investments in some developing countries and for US investments in European countries immediately after the Second World War, its applicability to current US-European investment patterns is somewhat doubtful. In the latter case, both parties would appear to have adequate capital resources, since even while US investment in Europe is increasing, the investment of European firms in the United States and elsewhere is growing simultaneously. There are indeed large capital movements within the group of developed countries stimulated by investment opportunities

---

[1] Behrman, op. cit., pp. 13-14.

[2] Ibid., p. xiii.

[3] For a review of the costs and benefits of foreign investment (particularly by multinational firms) in developing countries, see UNCTAD, Secretariat: *Financial resources for development: Private foreign investment in its relationship to development*, United Nations Conference on Trade and Development, Third Session, Santiago, Chile, April 1972 (Geneva, doc. TD/134, 17 Nov. 1971; mimeographed).

arising from factors other than capital shortage in any absolute sense. In this situation the resources of the multinational enterprise in managerial know-how and technology become increasingly significant, as will be explained later.

For the home country, investments abroad are of some concern because of their effects on the country's balance of payments. Such effects are difficult to trace, however, largely because it is not possible to know what alternative business patterns might have developed if the foreign investment had not been made (would the market in the host country have been served by exports from the home country? or by an indigenous firm? or by a competitor from another country?). Further, in making such calculations, account must be taken not only of the original capital investment and of the estimated decrease of exports from the home country but also of such unknown factors as the future flow of repayments to the home country, the use of foreign earnings and foreign capital for the foreign operation, and the potential for increased exports of related products from the home country as the foreign affiliate becomes established.[1]

For a host country, the capital inflow associated with a multinational firm's new facility provides an immediate gain, with continuing positive effects arising from increased exports and/or reduced imports. However, the benefit from increased exports to the host country's balance of payments may be considerably reduced by capital outflows for imported raw materials and equipment necessary to produce the goods for export. Earnings repatriation may also have an adverse effect.[2]

In a broader sense, there is the question of whether classical economic theory is relevant to current conditions. As pointed out by the US Department of Commerce, traditional thinking holds that "commodities move internationally while productive factors do not".[3] But productive factors such as technology and managerial ability do move internationally, and since these movements arise in large measure from the decisions of multinational enter-

---

[1] These difficulties are discussed in some detail in US Department of Commerce: *Studies on US foreign investment*, op. cit., I: "Policy aspects of foreign investment by US multinational corporations", Chapter V: "The impact of the multinational corporation on the balance of payments", and in W. B. Reddaway *et al.*: *Effects of UK direct investment overseas. Final report*, University of Cambridge, Department of Applied Economics, Occasional papers, No. 15 (Cambridge University Press, 1968), Part IV, pp. 209 ff. Both sources draw on a number of technical research projects.

[2] For further details in this connection, see UNCTAD: *Financial resources for development . . .*, op. cit.

[3] US Department of Commerce: *Studies on US foreign investment*, op. cit., I: "Policy aspects of foreign investment by US multinational corporations", Chapter I: "The multinational corporation: An overview", p. 7.

prises, their operations call traditional assumptions into question. The implications for national economic systems are not yet clear.[1]

Technology transfer

The multinational firm has been a principal though not the sole vehicle for the transfer of technology. The significant role of multinational firms in this process can be seen as a two-way flow between home and host countries. Technological capability is most usually transferred from the central headquarters of the firm to its affiliates abroad, in the form of managerial know-how, production techniques, new products and processes, and patent licensing. Such transfers raise the technological capabilities of the host countries in general and, more specifically, provide an impetus to technological improvements in indigenous supplier and competitor firms. At the same time, a too rapid jump in technology carries the danger of adverse effects on local producers in an industrialised country, while in a developing country these adverse effects are aggravated by the replacement of artisan workshops and cottage industries by mass-production techniques.

For the firm, the transfer permits research and development costs to be spread over an increased scale of operations, with consequent market and earnings advantages. But benefits for the firm are not necessarily benefits for the home country. The more rapidly a country's advanced technology is adopted for use abroad (whether by the multinational firm or other business units), the more quickly does it lose the related competitive advantages in the international market; the multinational hastens this process.

The second type of technology transfer is a reverse flow, from the host to the home country. It is not unusual for a multinational firm to purchase an operating company for the purpose of acquiring its advanced technology.[2] Nor is it unusual for a multinational firm to establish research centres in association with foreign plants and thus gain from foreign innovative abilities. In these cases, as in those previously examined, an understanding of the ramifications of technology transfers must consider the separate, and sometimes

---

[1] Professor Johnson challenges the traditional concept that views "liberality of international economic relations in terms of freedom of trade in commodities", and writes: " . . . we have evolved beyond international trade into international businesses". He refers to the "framework of fair international trade" (GATT) and notes that "there is no internationally agreed code and no international regulatory institution to govern the conduct and define the rights of international business". See Harry G. Johnson: *International economic questions facing Britain, the United States and Canada in the 70s* (London, British-North American Committee, 1970), p. 11.

[2] Nestlé's takeover of the frozen-food firm Findus and Bayer's acquisition of the paint-manufacturing firm Nordsjö, both in Sweden, are cases in point. See "Multinational give and take", in *Sweden Now* (Stockholm), Jan. 1972, pp. 30-31 and 49.

conflicting, interests of the multinational firm, the home State and the host States in which it operates.

International trade

As multinational firms develop an integrated group of production facilities around the world, they provide opportunities for countries to share in the growing volume of international trade, even while new trade patterns develop. While some forms of international subcontracting have proved feasible, there are limitations on the ability of indigenous firms in the host country independently to develop domestic production that can eventually be integrated into a multinational corporation's final product by means of subcontracting. Such production comes more easily from a foreign affiliate of a multinational firm which, although contributing only marginally or indirectly to the development of local industry, does have a beneficial effect on the country's economy through the expansion of its exports.[1] In other situations the multinational introduces capital and technology for the development of natural resources or may offer long-term purchase commitments, without which the resource development would be economically unfeasible.

But with the growth of multinational enterprise has come a change in the basis of international trade. Classical theory suggests that such trade develops from the natural and comparative advantages of different countries, implying competitive prices as an underlying assumption. Under current conditions, however, it is possible that significant amounts of international trade arise from sales within a multinational firm at internal company transfer prices, which could differ from those arrived at by independent buyers and sellers. The implications of this development have not been empirically investigated —in part because information on company pricing policy is not available—but the potential exists for centralised decisions affecting tax, income and other economic issues.[2]

THE MOTIVATION OF MULTINATIONAL OPERATIONS

The organisation of business units operating in more than one country is not particularly new. Trading operations have for long been multinational in scope. Already in the eighteenth century European investment in foreign operations was taking place. In the first half of the nineteenth century, a total of some 15 US entrepreneurs undertook ventures in Canada, England, Mexico,

---

[1] See Vernon, op. cit., p. 104.
[2] Ibid., pp. 137-140.

Hawaii and South America, in such fields as banking, textiles, machinery manufacturing, mining (iron, copper and precious metals), transportation (steamboats and a stagecoach line), printing and paper making.[1]

It is not difficult to compile a list of reasons for the increase of foreign direct investment in the ensuing years and even to note some of the special factors leading to the rapid growth rate of recent decades. While some factors undoubtedly lie in the personality of individual business leaders and others may be traced to a firm's history of foreign operations, the majority are economic in character.

In broad terms, foreign investment decisions have been described as "offensive" when they are undertaken in search of increased markets and profits, and "defensive" when motivated by the desire to retain specific markets or maintain a relative share of the market as a whole. Any one decision may, of course, develop from a mixture of motives.

Certain industries are by nature international. These include the petroleum, mining and plantation industries, where the raw material resources are located abroad. The exploitation of these resources requires international investment of capital and the application of technology not available in the host country. These ventures—whether in mining, oil exploration or plantations—are commonly undertaken to provide a source of raw materials for home country processing, that is, the foreign operation is part of a firm's move towards vertical integration.

The foreign investments of oil companies in the late nineteenth century involved the integration of operations, since the firms were expanding into marketing operations in order to sell domestically produced oil in competition with foreign oil firms. It was essentially after 1900 that European and US petroleum firms developed oil wells and production facilities abroad, and the petroleum industry is today a prime example of multinationalism, with major firms operating on a global basis in oil extraction, processing and marketing.[2]

In manufacturing industries, decisions to undertake operations abroad have until recently been principally related to market considerations rather than to an interest in integrating activities or to other factors. Markets that are first developed through exports from the home country grow over time to such size that they can be better served from facilities in the countries or regions concerned. Market considerations also underlie a firm's decision to

---

[1] Mira Wilkins: *The emergence of multinational enterprise: American business abroad from the colonial era to 1914* (Cambridge (Massachusetts), Harvard University Press, 1970), pp. 17-18.

[2] For a detailed history of this development, see Edith T. Penrose: *The large international firm in developing countries: The international petroleum industry* (London, George Allen and Unwin, 1968).

follow a major competitor or customer into operations abroad or to acquire a foreign firm with special technological capabilities.

In considering market factors, long-term objectives may sometimes predominate. For example, the current scale of production of automobiles in a number of developing countries is reported to make operations unprofitable, but firms have introduced and retained facilities in order to have a better opportunity to share in the anticipated market expansion. The spurt of US affiliates in EEC countries has been explained in part by the desire of such firms to become established in a rapidly growing market and to avoid possible EEC trade barriers.

In addition, locally produced goods are often likely to find greater acceptance than imported products, and as a firm develops the market for some items, it frequently finds easier entry for its other products.

Factors in the home market also influence firms to turn toward investment abroad. Competition, for example, may keep a company from expanding, or the market may appear to be saturated or declining. Legislation sometimes places limits on expansion. More positively, the transfer of technological developments—products or technology—to operations abroad contributes to over-all earnings by spreading the major research and development costs over a larger market area.

The list of motivational factors mentioned above is far from complete and has concentrated mainly on market considerations. The diversification of product lines to lessen risk can also stimulate overseas expansion, as can the possibility of utilising licences held by foreign firms. Cost factors naturally play an important role in such decisions, including the level of existing or anticipated tariff barriers, raw material costs, transportation expenses and labour costs. The last-mentioned factor is, of course, of special interest to this paper and includes considerations of labour availability in terms of adequate numbers, requisite skills and, if these skills are not present, the trainability of such labour as is available. Within the broader context of industrial relations, labour as a cost factor must also be considered in general terms of labour unrest and labour peace, which have a bearing on the actual, as opposed to potential, utilisation of planned plant and equipment. In this connection, labour turnover rates and absenteeism also play a part. Finally, a favourable investment climate in general may motivate investment abroad and may include, in addition to the above-mentioned factors, such considerations as the political stability of a potential host country or advantageous currency exchange rates.

An explanation of the very rapid growth rate of multinationals in the past two decades lies partly in these factors, any or all of which become effective in the context of the special circumstances prevailing at a given point in time and in a particular place. For example, as European countries rebuilt their economies following the Second World War, the United States promoted the outflow of capital and technology. Later the formation of European economic blocs (EFTA and EEC) occurred at the same time as rapidly rising consumer incomes created an accelerated demand in industrial sectors in which US firms held a technological advantage. These factors prompted US firms to establish European operations, and even when US policy on capital outflows became restrictive in 1965, entry was possible (indeed eased) through European-held dollar balances, or Eurodollars. Such investments in turn stimulated additional investments as the US firms responded to the need to follow customers and competitors and to the availability of foreign-generated funds for further expansion.

Of probably equal significance, however, is the fact that in this period advances in transportation, communication and data processing opened up new possibilities for integrating a firm's operations on a multinational basis.

The confluence of these factors in the 1950–70 period raises questions about the future rate of growth of multinational firms, at least in the European market. Whereas past growth was predominantly based on market considerations, there are indications that considerations of cost and integrated operations (whereby subsidiaries each specialise in certain components of a product, exchange them, supplement one another's production and so on, all being co-ordinated from a central point in order to minimise costs, among other reasons) are becoming increasingly significant. Instead of new plants being established in high-income areas with expanding markets, the next decade may see an accelerated growth of multinational enterprise in developing countries, with emphasis on exporting semi-finished or finished products rather than on supplying a local market. This trend is evident in certain industrial sectors, such as apparel, electronics, plastics, and photographic equipment, but could very well spread more widely. However, in view of the lack of information, including statistical data, and even of a precise definition of the phenomenon under study, additional predictions of the development of the multinational corporation are impossible.

The multinational corporation is a highly complex business institution and has brought into question international economic theory and the basic assumptions on which it rests. It is no wonder, then, that this phenomenon has generated the emotional responses it has, both favourable and otherwise, in all areas on which it has touched—political, fiscal, economic and, not least, social. This chapter has merely attempted to provide some broad background information on the economic aspects of the multinational corporation. The remainder of the paper deals with the subject of the meeting, namely the relationship between multinational corporations and social policy.

2. THE IMPACT OF MULTINATIONAL ENTERPRISES ON MANPOWER

While the economic aspects of direct investment by multinational enterprises have already received considerable study, albeit often based on limited information, relatively little attention has been paid to the way in which these transfers of capital and technology may affect the workers in either the host or the home country. Employment questions, although perhaps not entirely ignored, have been neglected, and knowledge in these areas is insufficient. The international business community tends to look upon comparative advantage and free trade as fundamental principles, the application of which will ensure the optimum allocation of the world's resources, including manpower. Manpower thus tends sometimes to be regarded as primarily a cost factor reflected in wages and other labour-related expenditures. Such an approach is inadequate, for it does not take into consideration the impact of the multinational corporation's activities on the various aspects of the manpower question, such as employment levels, the structure of the labour force, training, and management development. Understandably, reliable information has been difficult to obtain from sources extraneous to the firm, and material gathered and analysed by the firm is often treated by it as confidential, since it is considered to be information upon which the success of the firm's world-wide corporate strategy rests.

EFFECTS IN THE HOME COUNTRY

Employment levels and structure

Although the possible impact of multinational corporations on employment has not yet been given very much attention in a majority of the developed countries, serious investigation has begun in the United States, the results of which may well prove to be relevant elsewhere. Some hold the view that the employment problems associated with direct investment abroad can and should be differentiated from those commonly resulting from structural change or the ups and downs of market demand. However, this view is contested by many. While no attempt is made here to assess the validity of either opinion, a brief summary of the situation in the United States is given below and may throw light on why direct investment abroad is thought by some to have a unique effect on employment in the home country.

The position of the American Federation of Labor and Congress of Industrial Organizations (AFL-CIO), is as follows [1]:

The United States position in world trade deteriorated in the 1960s, with adverse impacts on American workers, communities and industries. The deterioration threatens to continue in the 1970s. . . .

Exports from the nations of the world rose from approximately US$61,000 million in 1950 to about US$238,000 million in 1968—a nearly fourfold increase—according to the United Nations. But US exports increased at a slower pace. As a result, the US share of rapidly expanding world exports continued to decline, from 16.5 per cent in 1950 to 15.9 per cent in 1960 and 14.3 per cent in 1968. . . .

While US exports continued to increase—although at a much slower rate than most other industrial countries—imports also rose. In most of the latter 1960s, imports increased much faster than exports. . . .

The US trade position has been changing in composition, as well as in over-all volume. The growth of rapidly rising imports has been primarily in manufactured and semi-manufactured goods—parts and components, as well as finished products. . . .

During the 1960s, the expansion of manufactured exports was strongest in products based on advanced technology, such as computers, jet aircraft, control instruments and some organic chemicals. Such industries are generally capital-intensive, with relatively few production and maintenance workers for each dollar of production.

The rapid expansion of manufactured imports in the 1960s was particularly great in several products for which the US had previously been a world leader—such as steel, autos, machinery and electrical products (including TV, radios, telecommunications apparatus). Imports of these products, in the 1960s, joined with the continued rise in imports of other products that had previously posed import problems—such as shoes, textiles, clothing, glass and leather goods. These industries are mostly labour-intensive—with sizeable numbers of production and maintenance workers per dollar of output. . . .

Detailed information on the job impact of imports is not available. There are jobs involved in the transportation and distribution of imports. Also, there are job

---

[1] Extracts from a statement by Nathaniel Goldfinger, Director, Department of Research, American Federation of Labor and Congress of Industrial Organizations, on US trade policy, before the Joint Economic Committee of the US Congress, 18 March 1970. A more recent statement by Mr. Goldfinger ("A labor view of foreign investment and trade issues") can be found in *United States international economic policy in an interdependent world*, Papers submitted to the Commission on International Trade and Investment Policy [the Williams Commission] and published in conjunction with the Commission's Report to the President, Compendium of papers, Vol. I (Washington, DC, US Government Printing O\ce, July 1971), Part II: "Major issues", section 8: "Investment and production on a globa scale: Impact on the US economy", pp. 913-928.

losses, due to imports that compete with US-made products. Moreover, the labour-intensive nature of much of the great import expansion of the 1960s indicates significant losses of job opportunities, particularly for semi-skilled and unskilled production workers—at a time when such job opportunities were sorely needed. And the shift of imports to relatively sophisticated products also indicates the loss of skilled industrial jobs. . . .

. . . In the 1950s, according to foreign trade experts, only about 30–40 per cent of imports were considered competitive with US-made products. By 1966, according to a report by Secretary Shultz to the Joint Economic Committee of Congress, about 74 per cent of the much greater volume of imports were "nearly competitive with domestic products". . . .

Temporary factors in the 1960s can explain only part of the deterioration of the US trade position. The rising price level in the US since 1965 and the boom of business investment in new plants and machines undoubtedly contributed to the sharp rise of imports and the deterioration of the US position.

But there are basic underlying causes of the deterioration of the US trade position. Temporary factors . . . merely aggravated them.

The AFL-CIO statement goes on to list "the basic causes of the deterioration of the US position in world trade"—

(1) the revival, by the late 1950s, of industrial economies that had been shattered during the Second World War;

(2) the emergence, in the 1960s, of trading blocs, such as the European Common Market with its inward-looking protectionist tendencies;

(3) the spread of managed national economies, in which there are complex governmental economic arrangements to spur exports and to bar or hold down imports;

(4) the internationalisation of technology, which has been reducing or eliminating the former US productivity lead in many industries and product lines;

(5) the sky-rocketing rise of foreign investments of US firms, which—

accompanied by licensing arrangements, patent agreements, etc., of US companies with foreign firms—has contributed substantially to the internationalisation of technology and its deteriorating effects on the US trade position. . . .

Foreign subsidiaries of US firms and foreign companies using US licences, patents, etc., with US technology—and, thereby, with productivity levels that are close to those in similar US plants—can take maximum advantage of lower wage and fringe benefit costs and produce goods at lower unit costs. Both directly and indirectly, the sharp rise of foreign investments, licensing arrangements, etc., of US firms has cost American jobs. To some degree, it has meant the export of US jobs to subsidiary plants in foreign countries; to some degree, it has resulted in the loss of exports to third countries; to another degree, it has meant the increase of imports from foreign subsidiary plants to the US—with a further loss of jobs. There is no precise information on these impacts, but the fact of job loss is clear;

(6) the rapid spread of multinational corporations—

usually US firms with plants, offices, sales agencies, licensing arrangements, etc., in as many as 40 or more countries—is a new factor of growing importance in the deteriorating US position in world trade. They can manipulate the location of operations, depending on labour costs, taxes and foreign exchange rates. They can juggle exports, imports, prices, dividends, from one country to another within the corporate structure. . . .

The spreading operations of US-based multinational companies are an important factor in both the surge of manufactured imports into the US and the absolute slow-down or the slowing rise of US exports in many product lines. . . .

The AFL-CIO statement declares—

Capital is mobile—investments can be moved out of an unprofitable business to other industries, companies and countries. . . . In contrast, workers have great stakes in their jobs and communities—skills that are related to the job or industry, seniority and seniority-related benefits, investment in a home, stake in the neighbourhood, schools, church, etc.

In a special study commissioned by the Industrial Union Department of the AFL-CIO in 1971 the claim was made that some 500,000 job opportunities were lost between 1966 and 1969, owing to the United States' changing trade patterns, including in particular the exports of US subsidiaries abroad.[1] This figure represented the increase of 700,000, over the three-year period, in the number of jobs which would have been required to produce the goods to replace the imports competing with domestic products, less an increase of 200,000 jobs attributable to higher exports from the United States.

As further evidence of job loss, the President of the International Union of Electrical, Radio and Machine Workers in the United States presented a paper to a recent meeting organised by the Organisation for Economic Co-operation and Development, which showed that between 1966 and the first half of 1971 employment in the United States fell from 169,400 to 131,700 in the manufacture of radio and TV receiving sets and from 374,200 to 317,700 in the electronic components and accessories industry. This paper also listed a number of US firms which had announced the shut-down of plants and laying off of workers in the United States, while at the same time similar production was being undertaken in factories abroad.[2] The industries dealt with in this paper are among those for which recourse can be and is had to tariff exemptions under items 806.30 and 807.00 of the Tariff Schedules of the United States, which were mentioned in Chapter 1.[3]

---

[1] Stanley H. Ruttenberg and Associates: *Needed: A constructive foreign trade policy*, A special study commissioned and published by the Industrial Union Department, AFL-CIO (Washington, DC, October 1971), pp. 62-63.

[2] Organisation for Economic Co-operation and Development, Social Affairs Division, Programme for Employers and Unions, Regional Trade Union Seminar on International Trade, 7-10 December 1971: *Part III*, (c): *A case study of the electronic sub-assemblies and components industry*, by Paul Jennings (Paris), pp. 5 and 15.

[3] In 1969, metal products (office machines, TV receivers, TV apparatus, radio apparatus and parts, phonographs, semi-conductors and electronic memories) accounted for 94 per cent

In accordance with this assessment of the situation, a majority of workers' organisations in the United States have developed an increasingly negative attitude towards movements of capital and technology from domestic operations to foreign locations by multinational corporations and have pressed for legislative action such as the Foreign Trade and Investment Bill of 1972[1] to protect the international trade position of the United States. At the same time, however, the US trade union movement has specifically denied that it has become protectionist or isolationist in its views on international trade. Rather, it has maintained that the conditions of international trade have altered, so that the "rules of the game" now need to be rewritten in order to render these conditions equitable again.

This position has been strongly objected to by US business, and in 1971 and 1972 several studies were prepared and published by various business groups.

Some these of studies, such as the one that was released by the National Association of Manufacturers (NAM) early in 1972[2], were based on an analysis of existing information relating to the points brought up by the trade unions. Others were based primarily on the replies to questionnaires sent to member business organisations.[3]

At about the same time the Government of the United States, which had been investigating the whole question of international trade and, more specifically, the impact of US multinational corporations, also began publishing

---

of the total value of imports under item 807.00. Most of the remainder consisted of toys, scientific instruments, body-supporting garments and women's outerwear. The principal articles entered under item 806.30 were (in order of the total value of imports): parts of aircraft (primarily wing and tail assemblies and fuselage panels); aluminium sheet and strip, rods, and pipe and tube; semi-conductors; copper and brass strip, pipes and tubes, rods, and wire; parts of steam turbines, boilers, and auxiliary equipment; aluminium foil; and parts of internal combustion engines. See US Tariff Commission: *Economic factors affecting the use of items 807.00 and 806.30 of the Tariff Schedules of the United States*, Report to the President on Investigation No. 332–61 under section 332 of the Tariff Act of 1930 (Washington, DC, TC Publication No. 339, Sep. 1970), pp. 36 and 79.

[1] This Bill, known as the Burke-Hartke Bill, would regulate US-based multinationals, raise the taxes on their foreign operations in a variety of ways, control capital outflows, limit the transfer of US technology, and control certain imports by means of new quotas.

[2] National Association of Manufacturers: *US stake in world trade and investment: The role of the multinational corporation* (New York, n.d.).

[3] See, for example, "Labor's charges that multinational corporations hurt economy refuted in national Chamber survey", in *News* (Washington, DC, Chamber of Commerce of the United States), 15 Feb. 1972; Emergency Committee for American Trade: *The role of the multinational corporation (MNC) in the United States and world economies*, Based on an analysis of the International Economic Subcommittee of the Emergency Committee for American Trade of the domestic and international activities of 74 US corporations, two vols. (Washington, DC, Feb. 1972) (the second volume is entitled *Individual industry analyses*); and National Foreign Trade Council: *The impact of US foreign direct investment on US employment and trade: An assessment of critical claims and legislative proposals* (New York, Nov. 1971).

studies in an attempt to clarify the pressing issues in this area. As the root cause of many of the issues raised, including those of employment, lay in international trade, a majority of these studies were carried out by the US Department of Commerce, the US Tariff Commission or specially commissioned bodies.[1]

Essentially the counter-arguments put forward by the various business organisations divide into two types. In the first type it is maintained that within the context of present-day international trade and competition the US firm has no choice but to go overseas for investment and production. The second type of argument is directed towards accusations against the multinational corporation and seeks to show that the information and data used by the trade unions have been incorrectly interpreted and that in fact the multinational firm is a positive element in the US balance of trade, that it creates jobs rather than reduces them and that its activities help to keep US industry competitive.

Those using the first type of argument assert at the outset that criticism should not be applied indiscriminately to all multinational corporations. "The problems in textiles and shoes are entirely different from the problems in pharmaceuticals or petrochemicals. The motivations for going international are different for each industry and even for each corporation." [2] The study by the National Foreign Trade Council (NFTC) points out: "There is nothing complex or mysterious about the phenomenon of US direct foreign investment since World War II: economic and political conditions for investment improved; US and other governmental policies supported it; and tariffs and non-tariff barriers made it necessary." [3] Furthermore, the employer studies hold that foreign markets would have been lost without the establishment of foreign subsidiaries and that exports are actually increased, at least in the long run,

---

[1] See, for example, *United States international economic policy in an interdependent world*, op. cit. (the Williams Commission Report); Peter G. Peterson (Assistant to the President for International Economic Affairs; Executive Director, Council on International Economic Policy): *The United States in the changing world economy*, Vol. I: *A foreign economic perspective* (Washington, DC, US Government Printing Office, Dec. 1971) and idem: *The United States in the changing world economy: Statistical background material* (Washington, DC, Dec. 1971) (the second of these documents provided the basis for briefings to the President of the United States and the Council on International Economic Policy during the year 1971); US Department of Commerce: *The multinational corporation*, Vol. I: *Studies on US foreign investment* (Washington, DC, Mar. 1972); US Tariff Commission: *Economic factors affecting the use of items 807.00 and 806.30 of the Tariff Schedules of the United States*, op. cit., and idem: *Competitiveness of US industries*, Report to the President on Investigation No. 332–65 under section 332 of the Tariff Act of 1930 (Washington, DC, TC Publication No. 473, Apr. 1972).

[2] National Association of Manufacturers: *US stake in world trade and investment . . .*, op. cit., p. 16.

[3] National Foreign Trade Council: *The impact of US foreign direct investment on US employment and trade . . .*, op. cit., p. 3.

by the export of products complementing the lines manufactured overseas, as well as through the shipment of parts and components required by the foreign subsidiaries, although in the short run there may be some export displacement, with the foreign subsidiaries producing goods previously exported from the United States. The employer studies also point out that imports into the United States from foreign subsidiaries are a very small proportion of total US imports. They admit, however, that in a few particular cases the imports in question have increased, both absolutely and relatively. For example, the study published by the NAM states [1]—

This is not to say that imports from US affiliates in certain industries, such as electronics, have not increased. They have. In these industries the problem is different. Foreign firms in these industries enjoy such large cost advantages in certain product groups that it is impossible for US firms to compete for the US markets. Faced with the choice of losing the domestic market or producing abroad and exporting to the US, many firms have chosen the latter.

In rebutting the arguments put forward by the trade unions, the Emergency Committee for American Trade summarised its findings as follows [2]:

... during the ten-year period covered by the survey, American multinational companies have—

increased their domestic employment (exclusive of employment gains through acquisition) more rapidly than the average manufacturing firm. Their rate of new job creation was about *75 per cent* greater than that of all other manufacturing firms;

increased their investment in domestic plant and equipment more rapidly than other US manufacturing firms and more rapidly than their foreign investments;

increased their domestic sales *more* rapidly than the typical US manufacturing firm;

increased their sales from domestic facilities *twice as much* as from their overseas operations;

exported a growing proportion of their domestic production. Their ratio of exports to domestic production in 1970—10.8 per cent—was *double* that of the average US manufacturing firm;

accounted for a *small* and (except for US-Canadian automobile trade) *declining* proportion of total US imports.

These findings were supported by the study made by the Chamber of Commerce of the United States, which found that between 1960 and 1970, as regards the firms surveyed [3]—

US multinational corporations increased domestic employment at a significantly higher rate (31.1 per cent) than the national average (12.3 per cent);

---

[1] National Association of Manufacturers: *US stake in world trade and investment . . .*, op. cit., p. 29.

[2] Emergency Committee for American Trade: *The role of the multinational corporation in the United States and world economies*, op. cit., p. 5.

[3] *News*, 15 Feb. 1972.

US multinational corporations increased exports by 180 per cent, while the national
average grew by only 53.5 per cent;

major reasons for US multinational corporations locating plants in foreign countries
are to retain foreign markets and to overcome trade and tariff barriers, not for
increasing exports to the US. Less than 10 per cent of such production is imported
into the US.

Both the NAM study and the NFTC study generally agreed with these
conclusions.

The NFTC survey found that both US employment and exports in responding
companies have generally risen. The findings support the conclusion that foreign
direct investment tends to expand trade and create employment in the United States,
even though this may involve some shifts in the structure of employment in this
country. The evidence, moreover, indicates that such shifts as they occur are likely
to be toward industries of higher technology.[1]

A study released by the US Department of Commerce tends to agree
with the employer analysis that direct foreign investment does not result in
job loss, stating: "A reasonable interpretation of available evidence leads
to the conclusion that US foreign direct investment is not contrary to the
interests of US workers but may, in fact, be a positive factor in stimulating
US employment and economic activity."[2] A study by the US Tariff Commission on the employment effects of items 806.30 and 807.00 of the Tariff
Schedules (on which the Department of Commerce study rested in part)
indicated that employment in foreign assembly operations utilising these
provisions was about 121,000 in 1969. While acknowledging that the effects
of the repeal of the items in question on US employment could only be
estimated, the Tariff Commission put forward the view that—

Only a small portion of these jobs would be returned to the US if items 807.00 and
806.30 were repealed. On the other hand, these provisions now provide employment
for about 37,000 people in the US . . . repeal would probably result in only a modest
number of jobs returned to the US, which likely would be more than offset by the
loss of jobs among workers now producing components for export and those who
further process the imported products.[3]

The Tariff Commission's estimate was based on the assumption that
there would be no change—in the form of import restrictions—in existing
conditions, whereas one of the aims of the US trade union movement is,
precisely, to bring about just such a change.

---

[1] National Foreign Trade Council: *The impact of US foreign direct investment on US
employment and trade* . . ., op. cit., p. 10.

[2] US Department of Commerce: *The multinational corporation*, Vol. I: *Studies on US
foreign investment*, op. cit., I: "Policy aspects of foreign investment by US multinational
corporations", p. 28.

[3] US Tariff Commission: *Economic factors affecting the use of items 807.00 and 806.30
of the Tariff Schedules of the United States*, op. cit., pp. 232–233.

Thus the effect of the multinational corporation's activities abroad on employment in the home country is a crucial issue. In the past, when imports into the home country were low or of a non-competing nature, or were balanced with exports, the possible impact of multinational operations on home country employment did not arouse much attention. The commercial activities connected with multinational operations were regarded as normal trade; even when their distinctive corporate nature became apparent, the commodities involved—minerals, petroleum and plantation products—constituted the raw materials for the home country's manufacturing industries and were therefore acceptable to its workers. Now the manufacturing multinational corporation has come to be regarded by trade unions as one of the primary causes of job loss in the home country, and its expansion abroad is thought to reduce employment there directly in two ways: first, through imports of goods which, it is claimed, would otherwise have been manufactured in the home country, and secondly, through the export of goods for foreign markets by the subsidiaries located abroad rather than by plants in the home country. These developments, it is felt, would possibly not have become disruptive of domestic employment without the simultaneous transfer abroad of capital, management techniques, technology and distributive skills by the multinational corporation. Even then, they might not necessarily have become a subject of dispute if they had occurred in a home country with relatively full employment. The fact that Western Europe as a whole has enjoyed a long period of relatively full employment while the United States has had rising unemployment may partly explain why the activities of the multinational corporation and their impact on employment levels have yet to receive anything like the degree of serious investigation in Western European countries that they have been subjected to in the United States.

Yet Western Europe may not be immune from problems similar to those experienced in the United States. It was recently reported that the manufacturers of Rollei photographic equipment, in the Federal Republic of Germany, were able to reduce their prices by some 25 per cent and thus to compete once more with Japanese products in the traditional Rollei markets. This was achieved through lower production costs at the newly established Rollei factory in Singapore, and future plans call for the transfer abroad of at least two-thirds of the firm's total production.[1]

In 1971 Zeiss Ikon was said to have "based its August announcement that it was giving up amateur camera production on the impossibility of producing anything other than the most sophisticated type on a competitive basis in the Federal Republic of Germany". The article reporting this fact compared

---

[1] *Wall Street Journal* (New York), 11 May 1972, p. 1.

Rollei with Zeiss Ikon, the one succeeding by transferring production abroad, the other partly withdrawing from the market because it had "consistently refused to take the road to the Far East".[1] With regard to AEG-Telefunken, the article, which was based on an interview with this firm's managing director, reported: "Now AEG, Germany's best-known radio and tape recorder manufacturer, has given notice that it is up against the same sort of problem. It is too early to say how many of its products will go the way of Zeiss cameras, but there is no doubt that some of them will go by the board and others may well either be assembled from parts manufactured abroad or even be imported under licence. . . ." To show the extent of import penetration in the Federal Republic of Germany, "AEG has produced a rough projection of the share imports will gain in the West German popular electronics market by 1980. To select just a few examples: pocket radios are 100 per cent imported and will remain so; mono radios (58 per cent imported in 1970, 100 per cent as early as 1975); black and white TV will be 85 per cent covered by imports in 1975; cassette tape recorders (98 per cent in 1971, 100 per cent by 1975) . . .".

Early in 1972 Philips Electrologica GmbH, the subsidiary of Philips (Netherlands) in the Federal Republic of Germany, announced the closing of its desk calculator plant because of a reduction in sales due to Japanese import competition.[2]

Up to this point consideration has been given to the effect of multinational operations on employment levels only. Such operations, however, also tend to have an effect on the structure of the labour force within the home country.

Generally speaking, in the developed countries (and most if not all multinational corporations are based in developed countries) the burden of unemployment falls most heavily on workers of low skill and educational attainment, while employment opportunities continue to expand at the opposite end of the skill and educational spectrum. This is a continuous process and represents an upgrading of the labour force as higher levels of technology are used and customer preferences change—provided there are adequate opportunities for retraining and re-employment. Manufacturing processes or lines of industry which are innovational, skill-demanding, highly technological and capital-intensive, such as aircraft, electronics and others, tend to remain where they were established and developed, while the low-skill, labour-intensive manufacturing processes or product lines, such as mass-production methods used in the consumer goods industries, are profitably transferred to other locations where costs are lower. This is especially common when a

---

[1] *Financial Times* (London), 15 Dec. 1971, p. 7.

[2] *L'Usine nouvelle* (Paris), 9 Mar. 1972, p. 117.

production process can be physically broken down into its constituent elements and the labour-intensive elements can be carried out elsewhere. When they are not transferred, they are eventually eliminated by automated processes. Low-skilled workers are then reabsorbed into the labour market with the same or a higher level of skill, once they have been retrained. This is a highly simplified model, showing how the structure of the labour force in the home country changes over time. Because of the constantly shifting nature of the labour force structure, developed countries are continually faced with problems of readaptation, retraining and relocation of workers displaced by this process. In recent years, as the pace of technological change has accelerated, these problems have grown in size and complexity. Governments and employers' and workers' organisations have, with a greater or lesser degree of success, learned to deal with them at the national level. When this situation occurs in an international framework, the complexity of the problems is magnified.

When imports into the home country are non-competitive (that is, when the goods in question are either not produced at all in the home country or only in quantities insufficient to meet demand), employment is unaffected. When, however, the goods imported are of a competitive nature, workers and their skills are involved, for by definition these goods could have been produced in the home country. US workers' organisations have long complained about this form of competition in such product lines as shoes, textiles, clothing, radios, and TV sets, but now they see a further threat in the form of increasing imports of sophisticated, high-technology products. This, the workers' organisations believe, has been due to the rapid dissemination by multinational companies of US technology throughout the world, which, when coupled with productivity rates equalling or only slightly below those in the United States, turn what were once non-competitive goods into competitive goods, with a consequent loss of jobs and skills in the United States. Thus there may be a narrowing of the manufacturing base of the home country and "the question asked by the unions is whether the internationalisation of production may accelerate the reduction in jobs in manufacturing, and thus leave less diversity in jobs and production".[1]

The effect of the various capital and labour combinations in the production of goods, especially consumer goods, has not been investigated enough to reveal whether there are practical optima which could influence decisions to transfer operations abroad or whether firms have over-reacted and turned to foreign production even in cases where they would have been better or equally well off had they remained in the home country.

---

[1] Robert d'A. Shaw: "Foreign investment and global labor", in *Columbia Journal of World Business* (New York), July-Aug. 1971, p. 58.

Manpower adjustment

Though it is not clear to what extent, if any, the foreign operations of multinational corporations result in a net loss of over-all employment opportunities in the home country, it is safe to say that they can generate structural dislocations in the workforce of particular sectors of industry, especially if production requiring the employment of unskilled and low-skilled workers is concentrated abroad, while production involving a high degree of specialisation remains in the home country. A study prepared by the Bureau of Labor Statistics of the US Department of Labor for the Commission on International Trade and Investment Policy (the Williams Commission) concluded that—

in the aggregate a reasonable estimate of the employment displacement of imports is modest when viewed in the perspective of employment changes which normally take place in our dynamic economy. However, imports may have significant employment effects on specific industries, plants, and geographic areas of the country.[1]

In such circumstances manpower adjustment becomes an issue of some importance.

Although the potential adverse impact of competition from imports of foreign goods on business firms has long been recognised in the United States, it was not until the passage of the Trade Expansion Act (TEA) of 1962 that attempts to cover the adjustment problems of workers as well as those of business firms were made. Prior to 1962 the President of the United States could provide increased protection against imports where an industry needed time to adapt its products or its methods to new conditions. The TEA went a step further and opened up the possibility of providing direct assistance to firms or groups of workers to enable them to make the necessary adjustments. For eligibility for adjustment assistance to be established, the following two criteria had to be satisfied: the increased imports must have been the major factor causing injury to the industry, firm or group of workers; and increased imports causing injury to an industry, firm or group of workers must have resulted in major part from concessions granted under trade agreements.

Adjustment assistance for workers under the Act consists of—

(1) trade readjustment allowances which replace unemployment insurance. The weekly allowances are set at 65 per cent of the worker's previous average weekly wage, with a ceiling of 65 per cent of the average weekly wage in manufacturing. These allowances are payable for 52 weeks (not necessarily consecutive) but may be extended a further 26 weeks to com-

---

[1] *United States international economic policy in an interdependent world,* Compendium of papers, Vol. I, op. cit., p. 506.

plete a training programme. If the worker had his sixtieth birthday prior
to his original lay-off he is automatically eligible for 65 weeks of benefits;

(2) full access to counselling, job referral, testing and training programmes
available in his area;

(3) relocation allowances (full moving expenses of the worker and his family
plus a cash amount equal to 2½ times the average weekly manufacturing
wage) if there is no suitable job in his area and there is a suitable job in
another city. No worker can be compelled to move. Unlike refusal to
accept appropriate training, refusal to move is not a reason for losing
eligibility for assistance.[1]

Referring to the adjustment assistance programme, and in particular to
the criteria for eligibility, the Williams Commission stated that in practice
the two criteria were extremely difficult to meet as the Tariff Commission
(which was charged with determining eligibility) interpreted the Act to mean
that increased imports had to be the more important cause of injury than all
other causes combined and similarly gave a rigorous interpretation to the
second criterion. The Williams Commission further pointed out that because
of the difficulties in meeting the two criteria, no affirmative findings of serious
injury had been made between passage of the TEA in October 1962 and
November 1969.[2] Between November 1969 and August 1971, however, 51
petitions were certified, representing 20,660 workers.[3]

In a study by the National Planning Association, the US approach to
adjustment assistance was described as "an *ex post facto* approach, aiming to
repair actual damage and not to anticipate it". The study described what
were felt to be two basic weaknesses of the programme, the first being the
difficulty in distinguishing the degree of importance of the adverse effects of
import competition among the various factors entering into the problems of
an industry or business firm. The second rested on the observation that—

The larger the adjustment problem, the more the *ex post facto* approach becomes
too little and too late. When substantial segments of an increasing number of
industries require help, the task goes beyond that of facilitating the adjustment of

---

[1] For a detailed description of the adjustment assistance programme for both workers
and firms, see "Adjustment assistance", by Stanley D. Metzger, "Trade adjustment assistance", by Marvin M. Fooks, "Adjustment assistance for US firms", prepared by the Bureau
of Domestic Commerce, Department of Commerce, and "Adjustment assistance for workers",
prepared by the Department of Labor, in *United States international economic policy in an
interdependent world*, Compendium of papers, Vol. I, op. cit., Part. II: "Major issues",
section 3: "Governmental responses to competition from imports", pp. 319–394.

[2] *United States international economic policy in an interdependent world*, Report to the
President submitted by the Commission on International Trade and Investment Policy
(Washington, DC, US Government Printing Office, July 1971), p. 50.

[3] National Planning Association: *US foreign economic policy for the 1970s: A new approach
to new realities*, A policy report by an NPA advisory committee, Planning Pamphlet No. 130
(Washington, DC, Nov. 1971), p. 198.

individual firms and small groups of workers. Rather, it becomes one either of modernising entire industries, or large portions of them, with the many different kinds of changes that may be required, or of creating employment opportunities on a large scale, which usually involves the development or redevelopment of entire communities or local regions.[1]

US trade union representatives have been especially critical of this programme, often referring to it as "burial insurance".[2] With regard to the level of benefits, the United Automobile, Aerospace and Agricultural Implement Workers of America (UAW), in a hearing of the US Tariff Commission on 11 May 1970, referred to the "miserly benefits provided in the TEA" and pointed out that the maximum TEA benefit existing at the time was US$85 per week, substantially less than benefits paid under the UAW supplemental unemployment benefit (SUB) plans to workers affected by ordinary lay-offs. In offering specific examples, the union stated—

A laid-off General Motors assembly line worker, with a wife and two children, for example, would receive $114.96 per week in unemployment benefits under the SUB plan. A laid-off die maker in the same company with a similar family would receive $154.88 per week.

Comparing these examples with the above-mentioned maximum TEA benefit of US$85 per week, the union stated that the TEA amount would represent 55.9 per cent of wages to the assembly-line worker (having a current wage of US$152 per week) and only 41.3 per cent to the die maker (having a current wage of US$205.60 per week).[3] On another occasion the Director of Special Projects and Economic Analysis of this union stated—

Those who argue that existing adjustment assistance benefits are "adequate" should be asked if they would accept 35 or 40 per cent of market value as adequate compensation if their homes were condemned so that the land might be used for public purposes. When fringe benefits as well as wages are taken into account, 35 or 40 per cent of normal compensation is what present maximum adjustment assistance benefits amount to for typical workers in major industries.[4]

The study commissioned by the Industrial Union Department of the AFL-CIO from Ruttenberg and Associates said: "The Trade Adjustment Act of 1962 was enacted to provide this kind of assistance [to retrain workers displaced by import competition and to re-establish dislocated businesses]. It was a cruel hoax."[5]

---

[1] National Planning Association: *US foreign economic policy for the 1970s...*, op. cit., pp. 208–209.

[2] Statement by Donald K. Kendall, Chairman of the Emergency Committee for American Trade, in *News Release* (ECAT), 24 Feb. 1972, p. 4.

[3] *Statement of United Automobile, Aerospace and Agricultural Implement Workers of America (UAW) in hearings of United States Tariff Commission on assembled and processed articles, 11 May 1970* (Washington, DC, UAW), pp. 3–4.

[4] National Planning Association: *US foreign economic policy for the 1970s ...*, op. cit., p. 52, footnote 19, statement by Nat Weinberg.

[5] *Needed: A constructive foreign trade policy*, op. cit., pp. 110–111.

The Williams Commission in its report recognised the disruptive effects of economic change in general and the specific dislocations due to foreign competition. It stated—

Workers have acquired substantial stakes in their skills, jobs, homes and communities. They have acquired valuable seniority and pension rights. They are unwilling to bear disproportionately the costs of changes that benefit society as a whole; they look to the government to protect their stakes. Governments have had to assume greater responsibilities for ensuring high levels of employment, social stability, a healthful environment, and other social objectives.[1]

However, while the trade unions tended to dismiss the TEA programme as an inadequate response to the problems of foreign competition, the Commission felt the existing programme should be improved by instituting a series of administrative or legislative changes aimed at remedying its principal shortcomings. These changes included: adequate amounts of assistance available as quickly as possible after eligibility had been certified; greater incentives, including wider benefits, to accept training or relocation; making allowances available for the full period of retraining in addition to retroactive allowances paid during a period of unemployment while awaiting retraining; giving qualified workers the opportunity to pursue technical, professional or academic as well as vocational training; relaxation of the requirement concerning previous work and earnings, thereby enabling recent entrants into the labour force to qualify for the programme; provision of family health benefits for workers in the programme; and provision of subsidies to allow older workers not yet eligible for full social security benefits to enter the social security programme without reduction of benefits. The Commission also stated that a way must be found to protect the pension rights and health and welfare benefits of workers who had to change jobs.[2]

This view was echoed by the Chairman of the Emergency Committee for American Trade (ECAT) on the occasion of the release of its study on 24 February 1972. Mr. Donald M. Kendall said—

It takes no great imagination to realise that international competition causes hardships for some workers in some industries in the United States. The real problem, however, is much greater. In our changing economy, a young person can spend years learning a skill only to find out ten years later that there is no need for it. Because the economy has passed his or her skill by is no reason for the person to be passed by. We must look forward to a time when retraining and relocation are a way of life, a way to a better life, to an upgrading of a person's competence and satisfaction in his or her career. It is inexcusable that instead of a national programme of industrial adaptation that would allow the worker to retain pension and other rights, our economy offers only inadequate training or the dole. It is easy to understand why labour leaders call the present system of adjustment assistance "burial insurance".

---

[1] *United States international economic policy in an interdependent world*, Report, op. cit., p. 7.

[2] Ibid., p. 56.

Mr. Kendall recommended that, as a first step toward a programme of industrial adaptation, the Government initiate a study of all existing programmes. "I think we will find," he said, "that the United States is already far along the road to such a programme, but we are moving by means of overlapping, lopsided, and even conflicting programmes spread casually among dozens of federal, state, and industry actions." [1]

Other than the United States, there are few countries in which competition from imports has required special action on the part of the government. Sweden is one of these.[2] During the 1968 central collective bargaining session in that country, employers in the textile, garment-making and hand-made glass industries stated that they could not give their workers the kind of wage increase which both they and the central trade union organisation (LO) wished, unless there was a moderation of the inflow of imports, partly from developing countries, competing with the output of these industries. On the trade union side, a move towards protection would run contrary to the LO's persistent and strong advocacy of a policy of free trade. However, in the circumstances a "temporary" set of protective measures was supported by the national trade union federations involved. A joint study was then made of the likely prospects of the industries concerned. It was claimed that, because of its labour-intensive nature, the garment-making industry would not survive unless it underwent profound changes. A precondition of its survival was a deliberate switchover to the fashion trade or to other high-quality manufacture; a necessary condition of the success of this approach was the development of a larger market than could be provided by domestic demand alone, and for this strategy to work, great emphasis was needed on marketing and selling, as well as effective management in terms of design and production. The scale of manufacturing units in this sector would have to be enlarged, or, at the least, there would have to be co-operation and co-ordination in the design, production and marketing activities of small manufacturers. As regards textiles, the study claimed that there was considerable scope for capital intensity in the production process and that high-quality fabrics were likely to have good opportunities in export markets. The study recommended that while structural changes were intensified and steps were taken to improve managerial skills, the pressure of imports had to be reduced; but it was a basic premise of the analysis that restraints on imports would be abandoned

---

[1] *News Release* (ECAT), 24 Feb. 1972, p. 4.

[2] The information in this paragraph is taken from Organisation for Economic Co-operation and Development, Social Affairs Division, Programme for Employers and Unions, Regional Trade Union Seminar on International Trade, 7–10 December 1971: *Part IV (a) and (c): Trade union attitudes: Problems of adjustments in developed countries due to trade with less developed countries*, by Santosh Mukherjee (Paris), pp. 18–20.

as soon as these remedial measures had been completed with financial assistance from the Government. As a result, the Government took two steps: legislation was enacted in 1970 which provided for the grant of public money to help bring about the necessary changes in the industries concerned; and through informal discussions, the Government obtained the agreement of exporting countries to a voluntary reduction in the growth rate of their exports to Sweden. The legislation provided that the allocation of the money was to be spread over a four-year period. About 54 per cent of it was to be spent on activities specifically designed to bring about an increase in exports, such as the development of joint sales organisations covering a number of small firms, as well as market research and publicity in potential export markets. Another 21 per cent was to be set aside to provide export credit guarantees, while a quarter of the total funds was to be used for the adaptation and the adjustment training and education of the people in the industries concerned. The legislation went into great detail as to how the funds were to be used: for example, it laid down that a total of 1,440 people should be given training in sales and export techniques. The logic of the Government's measures was that if, at the end of the four-year period, the industries concerned had not been able to reshape themselves, then restrictions on imports would be lifted and the firms manufacturing the products in question would have to go out of business.

In this discussion of the manpower adjustment programmes of the home countries of multinational corporations other than the United States, the frame of reference is limited to Canada, Japan and seven or eight countries in Western Europe.[1] Apart from Canada, where the approach to the adjustment problem is somewhat similar to that in the United States, all of these countries deal with manpower adjustment in the broader context of continuous industrial modernisation and development, and all of them place greater emphasis on comprehensive manpower policies. According to one authority—

The most noteworthy difference between national manpower policies in the United States and those throughout Western Europe is that manpower considerations are far more basic to over-all economic and social policies in the latter countries. In fact, manpower policies characteristically dominate the broader economic and social policies of many of the Western European countries.[2]

Even Canada began moving during the 1960s towards the broader European approach to adjustment through industrial and regional development, estab-

---

[1] The information on adjustment programmes in the various countries is taken from National Planning Association: *US foreign economic policy for the 1970s . . .*, op. cit., pp. 202–207.

[2] John C. Shearer: "Manpower environments confronting American firms in Western Europe", in Alfred Kamin (ed.): *Western European labor and the American corporation* (Washington, DC, Bureau of National Affairs, 1970), p. 377.

lishing programmes designed to foster and assist Canadian industries to expand research and development activities and to help meet the costs and risks involved in introducing new products and methods, through subsidies, loans, tax benefits and technical assistance.

With regard to the remaining countries in Western Europe and Japan, the official programmes designed to stimulate and assist industrial and regional development and the modernisation of industry parallel each other, although varying in degree of emphasis from country to country. For example, France, Italy and Japan largely rely on national economic planning to achieve their desired goals, while the Federal Republic of Germany has strongly emphasised reliance on private initiative and competitive market forces. All these countries have a full range of instruments for facilitating economic adjustment and fostering the development of firms and industries, such as subsidies and loans, tax concessions, technical assistance, training programmes and the use of government purchasing. Other than the United States, only the Federal Republic of Germany has a special programme for facilitating adjustment to import competition, under which low-cost, guaranteed loans are available to companies for the purchase of new capital equipment. However, it appears that owing to the multiplicity of other aids to modernisation and adaptation, comparatively little use has been made of this programme. No special programme exists in the United Kingdom to assist industries to adjust to import competition, although the Government has been reported to be concerned about the impact of imports on domestic producers, especially in the textile industry. Here the Government has compensated companies for reducing their productive capacity, encouraged mergers and provided financial and technical assistance to help the remaining firms to become more efficient.

Within the framework of the European Economic Community as a whole, the main source of adjustment assistance to workers is the European Social Fund. Although the Fund, when set up in 1958, was not intended to deal with workers affected by trade liberalisation or the activities of multinational corporations, it may nevertheless now have application in this area. For example, the "Introduction to the Report on the Development of the Social Situation in the Community in 1971" [1] stated that the development of employment was still affected by different factors, partially linked to the functioning of the Common Market, among which were the increase in world competition resulting in a new distribution of labour, this time on a global level, and the

---

[1] See *Bulletin of the European Communities* (Brussels, Commission of the European Communities), 1972, No. 3, Part One: "Features and documents", pp. 26–32. See also *European Community* (Brussels, European Community Press and Information), June 1971, p. 19, and Nov. 1971, p. 4.

growing influence of multinational enterprises on the employment market because of their investments, the orders they place and the location of their establishments.

The Fund was revised by the Council of Ministers in 1971 and came into operation in its new form on 1 January 1972. As revised, it will help to retrain workers, resettle them and their families, provide unemployment allowances, and inform workers of job vacancies. Like the old Fund, the revised Fund will spend most of its resources in the Community's development regions, where the worst unemployment and redundancy problems exist. Instead of acting as a passive "clearing-house", financing half the cost of retraining and redeployment programmes initiated by the governments of member countries, the Fund will now play a more active role in retraining workers threatened with redundancy before their existing jobs actually disappear. The Fund will act in two ways: (1) it will help workers whose jobs may be threatened as a direct result of continuing integration in the Community, by covering the cost of retraining and, in certain circumstances, income support during retraining, and also resettlement, where necessary; and (2) it will, jointly with the government concerned, pay for retraining and resettlement in areas of structural unemployment not resulting directly from the Community's existence. The principle of an incomes guarantee under this second set of measures has also been approved, though this part of the scheme will not come into force immediately. The Council of Ministers also agreed that the two sides of industry should in future be more closely associated with the running of the Fund.

In addition to national programmes of manpower adjustment assistance and, in the case of the European Economic Community, regional programmes, there exist in many home countries of multinational corporations programmes negotiated between firms and trade unions. In the United States the United Automobile Workers' supplemental unemployment benefit scheme, mentioned earlier in this section, is an example. However, most if not all non-governmental programmes are designed either to cover redundancy in general, regardless of the cause, or the specific case of employment termination or lay-off due to technological change. No information is available on schemes which may have been negotiated to cover more specifically redundancies and dislocations arising in connection with the operations of multinational corporations.

Measures to reduce the cost to workers of adjustment to change vary widely in their details. A study of actual cases of plant closure by multinational corporations in the home country, or of reductions in the labour force of their plants, would no doubt help to reveal what kinds of special measures would be suitable in such cases. The Conventions and Recommendations adopted by the International Labour Conference [1] lay down standards and principles and indicate certain general measures which could appropriately be applied to manpower adjustment programmes.

The foregoing is not intended to provide a complete catalogue of the kinds of adjustment assistance that may be provided. The problems of adaptation to import competition in the home country are similar to those of adaptation to other structural changes, which occur continually in advanced economies. The degree in which the problems differ and call for specific answers can only be discovered by detailed analysis of the structural dislocations to which the operations of multinational corporations may give rise.

EFFECTS IN THE HOST COUNTRY

Foreign direct investment almost inevitably affects employment in the host country, but the extent of its impact and the particular aspects of employment on which it has the greatest effect vary widely, depending, among other things, on the level of industrialisation achieved by the host country. In an industrially advanced country the question of whether the investment represents, on the one hand, the takeover of an existing firm or, on the other, the setting up of new production capacity, is much more important than the questions of whether it has an impact on income distribution in the host country and of what level of technology it brings in—two questions that are often of vital interest to a developing country. This does not mean that each question is exclusively a matter for one or the other type of host country. Indeed, technology, for example, has been a much discussed issue in Western Europe [2] for the past decade, especially in relation to US multinational corporations and the question of whether they bring more or less new technology into

---

[1] The relevant Conventions and Recommendations are: the Employment Service Recommendation, 1948; the Vocational Guidance Recommendation, 1949; the Social Security (Minimum Standards) Convention, 1952; the Vocational Training Recommendation, 1962; the Termination of Employment Recommendation, 1963; and the Employment Policy Convention and Recommendation, 1964. For the texts of these instruments, see ILO: *Conventions and Recommendations adopted by the International Labour Conference, 1919–1966* (Geneva, 1966).

[2] See, for example, Organisation for Economic Co-operation and Development: *Gaps in technology: General report*, Report prepared for discussion by the participants at the Third Ministerial Meeting on Science of OECD Countries, March 1968 (Paris, 1968); the sector reports on scientific instruments, electronic components, electronic computers, plastics, pharmaceuticals, non-ferrous metals and machine tools, published by the OECD in its Gaps in Technology between Member Countries series; and studies published by the Commission of the European Communities, such as *L'industrie électronique des pays de la Communauté et les investissements américains*, Etudes, série Industrie, No. 1 (Brussels, 1969) and *La recherche et le développement en électronique dans les pays de la Communauté et les principaux pays tiers*, Etudes, série Industrie, No. 2 (Brussels, 1969).

European host countries than they take out. However, the appropriateness of the technology brought into a European host country by the subsidiary of a US multinational is hardly, if ever, a subject of discussion, whereas in developing countries the level of technology brought in by a multinational corporation's subsidiary—in particular, its capital or labour intensity—has been the focal point of a great deal of discussion in recent years.[1]

Employment generation

It can be argued that foreign investment brings benefits to the host community which, like employment itself, are both economic and social. These benefits may be direct or indirect and may be evident immediately, in the short run, or not for some time. The negative effects on the community when a multinational employer shuts down or transfers operations are of a similar order. As in so much concerning the activities of multinational corporations, there are many individual examples, but little objective research has been carried out. Even the basic economic magnitudes are elusive. In this section some examples are given which illustrate, though incompletely, the impact of multinational corporations on employment. While they provide no measure of the changes over time in local employment growth, or of the secondary impact on employment in the community and on other aspects of manpower, they do at least show the multinational corporation as an economic and social force in the host country.

A group of 18 foreign manufacturing and banking firms operating in the Campinas area of Brazil attempted to determine the net benefits derived by the country from their activities. The most important impact was that on employment: the 18 subsidiaries and their suppliers employed 40,595 workers, who themselves directly supported another 161,000 Brazilians. The total annual payrolls were calculated to be 13,200 million cruzeiros; the total purchasing power created was 37,000 million cruzeiros; total taxes and social charges paid were 11,500 million cruzeiros. The total savings in foreign exchange during the year under study amounted to US$125.6 million (calculated as the amounts that would have been spent to import products equivalent

---

[1] See, for example, the series of research reports published by the United Nations Institute for Training and Research dealing with the question of enterprise-to-enterprise arrangements in the transfer of technology and skills to developing countries; Organisation for Economic Co-operation and Development: *The transfer of technology*, by Edward P. Hawthorne (Paris, 1971); W. Paul Strassmann: *Technological change and economic development: The manufacturing experience of Mexico and Puerto Rico* (Ithaca (New York), Cornell University Press, 1968); and Jack Baranson: *Industrial technologies for developing economies*, Praeger special studies in international economics and development (New York, Praeger, 1969).

to the firms' production, plus the firms' total exports less imported components and equipment).[1]

In the United Kingdom, Professor Dunning found that the main advantage of the participation of US firms was that it offered a package deal of new products, money capital, knowledge, the training of labour in new skills, access to new markets and the escalation of competitive levels in the country.[2] With specific regard to employment in one of the United Kingdom's development areas, he quoted the Scottish Council as stating that a substantial number of North American firms had been attracted to Scotland, that the investments of these enterprises amounted to US$162 million in 1966 and that in that year they accounted for 8.3 per cent of all manufacturing employment and 24 per cent of manufactured exports. Their rate of growth of output was more than three times that of domestic firms.[3] Writing in March 1971, Professor Dunning stated that, directly or indirectly, US firms had added to total employment in the United Kingdom. In the less prosperous areas of Wales, Scotland and north-east England it was estimated that they were providing jobs for about 125,000 people, who would otherwise have remained unemployed.[4]

Magnitude of employment

According to one estimate, US-controlled foreign subsidiaries engaged in manufacturing and extraction employed about 49,000 US nationals and some 5.5 million local workers in 1966.[5] The US Department of Commerce reports[6] that majority-owned foreign affiliates of US manufacturing corporations employed in 1966 slightly over 3 million workers, of whom only 10,594 were

---

[1] Business International: *National governments and international corporations*, Paper prepared by Business International for the Business International Roundtable, Geneva, July 1967, excerpted from the briefing paper on "Corporate planning today for tomorrow's world market" for the Business International Roundtable for Chief Executive Officers, Bermuda, December 1966.

[2] John H. Dunning: *The role of American investment in the British economy*, with two case studies by W. G. Jensen, PEP broadsheet No. 507 (London, Political and Economic Planning, Feb. 1969), p. 151.

[3] Ibid., p. 123.

[4] John H. Dunning: "US direct investment in the United Kingdom and national economic objectives", in *Quarterly Review* (Rome, Banca Nazionale del Lavoro), Mar. 1971, p. 51.

[5] Raymond Vernon: *Sovereignty at bay: The multinational spread of US enterprises* (London, Longman, 1971), p. 156.

[6] US Department of Commerce: *US direct investments abroad, 1966*, Part II: *Investment position, financial and operating data*, Group 2: *Preliminary report on foreign affiliates of US manufacturing industries*, A supplement to the *Survey of Current Business* (Washington, DC, Jan. 1972), p. 61.

Table 10. Employment in majority-owned foreign affiliates of United States manufacturing corporations, by industry, 1966

Industry	US employees	Foreign employees	Total employment
Food products	472	238 981	239 453
Paper and allied products	190	92 600	92 790
Chemicals and allied products	1 070	331 113	332 183
Primary and fabricated metals	527	213 407	213 934
Non-electrical machinery	774	379 511	380 285
Electrical machinery	406	388 498	388 904
Transportation equipment	869	459 528	460 397
Other	6 286	897 141	903 427
All industries	10 594	3 000 779	3 011 373

Source: US Department of Commerce: *US direct investments abroad*, 1966, Part II: *Investment position, financial and operating data*, Group 2: *Preliminary report on foreign affiliates of US manufacturing industries*, A supplement to the *Survey of Current Business* (Washington, DC, Jan. 1972), p. 61.

US nationals. Some 717,832 of the 3 million, or 23.8 per cent, were employed in developing countries, while 76 per cent were working in economically advanced countries. Table 10 shows employment in subsidiaries of US multinational manufacturing corporations in 1966, broken down by industry. These figures give an indication of the magnitude of employment in the foreign subsidiaries of US manufacturing firms, but they do not throw any light on changes over time. One study on Latin America, using data from a 1960 Department of Commerce document, estimated that in 1957 US affiliates in Latin America (excluding Cuba) employed a total of 319,000 workers in manufacturing.[1] By 1966 the number of foreign employees in the Latin American affiliates of US manufacturing companies had reached 534,233, an average annual increase of slightly over 8 per cent.[2] This is evidence of an employment-generating effect, at least in one developing region of the world. In a survey carried out in 1966 by the American Chamber of Commerce in the United Kingdom, it was estimated that total employment in 161 US manufacturing subsidiaries in that country was 404,000.[3] In 1970 the number of people employed in 270 US industrial subsidiaries in the United Kingdom was said to be 481,268, an increase of 25,858 over the figure for 1969.[4] However, the

[1] Herbert K. May: *The effects of United States and other foreign investment in Latin America*, An interim report to the Council for Latin America, 27 December 1969 (New York, Council of the Americas, third printing, Jan. 1971), p. 59.

[2] US Department of Commerce: *US direct investments abroad, 1966*, loc. cit.

[3] Dunning: *The role of American investment in the British economy*, op. cit., p. 128.

[4] American Chamber of Commerce (United Kingdom): *American manufacturers in the United Kingdom: Exports, employment, research, 1970*, A summary based upon replies from 270 American industrial subsidiaries in the UK (London, n.d.).

US Department of Commerce figure for employment in subsidiaries of US manufacturing firms in the United Kingdom in 1966 was 582,269.[1] These examples illustrate the difficulty of assessing accurately the effect of subsidiaries on employment in the host country.

Although it is clear that foreign direct investment does generate employment in the host country, this does not necessarily mean that the employment would not have been generated without the presence of the foreign investment. It is conceivable that in certain cases domestic producers might have played the same role as the foreign subsidiary in this respect. Moreover, in a host country with virtually full employment, a foreign subsidiary establishing new production facilities can only employ the local workers it needs by outbidding domestic firms—which could possibly arouse resentment and drive marginally profitable domestic firms out of business. The latter result might not, however, be bad in the long run, inasmuch as outdated (and presumably uneconomic) methods would be replaced by modern and efficient methods, as was reported to have occurred in France.[2]

Labour availability

When setting up a subsidiary, the multinational corporation is likely to carry out a wage survey at the potential location of its subsidiary in order to determine the going rates for the various jobs and skills it needs, and then to compare the results with the total it is willing to spend on the subsidiary's workforce. This may influence its decision with regard to the type of technology to be used by the subsidiary, the number of workers to be recruited, and other matters.

The question of how a firm determines the degree of labour availability is a crucial one but difficult to answer with any precision. It was reported that for the General Motors Company "the availability of labour was the biggest factor in picking Antwerp for a new plant".[3] Whatever else this may mean, it would seem to imply that the company expected to be able to recruit and continue to employ the number of workers it needed, at a total cost remaining within limits that would enable the company to realise the expected profits from the foreign operation. The concept of labour availability is fluid: one firm may consider a labour market too "tight"; another, even in the same line of production, may find that the manpower situation is suited to its

---

[1] US Department of Commerce: *US direct investments abroad, 1966*, loc. cit.

[2] Gilles Y. Bertin: "Foreign investment in France", in Isaiah A. Litvak and Christopher J. Maule (eds.): *Foreign investment: The experience of host countries*, Praeger special studies in international economics and development (New York, Praeger, 1970), pp. 105 and 116.

[3] *Business Week* (New York), 12 Feb. 1966.

needs. Moreover, the adequacy of labour factors is not likely to be judged in isolation but rather within the context of the expected over-all profitability of the subsidiary or even of the multinational corporation's activities as a whole. Whatever a particular company's notion of manpower availability may be, the labour factor is a key element in the pre-investment surveys carried out by multinational corporations.

Some considerations specific to industrialised host countries

The employment effect of business takeovers

Multinational corporations make foreign investments either by establishing new facilities or by acquiring existing firms, with or without participation by local firms or other foreign firms. New investment has clear economic advantages for the host country as long as there is neither full employment nor overcapacity in the sector of industry concerned: the immediate results tend to be employment expansion, regional economic stimulation, the establishment of supplies and services, improvements to current technology, external economies, and other efficiency- and employment-stimulating effects. As regards the acquisition of existing firms, however, the advantages, if any, are more difficult to ascertain. Possibly the key question to be asked here concerns the use to which the sellers put their new liquid funds.[1] If the sellers are nationals, familiar with the economic environment, they may venture into new productive activities. But the sellers may also be foreigners, as, for example, when one multinational corporation disposes of its foreign subsidiary to another. What actually happens in such cases is not known.

Another important question concerning the transfer of ownership is whether the original owner was in difficulty—perhaps faced with closure—and whether the new owner is able to overcome the problems in the short or the long run. If the answers to both questions are in the affirmative, this means that economic and employment losses have been averted and that imputed savings have been made in the social expenditures of individuals and the government, who would otherwise have had to draw on whatever reserves were available in order to face the inevitable hardships.

With specific regard to employment, one of the most frequently expressed fears concerning the takeover of a host country facility by a multinational corporation is that the management will be replaced or that the new owners will institute reorganisation and rationalisation measures leading to redun-

---

[1] For an analysis of liquidity preference in such a situation, see Charles P. Kindleberger: *American business abroad: Six lectures on direct investment* (New Haven (Connecticut) and London, Yale University Press, 1969), pp. 94–99.

dancies in the workforce. The Government of France is reported to "screen investment projects so that they conform to the economic goals of the [national] plan and so that their activities conform to French standards with respect to exporting, research and development, employment policies and labour relations".[1] In the United Kingdom, when the Chrysler Corporation took over Rootes, the Government required certain guarantees from Chrysler to ensure that the firm retained a British outlook.[2]

Foreign investments in depressed areas

During the 1950s and early 1960s the governments of European countries that were in serious need of capital restricted its outflow and offered inducements to foreign investors. Special efforts were made to disperse industrial investments, particularly into areas of growing unemployment. The incentive programmes were generally designed to attract any potential investor, whether foreign or national, but it was foreign corporations that made the greatest use of them.[3] Some of the inducements are still in force, though modified.

The United Kingdom Board of Trade, for example, in addition to constructing and letting industrial and other premises, provided grants of 35 per cent of the cost of erecting or expanding buildings and cash grants of up to 40 per cent of the price of new equipment, special depreciation rates, and loans or grants for general purposes. Other government agencies assisted in training programmes, the transfer of workers and the provision of basic services.[4]

Belgium does not grant special advantages to foreign investments as such, but it does have industrial development legislation designed to stimulate economic recovery in the depressed regions of the country, such as the old coalmining areas. The assistance provided takes the form of a rebate on interest payments, interest-free loans, government guarantees, subsidies, the construction of industrial buildings, and tax exemptions. According to government figures[5], foreign investment represented 35 per cent of the total invest-

---

[1] Bertin, op. cit., p. 120.

[2] For details of the Government's requirements, see ILO: *General report*, Report I, Metal Trades Committee, Ninth Session, Geneva, 1971, p. 165.

[3] Jack N. Behrman: *Some patterns in the rise of the multinational enterprise*, Research paper No. 18 (Chapel Hill, University of North Carolina, Graduate School of Business Administration, Mar. 1969), p. 18.

[4] Ibid. The relevance of such measures as far as multinationals are concerned can be seen from the estimate made by Professor John Dunning in 1971, mentioned earlier in this chapter, that in the less prosperous areas of Wales, Scotland and north-east England, subsidiaries of US firms were providing 125,000 jobs for people who would otherwise have remained unemployed.

[5] Léon Derwa: "Foreign investment in Belgium", in Litvak and Maule, op. cit., pp. 66–75.

ment subject to this legislation between 1956 and 1967. The dire need for capital had been accentuated by the continued movement of industry from northern to southern France, which entailed the loss of their jobs for thousands of Belgian workers who had commuted daily across the border.[1]

In 1967 the Netherlands reintroduced incentives to attract industry into several depressed mining areas. Measures included grants equal to 25 per cent of fixed assets, subsidies covering up to the first 3 per cent of the interest on loans, and long-term loans.[2]

In France, despite a sometimes critical attitude on the part of the Government to some foreign investment plans, the provincial authorities have consistently favoured any firm that will increase employment. The willingness of foreign companies to set up facilities in depressed areas has gained the support of the provincial authorities in arguing the companies' case before the central Government. Both Texas Instruments and Fairchild Camera received a great measure of support from central and local officials when establishing their subsidiaries in southern France.[1]

The Government of the United States also offers inducements to invest in depressed areas. The aids provided are available to foreign investors, although there has been some questioning by Congress of the appropriateness of their use for foreigners. State and municipal governments have sought to attract foreign investments, and Alaska has relied significantly on investments from Japan to finance oil and gas exploration and development, and forestry and fishery operations.[2]

Although several of these incentives have been of real use in stabilising employment and providing new jobs in many areas, the effects on total employment, the utilisation of available skills and the costs of readaptation, for example, have not been comprehensively analysed. Nor has any over-all assessment been made of the extent to which multinational corporations react differently from domestic firms to inducements and incentives.

Some considerations specific to developing host countries

Developing countries and technology levels

In the economic progress of developing countries there is probably no other factor as important as the choice of technology for the production of goods. Technology has the greatest impact on employment: on the numbers

---

[1] Behrman, op. cit., p. 19.

[2] Ibid., p. 20.

employed, on the types of jobs offered and skills needed, on the diversification of product lines and consequently on the range of skills developed, and on the current and future structure of the labour force. Owing to its crucial role in the development process, more has probably been written about technology than about any other aspect, and a great deal is being learned about the transfer of technology to developing countries. However, this knowledge is to a large extent theoretical, and large gaps remain in our understanding of the subject, especially as regards the impact of technology on manpower in the developing countries.

The role of the multinational corporation in the development process is not clear. The Secretary-General of the United Nations, in a report to the Economic and Social Council on the findings of the third in a series of panels held to consider foreign investment, stated—

> The Panel considered that foreign investment carried out within the context of the host country's national development programmes or policies could confer many benefits on that country, including increased output and incomes, higher employment and productivity, the transfer of management and production techniques and expansion of exports and tax revenues.[1]

A report by the UNCTAD secretariat to the Third Session of the United Nations Conference on Trade and Development summed up the relationship between private foreign investment and development in the following terms:

> In recent years private foreign investment has played a substantial part in transferring capital and skills to the developing countries. But this is not necessarily the same thing as contributing to development. There are wide differences of opinion on the impact private foreign investment has had in the past, and on the part it might play in the future.... The basic problem ... is that the interests of foreign companies and host governments are not necessarily the same.[2]

Although the business practices of the subsidiary of a multinational corporation in a developing country have an important effect on the country's development and hence on its manpower policies, the subsidiary's most direct relationship to manpower is seen in its choice of technology.

Much of the technology introduced into the developing countries by the multinational corporation derives directly from the methods used by the corporation in its home country or by its subsidiaries in industrialised countries.

---

[1] United Nations: *Fiscal and financial matters: Promotion of private foreign investment in developing countries*, Report of the Secretary-General to the 53rd Session of the Economic and Social Council (doc. E/5114, 31 Mar. 1972; mimeographed), pp. 1–2.

[2] UNCTAD, Secretariat: *Financial resources for development: Private foreign investment in its relationship to development*, United Nations Conference on Trade and Development, Third Session, Santiago, Chile, April 1972 (Geneva, doc. TD/134, 17 Nov. 1971: mimeographed), pp. 2 and 4.

It is usually advanced technology, designed for large-scale production and reflecting the fact that in industrialised countries capital is cheap compared with labour. It may therefore be questioned whether the type of technology introduced into a developing country is always well adapted to the new environment. One authority considers that there may be a misuse of local resources in so far as "too much capital and too little labour are used, given the relative price and supply of those local factors".[1]

However, the choice of technology tends also to be dictated by the particular industry concerned and by the product itself, which limit the possibilities of substituting labour for machinery or otherwise making use of the abundant manpower available in the host country. A study published by the United Nations Institute for Training and Research (UNITAR) found that—

in many if not most large-scale manufacturing operations, the opportunity for choosing from among the available technologies a more economically efficient and at the same time labour-intensive technique is extremely limited. . . . There is a consensus that such successful modifications as have been made have resulted from disaggregating the production function and seeking out those operations that may be effectively modified, notably in the handling of materials in the plant. . . . Foreign firms have looked into the possibilities with reasonable care and have made adaptations mainly in materials handling operations and in construction operations as well as in the simpler repetitive operations in technologically unsophisticated forms of food processing, pharmaceutical packaging and the like.[2]

An example given in another UNITAR study related to a Japanese glass company operating a subsidiary in India which was about half the size of the company's plant in the home country but which employed three times as many workers by using manual methods for cutting sheet glass, transporting raw materials within the plant and crushing coal.[3]

Not nearly enough is known about the reasons for which multinational corporations choose a particular level of technology when setting up subsidiaries in developing host countries. For example, it was found that subsidiaries of US firms in the Philippines and Mexico did indeed use more capital per worker than their local counterparts, but this was accounted for by the heavier investment they made in buildings and inventories; the firms did not seem to use more equipment per worker than their local counterparts.[4] Similarly, a study of sample firms in Jamaica and Kenya showed that the scope for

---

[1] Vernon, op. cit., p. 181.

[2] Walter A. Chudson: *The international transfer of commercial technology to developing countries*, UNITAR research reports, No. 13 (New York, United Nations Institute for Training and Research, 1971), pp. 25–26.

[3] Terutumo Ozawa: *Transfer of technology from Japan to developing countries*, UNITAR research reports, No. 7 (New York, United Nations Institute for Training and Research, 1971), p. 13.

[4] R. Hal Mason: *The transfer of technology and the factor proportions problem: The Philippines and Mexico*, UNITAR research reports, No. 10 (New York, United Nations Institute for Training and Research, n.d.).

substituting labour for capital would be small in the short term, and should a local producer take over the production hitherto carried out by a foreign concern, it was assumed that he would choose the same or similar production techniques.[1]

The foregoing seems to indicate that the possibility of a multinational's subsidiary making an additional contribution to employment generation in a developing host country by increasing the labour intensity of its technology is a subject which needs far more investigation. At present, the ILO's World Employment Programme missions to a number of developing countries are throwing some light on the role played by foreign direct investment in developing countries, particularly with regard to the various aspects of manpower.

Vocational training

The training activities of multinational corporations vary greatly, depending on the country where their subsidiaries are located, the economic sector in which they operate (mining, manufacturing, plantations), the type of production process used (capital-intensive or otherwise), the level of skills required, the local employment market situation, whether or not the enterprise is newly established, and other factors.

From the information available, there is no evidence that the problems faced by multinational corporations in connection with training within the firm up to the supervisory and technical level differ very much from those faced by indigenous enterprises at an equivalent level of development and located in the same economic and cultural environment. For example, the subsidiaries of US multinationals operating in the industrialised countries of Western Europe have approximately the same training problems as domestic firms and use similar approaches to solve them. Accordingly, this section will deal primarily with the training activities of multinational corporations in the developing countries.

The multinational corporation has an important role to play in countries where indigenous enterprises at a similar or equivalent level of development do not yet exist or are relatively new. Very often the foreign subsidiaries serve as vehicles of technology and organisational know-how by introducing techniques and processes that are new in the countries concerned and by training local personnel to high levels of skill and in new occupations. It is

---

[1] Paul Streeten: *The flow of financial resources: Balance-of-payments effects of private foreign investment*, United Nations Conference on Trade and Development, Trade and Development Board, Committee on Invisibles and Financing Related to Trade, Fourth Session, Geneva, July 1970 (Geneva, doc. TD/B/C.3/79/Add.2, 21 May 1970; mimeographed).

widely held that in this way the multinational corporation could constitute an essential element in the industrialisation of developing countries. However, the extent to which the multinational corporation participates in the development of human resources in the host country depends on the type of activity engaged in by its subsidiaries and on the attitudes of these subsidiaries and of the multinational's headquarters.

In addition to the need for a subsidiary to make arrangements to ensure the continuous availability of a workforce that is adequate both in numbers and in levels and range of skills, training arrangements often have to extend to such basic matters as the adaptation of the worker to an industrial environment. In a country as far advanced in development as Brazil, for example, a multinational automobile assembly plant in Recife reported that it took from three to six months for a newly recruited worker to become fully effective.[1] It is, however, difficult to separate special training measures necessitated by the newness of the plant, its products or its manufacturing process from measures which would be normal in a plant of a given size, set up in a country or area that is subject to a given set of regulations and practices.

The role of multinational corporations in the training field was the subject of a pilot survey of the training, at all levels of the enterprise, given by such corporations based in Members of the Organisation for Economic Co-operation and Development (OECD). It was found that the number of persons from developing countries trained by these multinationals in the home countries of the corporations substantially exceeded the number of such persons undergoing officially financed training in those countries. Lack of data prevented an accurate assessment of the situation in the developing countries, but there were indications that the part played by the private sector (that is, by the subsidiaries of multinational corporations based in OECD countries) was very important as compared with the training financed in the developing countries by the governments of the OECD countries.[2]

In some countries the training activities of companies, including subsidiaries of multinational corporations, are linked to those of the government. For example, in Colombia industry obtains most of its skilled manpower by co-operating closely with the national vocational training body, the Servicio Nacional de Aprendizaje (SENA). The extent of this co-operation can be seen from the fact that all SENA students are sponsored by firms, and if the trainee is an apprentice the firm undertakes to pay him one-half the minimum wage of the country while he is in training. If the trainee is a worker

---

[1] Business International Corporation: *Brazil: New business power in Latin America* (New York, May 1971), p. 23.

[2] Organisation for Economic Co-operation and Development: *Pilot survey on technical assistance extended by private enterprise* (Paris, 1967), p. 23.

upgrading his skills, the firm pays him somewhat less than his regular wage. SENA apprentice training takes three years and consists of six-month periods of formal training alternating with equal periods of training on the job.[1]

In many cases large enterprises have their own training centres either in the host or in the home country. For example, at a pilot plant set up in 1961 in Utrecht (Netherlands) by Philips Gloeilampenfabrieken many of the conditions prevailing in Africa are simulated. Both Europeans and workers from developing countries are trained there, mainly in the production of radios, television sets and components. Special efforts are made to solve technical problems on the spot without sophisticated equipment or the advice of specialised technicians. Under the limited conditions of the pilot plant, use is made of simplified production methods, and in seeking to solve problems both staff and trainees have been forced to innovate.[2]

Apart from job-oriented training, the plants of a number of multinational corporations arrange for other types of training, normally shorter in duration and often provided in the undertaking during working time. Such training can include: induction training to familiarise new workers with the enterprise; further training to improve the general educational qualifications of existing personnel, with a view to meeting new training requirements in the future; the provision of supplementary knowledge and skills to increase a worker's versatility and occupational mobility; and supervisory training, with a view to the rapid replacement of expatriate staff. In some European countries the plants of multinational corporations also give language training for migrant workers; in developing countries language training may be required in some cases, but more frequent are literacy courses for workers at the unskilled and semi-skilled levels. At one time it was reported that the General Electric Company in Brazil provided basic literacy and arithmetic courses for employees, with the employee contributing half of the required time, while the company paid for the other half and met all the costs of the courses.[3]

In a series of case studies conducted by the Special Committee on the International Corporation of the International Chamber of Commerce it was found that "in general, the obstacles most frequently cited by companies as impeding their efforts to transfer technology arise out of shortcomings in the educational systems of the host country or in the linguistic ability of local employees". The report on the case studies stated: "In many developing

---

[1] Business International Corporation: *Solving Latin American business problems*, 1968–69 edition (New York, Aug. 1968), pp. 118–119.

[2] Idem: *Prospects for business in developing Africa* (New York, Aug. 1970), pp. 70–71.

[3] Theodore Geiger: *The General Electric Company in Brazil*, Ninth case study in an NPA series on United States business performance abroad (Washington, DC, National Planning Association, 1961), p. 61.

countries functional weaknesses in the educational system persist, which can, for example, mean that the basic education needed as a prerequisite for training in skills such as accountancy is lacking.'' [1]

The plants of multinational corporations have, as a rule, the same obligations as indigenous enterprises in the field of vocational training: they have to pay the same training levy, where such exists; they have to employ the same quota of apprentices; and they have to observe national training standards. In many cases it is reported that these plants go further than their legal obligations and engage in a variety of training activities in the host country, such as sitting on examination boards, working in and with vocational training councils and human resources planning bodies, and helping in the elaboration of training standards. In some cases subsidiaries have established schools or centres open to persons other than their own employees and have put their personnel and facilities at the disposal of technical schools and universities. These activities are based on business considerations. By increasing the educational levels and qualifications of its employees, the subsidiary contributes directly to the increase of its own productivity and to the efficient utilisation of its workforce. By entering into training activities of various kinds in the community, the subsidiary helps to form a pool of manpower qualified to the level required for future use in the firm.

The impact of the subsidiary of a multinational corporation on local undertakings can be, and often is, considerable but may not always be positive. The local firms sometimes complain that foreign subsidiaries poach their trained workers and attract the best graduates of the vocational training schools by offering better remuneration and fringe benefits.[2] However, the reverse can also happen, as illustrated by the case of a subsidiary in Ghana of the United Africa Company, distributor for Caterpillar equipment in that country. Here the firm originally recruited students from two of Ghana's top technical training colleges for a training programme designed for technicians and specialists. These students had high-school diplomas, possessed a good general knowledge and were in fact overqualified for the jobs envisaged for them. After two years of training they were greatly sought after, especially by government agencies, and, faced with the choice between attractive government posts and low-rung initial appointments in the firm, a good many left for government jobs.[3]

---

[1] International Chamber of Commerce: *The international corporation and the transfer of technology*, Report adopted by the Special Committee on the International Corporation, approved by the Executive Committee of the ICC (Paris, Apr. 1972), pp. 7 and 8.

[2] The question of multinational corporations and wages in host countries is taken up in Chapter 3 of this report.

[3] Business International Corporation: *Prospects for business in developing Africa*, op. cit., p. 71.

The complaint that subsidiaries of multinationals poach the better workers often leads the government of a host country to the conclusion that an additional training effort on its part is required, which in turn raises the question of who should pay for the additional effort needed.

It is sometimes asserted that because the training programmes of multinational corporations are designed to fulfil their own needs they do not necessarily suit the over-all needs of the host country. On the one hand, it is said that subsidiaries of multinational corporations which use capital-intensive equipment are likely to "overtrain" their workers, in the sense that these workers acquire skills and a degree of specialisation that are not needed elsewhere in the host country's economy. The question which then arises is what these workers would do if a reduction in the subsidiary's workforce or a plant closure became necessary. On the other hand, it has been suggested that in some cases multinational corporations train nationals of the host countries only at low levels of skill, which prevents them from entering occupations with better career prospects in the technical or managerial field. In both cases, as with so many aspects of multinational operations, the information necessary to obtain a balanced and complete view of the situation is lacking.

Generally speaking, it can be said that the subsidiaries of multinational corporations in developing host countries have had a beneficial effect on training, as a result of their own efforts to train personnel in the firms, their co-operation with government training schools and centres and with private industrial training schemes, their enforcement of quality control standards on suppliers (which necessitates training programmes in supplier industries), the example they set for local firms to follow, their contribution to the raising of general education levels, and their creation, in a given cultural environment, of the occupational attitudes necessary in an industrial society. Nevertheless, as has been shown by some examples cited in this chapter, there are instances where a subsidiary's training activities have given rise to difficulties and problems which deserve serious attention.

Management development

The nature of the management training and development provided by a multinational corporation in its subsidiaries may depend upon one or more of a number of factors.

Firstly, the size of the subsidiary may influence the costs and benefits of organising management training in the host country as compared with those of sending members of the staff for training in the country of the parent company.

A second factor is the strategy of the parent company, as reflected in the degree of decentralisation in its decision making. The more centralised the company's strategy is, the more the emphasis is likely to be on developing managers for subsidiaries to implement rather than to make policy. However, in view of the declared policy of many multinational corporations to pursue a programme of decentralisation, especially in personnel and other matters affected by local needs and requirements, the policy-making aspects of management development may be as important as the policy-implementing aspects.

A third factor is the level of technology employed by the subsidiary. The older multinational corporations, such as Unilever, Nestlé and British-American Tobacco, employ skills and technologies some of which are not particularly advanced and which can be acquired by technically trained national staff. On the whole, the strength of these older corporations lies in the over-all efficiency of their operations and their recourse to the large reservoir of staff, capital and management expertise found in international operations. Many of the new multinational corporations, on the other hand, employ more advanced technologies. For example, when IBM installed plants in Argentina, Brazil and Chile, it drew on the advanced knowledge of data processing derived from an investment of US$2,000 million in research. In such cases, an understanding in depth of the technology involved is important for effective top management, and the training and promotion of nationals would be affected accordingly.

A fourth factor of importance is the availability of local talent. A US corporation establishing itself in Europe would be able to recruit experienced and qualified persons for all grades of management. The chief executive in Europe is often a European. In a developing country local personnel with the necessary managerial background and experience may not be available. This would imply a larger initial proportion of expatriate managers and a different training problem.

These considerations, amongst others, will condition the range and depth of the management training offered to those employed by a multinational corporation in its subsidiaries. However, most multinational corporations appear to be aware of the need for continuous training at all levels, and their example has often stimulated management thinking in host countries. The practices of these corporations have frequently been held up as models for other businesses to follow. Their management practices and procedures not only are more advanced than those prevailing generally in developing countries but are often more advanced than those applied in some of the industrially developed countries. Their advantageous position stems primarily from the fact that their management practices adapt successfully to varying environments. Where a multinational has established a subsidiary, the managements of indigenous enterprises hear at first hand of new procedures, such as modern techniques of recruitment, selection and training, job analysis, organisation and inventory control, and frequently see them in operation. Some executives, following their training and a period of experience in the subsidiary of a multinational, may leave the firm and take positions with local companies, thus disseminating the modern management practices of the multinational's subsidiary.

Generally speaking, the multinational corporation runs courses for middle and junior management in the country in which its subsidiary is situated, supplementing them with training in other countries for selected personnel. ILO experience is that the multinational corporations send participants to the courses which are offered, with ILO assistance, by productivity and management centres, and that they generally support all such efforts to upgrade local management. They are also generous in placing lecture rooms, equipment and even visiting lecturers at the disposal of these centres. On the other hand, it has been reported that it is often difficult to secure places for outsiders on company courses.[1]

Most multinational corporations face the fact that expatriate staff must eventually be replaced by national personnel, either because of legislative requirements in some developing countries, which call for increasing proportions of local staff, or for reasons of cost, inasmuch as it is clearly cheaper to employ national staff than to retain expatriate staff with all the expense of removal, housing, education and repatriation allowances, and other items, all based on salary levels pegged to home country levels. Even when programmes for the replacement of expatriate staff are well administered and impartial, there seem to be inherent difficulties in this process. The national may make comparisons between his own formal academic qualifications and those of his expatriate counterpart and, finding himself to be at least equal in this regard, may fail to see that there are differences with regard to experience and other types of qualification. The expatriate executive may be cautious when discussing whether his national counterpart is ready to replace him. The subsidiary of a multinational corporation, in order to meet a prescribed quota of national staff, may recruit a national manager for a post for which he is not fully qualified. The new recruit will in fact merely be carrying out routine tasks and will not be in a position to develop his potential fully.

---

[1] An interesting exception is the Centre d'études industrielles at Geneva. Originally set up as a staff college for Alcan executives, it was converted by Alcan into a business training centre, providing courses open to all. Nestlé likewise set up a staff college for its executives in Lausanne, Switzerland, which has now been turned into a foundation for management development, known as IMEDE (Institut pour l'étude des méthodes de direction de l'entreprise), and which is also open to students from all over the world.

At a later date his promotion, or lack of it, will become a source of contention: on the strength of his present position he will be theoretically eligible for the next senior post, but in view of his limited qualifications he is unlikely to get it.

With regard to the promotion possibilities of national staff, do local managers move out of the subsidiaries and up into top positions at the multinational corporation's headquarters in the home country? Apparently not very frequently as yet. A study of 150 US firms, which was carried out in the mid-1960s, revealed that although 20.7 per cent of their total workforce was foreign, the proportion among their top corporate executives was only 1.6 per cent.[1] As one source puts it—

For the local national in the host country there are advantages in the multinational company with its prestige, its stability, its wide-ranging activities and perhaps its liberal personnel policies. But his is also likely to be a permanently subordinate position. Most of the companies had a policy of promoting local personnel to local executive positions, but hardly any appointed local nationals to their main board.[2]

With regard to the impact on the reserves of scarce skills available in the host country, the establishment of a multinational corporation's subsidiary in an industrially developed country will normally only have repercussions in the immediate vicinity of its operations. In a developing country, because of the relative size of the subsidiary, it may have a more widespread effect. Even so, the drain of scarce skills to the multinational corporation's subsidiary is often less than the drain of such skills to other countries with higher salary levels and better career opportunities.

It also appears that the multinational's subsidiary often provides managers with opportunities for promotion. In some areas, local enterprises fill their higher managerial posts only with persons from certain social groups, whereas the multinational's subsidiary in most cases gives more weight to ability.

The importance of the social group as a factor of recruitment and promotion in some developing host countries is one aspect of what may well be the most difficult problem to overcome when a multinational corporation establishes a subsidiary in a developing country: that of a potential clash between the social and cultural attitudes prevailing in the corporation and those of the host country. It is difficult to generalise about this matter because of the vast range of possible sources of conflict. For example, in the home countries of a large number of corporations there may be a generally (although not universally) held belief that length of service should not be the sole basis

---

[1] Sanford Rose: "The rewarding strategies of multinationalism", in *Fortune* (Chicago), 15 Sep. 1968, p. 180.

[2] Michael Z. Brooke and H. Lee Remmers: *The strategy of multinational enterprise: Organisation and finance* (London, Longman, 1970), p. 141.

for promotion of managerial personnel; but it may be difficult to put this principle into practice in a host country. The "earmarking for promotion" of managers may be partly determined by subjective judgements; consequently the promotion of a younger executive over an older one may be seen in the host country not only as an irrational act but also as an affront to the deep-rooted belief in promotion based on length of service, which may constitute an element of the cultural values of the host country. Similarly, the achievement of a high level of industrial development involves sudden and abrupt changes of working methods and the redeployment of management. This can have a traumatic effect on managers and workers in some developing countries, where there is a link between working and social life. Finally, the social life of the expatriate managers of a multinational's subsidiary may be conditioned by the life style of the home country, and it may not be easy to develop informal contacts between these managers and those of local origin. This in turn may affect day-to-day working relationships and lead to feelings of grievance and distrust on the part of both groups.

In sum, the multinational corporation can usually set an example of enlightened and effective management in a developing host country. It can also have a direct impact on the development of national management cadres in the host country, by training national managers in the firm, who later go into local firms or government service. Since the establishment, by a multinational corporation, of a subsidiary in a developing host country is preceded by months or even years of negotiation with the host government, there is ample opportunity to plan, in direct collaboration with the government, for management development and training that will be of benefit both to the firm and to the host country, provided that such collaboration and planning are based on fairness and a reciprocal respect for the aims of each party.

3. CONDITIONS OF WORK AND LIFE IN MULTINATIONAL ENTERPRISES

SOME PRACTICAL CONSIDERATIONS CONCERNING WAGE COMPARISONS

The very fact that a multinational corporation carries out operations in several different countries has created interest in inter-country comparisons of wage payments and labour costs. Such comparisons indicate differences in payments to workers who are performing similar operations in different countries and, when adjusted for living requirements and costs, draw attention to variations in living standards. They shed light on cost variations between countries and consequently on the relative competitive advantages of these countries.

Wage comparisons involve complex questions of both a conceptual and a practical nature. While wage rates are often more readily available, average hourly earnings are considered to be more relevant for studies designed to compare wage payments for similar work in different countries.[1] The collection of such statistics requires consideration of whether the job content of similarly designated occupations is actually comparable, and it involves the further question of calculating other benefits, which supplement the wage. Since these supplements may be national in scope (for example, family allowances), or plant-wide (for example, paid holidays), or may represent various combinations, perhaps even partially financed by employee contributions (for example, medical care and pensions), detailed and extensive calculations are required to yield a true picture of wage remuneration.[2]

Further technicalities are involved in converting wages paid in several different countries into a common monetary unit. Use of exchange rates

---

[1] ILO: *International comparisons of real wages: A study of methods*, Studies and reports, New series, No. 45 (Geneva, 1956), pp. 17–18.

[2] Ibid., p. 29.

yields a first approximation, but deeper analysis requires that "real wages" be calculated for the comparison, and this in turn involves an adjustment for the cost of purchasing a standard "market basket" of goods—a market basket differing markedly between countries.

This review of technical considerations suggests that technically sound inter-country wage comparisons require a range of detailed statistics of wages, prices and consumption which are seldom available, especially those applying to multinational corporations. Less rigorous comparisons will nevertheless provide an indication of wage differences, and as the order of magnitude of the difference increases, the degree of rigour needed (given reasonable attention to the major issues outlined above) becomes smaller.

A comparison of real wages considers the remuneration (in money and fringe benefits) of the worker and must be distinguished from a study of comparative labour costs. The latter deals with "items of cost borne by the employer . . . [some of which] cannot be regarded as workers' income at all, while others . . . may benefit only a small group of workers . . .".[1] Thus, in addition to wage payments and the costs of such benefits as bonuses, holidays and social security contributions, labour costs include such items as recruitment, training, subsidies to worker benefits, and other types of employer payments.[2] For purposes of comparing the competitive advantages of plants established in different countries, labour cost figures (which indicate costs per man-hour) represent a refinement on comparative wage statistics. More exact comparisons require an examination of output statistics to arrive at figures for labour cost per unit produced, while cost data for capital, raw materials, transportation and so on are needed to permit a complete comparison of cost differentials—and competitive advantages—among plants.

Given the difficulties of collecting sufficient official data for constructing technically accurate comparisons of operating costs among countries, is there any value in the preparation of wage and cost comparisons? It has already been suggested, with respect to real wages, that as the magnitude of inter-country differences increases, the requirement for rigorous treatment decreases. Similarly, the larger the size of the wage disparities, the greater the presumption of labour cost disparities, assuming similar equipment and a relatively similar organisational structure. It is perhaps worth noting at this point that a number of multinational corporations have not hesitated

---

[1] ILO: *Labour costs in European industry*, Studies and reports, New series, No. 52 (Geneva, 1959), p. 3.

[2] For a full list of the items included, see the International Standard Classification of Labour Cost annexed to the resolution concerning statistics of labour cost adopted by the Eleventh International Conference of Labour Statisticians, Geneva, 18–28 October 1966. The resolution is reproduced in *Bulletin of Labour Statistics* (Geneva, ILO), first quarter, 1967, pp. ix-xii.

to acknowledge lower labour costs in some plants, have pointed to such differences in partial explanation of production shifts they have made and have even argued that high labour cost plants face further production shifts if inter-plant differentials increase.

WAGE PARITY AND HARMONISATION OF CONDITIONS OF WORK

The importance of international comparisons of wages and conditions of work is evident in the increasing trade union demand for wage parity and harmonisation of conditions of work and fringe benefits. In recent years this issue has become a focus of trade union activities concerning multinational companies. So far, these activities have taken two forms: first, demands for parity between different plants of the same firm; and second, efforts at the international level to achieve more effective co-operation between trade unions, particularly unions representing employees of the same firm in different countries, with the object of pressing for harmonisation.

Demands by workers at one subsidiary or at one plant based on comparisons with conditions at other subsidiaries or plants of the same company follow naturally upon an awareness on the part of workers or their representatives of any significant differences. Such demands have been made sporadically for some time. In the automobile industry, for example, a survey covering Ford, General Motors and Chrysler operations in Canada and Europe showed that local bargaining groups did frequently use conditions at other establishments of the company as a basis for their demands. Thus data on wages paid by General Motors in the United States were used in wage claims against its Vauxhall subsidiary in the United Kingdom, and comparisons with sick pay and other fringe benefits in the United States were used at Chrysler's Rootes subsidiary in the United Kingdom. The General Motors Opel plant in France (at Strasbourg) and a Ford plant in Belgium (at Genk) received claims based on comparisons with conditions at the main subsidiaries of these companies in the Federal Republic of Germany. Up to the late 1960s, however, such claims were not "seriously pressed" or bargained upon at the European subsidiaries. General Motors, in fact, made a systematic effort to ensure "that no supranational General Motors pattern develops regarding workers' wages, benefits, and other employment conditions at overseas subsidiaries".[1]

---

[1] Duane Kujawa: *International labour relations management in the automotive industry: A comparative study of Chrysler, Ford and General Motors*, Praeger special studies in international economics and development (New York, Praeger, 1971), pp. 199–200 and 201. This study is based mainly on interviews with industrial relations staff in the three companies.

Since the late 1960s demands for parity have been seriously pressed, but they have most often aimed at parity within a country. Parity was a major issue in strikes at Ford in the United Kingdom in 1969 and 1971 and at Genk in 1968 and 1970. It has also been an issue in other industries and in other countries: two examples given in a report to the Ninth Session of the ILO Metal Trades Committee were the demands by workers at a Siemens plant in south-east Italy for parity with a plant in Milan and by shipyard workers at Kiel, in the Federal Republic of Germany, for parity with those in Hamburg.[1]

The demands at Ford in the United Kingdom fall into a larger pattern of discontent, not limited to multinational companies, arising from the payment of lower wages in the south-east and north of England and in Scotland as compared with the midlands. At both Ford and General Motors-Vauxhall the problem has been complicated by demands for parity with other companies, based on arguments that earnings in the plants of the two US subsidiaries, which have long used measured day-work systems, have fallen behind those of United Kingdom companies using payment-by-results systems. At the Ford plant at Genk the demands did have more of an international character, since they aimed at parity in wages and hours with a Ford plant at Cologne as well as with one at Antwerp: Cologne was the headquarters of the subsidiary to which the Genk plant belonged, the distance between the two towns is not very great, and many of the workers at Genk had been trained at Cologne.

The most significant example—and perhaps the only major one so far—of full achievement of international wage parity and uniformity of working conditions concerns US and Canadian automobile workers. Long a goal of the Canadian wing of the United Automobile, Aerospace and Agricultural Implement Workers of America (UAW), parity was first agreed upon in principle by the UAW and the Chrysler Corporation in 1967. The agreement called for full parity, that is payment for work done in Canada at the same rate in Canadian dollars as was payable in US dollars for similar work done in the United States, to be applied by 1970. The average differential at the time was 40 cents an hour. Similar agreements were subsequently reached with Ford and General Motors. Parity was made possible by several special circumstances: an integrated production structure and market (the way to parity was opened by an agreement between the US and Canadian Governments reached in 1965 to eliminate tariffs on shipments of new cars or parts

---

[1] ILO: *General report*, Report I, Metal Trades Committee, Ninth Session, Geneva, 1971, pp. 120–121.

by manufacturers); the domination of the Canadian automobile industry by
US firms; a relatively narrow difference in productivity; similar standards
of living and wage structures and levels; a single international trade union
representing workers in both countries; a strong interest in parity on the
part of the trade union leadership in the United States; and the close relationship between Canada and the United States. While parity was generally
welcomed by Canadian trade unions, it caused some anxiety in industry
and in certain government departments: fears were expressed that by tying
Canadian wages to US levels and by stimulating demands for parity in
industries where productivity might be significantly different, the agreement
might raise unit costs, threaten employment, aggravate inflation and damage
Canada's balance of payments. Defenders of the agreement argued that the
automobile industry and the UAW formed a unique case, that no demand
for parity was likely to be pushed to the point where a company or an industry
would be endangered, that the companies affected would make efforts to
equalise productivity and that where gaps in productivity could be overcome,
parity would be feasible. Immediately after the agreement had been signed,
demands for parity were seriously raised in negotiations between the United
Rubber Workers and the tyre and rubber manufacturers and between the
UAW itself and Massey-Ferguson (agricultural machinery manufacturers).
In neither case was parity achieved—Massey-Ferguson arguing that the extra
cost would be prohibitive for servicing its main US markets from Canada—
but in both cases the issue remained alive.[1]

The second level at which trade union interest in wage parity and harmonisation of conditions of work has been demonstrated is that of international
co-operation. Again, the UAW was a leader in promoting efforts to this end.
Its late President, Walter Reuther, said in 1964—

The corporations have internationalised and transformed the national economies
where once we worked and earned our wages into an international market for our
labours and our products. ... Today, we must stand together in international union
solidarity, or separately we will watch automation, relocation, and the erratic operation of the business cycle erode our standard of living in a process which will be
exacerbated by competition between workers of different countries at the expense
of their wages, working conditions and living standards.[2]

---

[1] David H. Blake: "Multinational corporation, international union and international
collective bargaining: A case study of the political, social and economic implications of the
1967 UAW-Chrysler agreement", in Hans Günter (ed.): *Transnational industrial relations:
The impact of multinational corporations and economic regionalism on industrial relations*,
A symposium held at Geneva by the International Institute for Labour Studies (London,
Macmillan, St. Martin's Press, 1972), pp. 137–172.

[2] Walter P. Reuther: "World-wide labor solidarity—Essential for developing international
co-operation", in *Bulletin* (Geneva, International Metalworkers' Federation), Nov. 1964,
p. 12.

One established form of international action by the UAW and certain other trade unions in the United States, notably the United Steel Workers of America, has been the strengthening of counterpart unions in developing countries, especially in Latin America and the Caribbean. But the main vehicles for systematic action at the international level have been international trade union federations and their industry departments. Activities aimed at harmonising conditions have included the regular collection and exchange of information not only on wages, conditions of work and fringe benefits but also on various aspects of corporation finances, the preparation of comparative studies, the organisation of meetings among trade unions representing workers in different subsidiaries of one company and, where possible, the arrangement of discussions between such trade unions and corporate management, the identification of priority areas, and the adoption of common bargaining objectives. Thus the International Federation of Chemical and General Workers' Unions and the International Metalworkers' Federation (IMF) have undertaken extensive research and information activities to facilitate comparisons among subsidiaries, between subsidiaries and the parent corporation and among corporations. The UAW has published a survey of automobile agreements in Latin America, and the IMF has carried out surveys of automobile agreements and of working conditions and plant practices in the agricultural implement industry in North America, Europe and Australasia. The International Federation of Commercial, Clerical and Technical Employees has begun establishing an occupational classification system to permit the comparison of salaries and conditions of work with a view to upward harmonisation. Permanent machinery for comparing conditions in the automobile industry, determining priorities and adopting objectives has been established in the form of world company councils within the framework of the IMF, and joint meetings of these councils were held in 1966, 1968 and 1971, at which central goals were formulated. The 1971 meeting adopted a declaration including a pledge "to support the efforts of the IMF directed to the upward harmonisation of wages and social benefits to the maximum degree possible and in the shortest time possible".[1] Numerous meetings concerning other industries and individual companies have been held under the auspices of various trade union federations. The companies have included Philips, General Electric, Shell, Nestlé, Grace and several others. At the regional level a meeting of the Caribbean Bauxite, Mine and Metalworkers' Federation held in 1971 adopted a number of specific objectives (including a 40-hour week wherever it was not already in force, extended annual vacations and vacation bonuses,

---

[1] Declaration of London IMF World Auto Company Councils, 23–25 March 1971, in *IMF Sector News* (Geneva, International Metalworkers' Federation), Apr. 1971, p. 14,

premiums for Saturday or Sunday work, paid educational leave and scholar-
ships, various fringe benefits, and equal pay for equal work regardless of
nationality, race or sex) as well as the general principle of upward harmonisation of wages and benefits in multinational aluminium companies in the
Caribbean.[1]

None of this activity implies that harmonisation on any truly international
scale, especially in respect of wages, is likely to be achieved in the near future
or that trade unions regard it as being more than a distant objective. What
seems more likely is an intensification of efforts to obtain uniform wage
rates and working conditions within countries. This will not, of course, be
limited to multinational companies, but the comparative information generated
in regard to such companies should furnish material for more precisely
formulated and better-supported demands. It is also probable that pressure
will increase for harmonisation at the regional or subregional level—for
example, in Europe, groupings within Europe, and the Caribbean—and
perhaps between Japan and Europe. Some development may occur in the
harmonisation of basic working conditions, such as hours of work, overtime
pay and annual holidays, the wider application of certain principles, such as the
integration of conditions of manual and non-manual workers, and the exten-
sion of specific practices, such as extra pay during annual holidays. The
international activity of trade unions in the near future may concentrate
more on such matters and on other problems of importance to particular
industries than on wages. In this connection the co-ordinator of the IMF
World Auto Councils has written that one of the purposes of the 1971 joint
meeting "was to make recommendations for priority of action in harmonisation of working conditions. The emphasis was put on conditions such as
employment security, speed of the production line, relief time and paid
holidays, etc., rather than wages as practical objectives more readily attainable
in the immediate future." [2]

Harmonisation of conditions of work will not be a phenomenon related
exclusively to multinational companies. In some fields parallel developments

---

[1] Declaration of the Caribbean Bauxite, Mine and Metalworkers' Federation, Fourth
Congress, Port-of-Spain (Trinidad), 14–16 Feb. 1971. For a general discussion of international
trade union activities, see Karl Casserini: "The challenge of multinational corporations
and regional economic integration to the trade unions, their structure and their international
activities", in Günter, op. cit., pp. 70–93, and "Summary of the symposium discussion",
ibid., pp. 353–422.

[2] Burton Bendiner: "Multinational unionism: IMF World Auto Councils at the London
conference", in *Free Labour World* (Brussels, International Confederation of Free Trade
Unions), June 1971, p. 14. A UAW official has argued that regional wage parity, particularly
in Europe, may be feasible within a decade in the metalworking industries and especially
in the automobile industry. See Guy Nunn: "World councils of employees: A challenge
to the supranational corporation?", in Alfred Kamin (ed.): *Western European labor and the
American corporation* (Washington, DC, Bureau of National Affairs, 1970), pp. 17–18.

are taking place in many countries and can be regarded as general trends: examples are the movement towards a 40-hour week and the introduction of a three-week and, more recently, a four-week holiday. Moreover, there are stimulants at the international level to greater alignment, such as standards adopted by the International Labour Conference and regional social policies promoted by the European Economic Community and the Council of Europe. Finally, there are consistent trade union demands not specifically directed at multinational companies and not expressly aimed at harmonisation which nevertheless contribute to harmonisation—again, the 40-hour week is an example.

WAGES IN HOST COUNTRIES

The second basic problem concerning wages in multinational corporations is that of comparing them with the wages paid by domestic employers. Most often the question is whether multinational corporations pay higher-than-average wages, and a common presumption is that they do. But data on this question are severely limited, extremely difficult to interpret and often inconclusive. Thus, with regard to the United Kingdom, a study on US investment, published in 1969, accepts the presumption that US firms pay better on average [1], while another study, published in 1972, suggests that this may be true of some industries but not of others and that the influence of foreign firms may lie more in determining the total sum involved in wage settlements than in rates of pay [2]; the Trades Union Congress's *Economic Review* for 1970 tends to support the view that the position varies between different industries but notes that US companies seem to give better fringe benefits.[3] A survey of US firms in Australia found that US-affiliated firms did pay more than others in the same industry but that almost all of them attributed this to local factors rather than to any deliberate policy.[4] A study based mainly on manufacturing plants in Latin America found that with some exceptions US firms tended to pay the legal minimum rates or slightly more but made little effort to apply high-wage, high-productivity policies.[5]

---

[1] John H. Dunning: *The role of American investment in the British economy*, with two case studies by W. G. Jensen, PEP Broadsheet No. 507 (London, Political and Economic Planning, Feb. 1969), p. 164.

[2] John Gennard: *Multinational corporations and British labour: A review of attitudes and responses* (London, British-North American Committee, Jan. 1972), pp. 29–33.

[3] Trades Union Congress: *Economic Review 1970* (London, Mar. 1970), p. 35.

[4] Donald T. Brash: *American investment in Australian industry* (Canberra, Australian National University Press, 1966), pp. 128–135.

[5] John C. Shearer: "Industrial relations of American corporations abroad", in Solomon Barkin *et al.* (eds.): *International labor* (New York, Harper and Row, 1967), p. 123.

Rather than attempting to discover a pattern applicable to multinational corporations generally, it may be more useful at this stage to consider particular policies and circumstances that influence wage levels in different companies.

A number of companies, for instance, do, as a matter of world-wide policy, pay wages somewhat above average, though not substantially so. Several firms surveyed in the study on US companies in Australia, cited above, responded along the lines that "parent company policy throughout the world is to pay wages '*at least* equal to the going rate in the local community —we don't have to be the leader, but we would certainly never lag behind".[1] To give another example, one of the large multinational companies follows in all its foreign operations a wage policy based on a thorough survey of local rates: wages and salaries are fixed so as to place the company around the eightieth percentile and thus to make it one of the leaders but not the leader.

A basic factor is the state of the labour market. Higher wages and benefits offered by companies setting up new operations or expanding or simply trying to recruit and retain labour in a tight market—especially trained workers—may come to be regarded by the workers as established rights, and there may be a tendency for the differential to be frozen. An example is the Ford plant at Genk, which had to pay higher wages on opening and to maintain them as it expanded, thus, according to one study, "creating a bitter resentment on the part of the nearby employers who were being pressured to raise their wages". As the wages in other companies went up, there were trade union demands for increases at Ford based at least partly on the argument that the Ford differential was traditional, reflected higher profitability and should be preserved.[2]

A company's wider interest may also result in the payment of higher wages where circumstances make it especially vulnerable. It has been stated that—

In January 1971 the British management of Chrysler conceded an inflationary wage claim despite very strong government pressure put on it. The claim happened to come just at the time the company was building up its supplies of the British-made Avenger, which was to be sold in the United States as the Cricket. For the sake of survival in America the company could not afford a lengthy show-down in Britain.[3]

Finally, the type of economic activity in which the company is engaged may itself be a decisive factor in determining the pattern of industrial relations

---

[1] Brash, op. cit., p. 131.

[2] Kujawa, op. cit., pp. 202–204. According to information from trade union sources, the demands of Ford-Genk were based on comparisons of wage rates paid in this plant with those paid in the Ford assembly plant at Antwerp and in the Ford-Cologne plant.

[3] Economist Intelligence Unit: *The growth and spread of multinational companies*, QER special No. 5 (London, second edition, 1971), p. 28.

and thus its wage policy. It has been argued, for example, that in the petroleum and mining industries the necessity for large, fixed investments leaves management less flexibility and discretion than it has in manufacturing, where it is geographically less bound. In the petroleum industry a combination of vertically integrated technology (which makes work stoppages extremely costly), low labour intensity, rising demand for products, and improvements in efficiency achieved by advanced technology and economies of scale makes it both desirable and possible to pay exceptionally high wages and to provide exceptionally good conditions of work. Mining has some characteristics in common with the petroleum industry, but there is generally a lesser degree of vertical integration, greater labour intensity, more price fluctuation and a greater possibility of stock-piling. The industry comprises many small companies as well as large ones. Work itself is arduous and takes place in difficult conditions. This combination of factors tends to produce hard bargaining punctuated by occasional bitter strikes. An exception is bauxite mining, in which there is a high degree of mechanisation and vertical integration: the companies tend to be more like oil companies in their industrial relations policies.[1]

There is no doubt that in the developing countries wages in petroleum and mining, in which productivity is usually much higher than the general level, do tend to be considerably higher than in other branches of activity. A recent study of foreign investment in these industries, based on experience in Latin America and to a lesser extent the Middle East, confirmed that "in virtually every developing country where mineral or petroleum production is an important industry, the average wage in the resource industry is substantially higher than that of any other industrial category".[2] An ILO report on incomes, wages and prices in Zambia noted that the earnings of Zambian miners were double those of wage earners outside the mines and nine times those of peasant farmers.[3] A study on multinational corporations in Jamaica found that wages in bauxite mining and alumina production, an industry which occupied less than 1 per cent of the country's labour force, far exceeded the national average for both skilled and unskilled workers. A special cir-

---

[1] This argument is taken from B. C. Roberts: "Factors influencing the organisation and style of management and their effect on the pattern of industrial relations in multinational corporations", in Günter, op. cit., pp. 109–112.

[2] Phillip E. Church: "Labor relations in mineral and petroleum resource development", in Raymond F. Mikesell et al.: *Foreign investment in the petroleum and mineral industries: Case studies of investor-host country relations* (Baltimore, Johns Hopkins Press, 1971), p. 82.

[3] ILO: *Report to the Government of Zambia on incomes, wages and prices in Zambia: Policy and machinery* (Geneva, doc. ILO/TAP/Zambia/R.5, 1969; mimeographed), pp. 9–13.

cumstance here was the influence upon labour relations exerted by close co-operation between local unions and the United Steel Workers of America.[1]

Such disparities between those who have employment in high-paying industries and other workers, coupled with the common disparity between an urban wage-earning minority and a rural majority consisting of small cultivators, accentuates a fundamental dilemma extending beyond multi-national companies but often exemplified in them: how to reconcile the principle of allowing workers to share in the productivity of the industry in which they are employed with the broader social objectives of reducing gross inequalities in incomes and living standards, expanding employment opportunities and generally enabling the entire population to benefit from the development of the productive resources of the country.

OTHER CONDITIONS OF WORK

As in the field of wages, so in regard to other conditions of work the subsidiaries of multinational corporations have, in general, the reputation of offering better standards than those usually found in the host countries: higher standards of safety, shorter hours of work, a five-day week, and better fringe benefits, especially in areas such as sick pay schemes, retirement plans, and allowances for education and transport.

In the late 1950s and early 1960s the National Planning Association of the United States conducted a series of case studies of selected subsidiaries of US corporations abroad (in one instance a Canadian corporation) in an attempt to assess their contributions to the host countries. General Electric's policies in Brazil were described as follows:

GE follows a policy of conscientiously complying with all the requirements of the country's labour and social welfare regulations. In most areas, the Company voluntarily exceeds minimum legal requirements because it believes that its employees are entitled to greater or more secure benefits, which in turn may contribute to improving labour productivity. In some cases, the Company has to compensate for the malfunctioning of the Government's welfare legislation.[2]

The study gives, among others, the following examples of this policy:

To combat absenteeism, GE offers its factory and office workers an extra day's pay for every week in which they have a perfect attendance record.
... when its workers are on sick leave, GE voluntarily pays the remaining two-

---

[1] Jeffrey Harrod: "Multinational corporations, trade unions and industrial relations: A case study of Jamaica", in Günter, op. cit., pp. 173–194.

[2] Theodore Geiger: *The General Electric Company in Brazil*, Ninth case study in an NPA series on United States business performance abroad (Washington, DC, National Planning Association, 1961), p. 64.

thirds of the employee's regular salary as a supplement to the one-third paid by the governmental institute.[1]

In the subsidiary of a multinational aluminium corporation in India the workers were reported to get an allowance covering the initial seven days of a "waiting period" which were not covered by the Workmen's Compensation Act; in one mining centre the company was the only major one which guaranteed minimum weekly earnings.[2]

In another study, it was stated with regard to wages in Mexico that according to most estimates the supplements (bonuses, allowances, social insurance, and a variety of payments in kind) ranged from 10 to 30 per cent of wages and salaries. In the sample, Mexican-owned firms tended to give supplements below 15 per cent of wages, while foreign subsidiaries gave above 25 per cent.[3]

Because of the very nature of its operations a multinational corporation is subject to various types of social security legislation. Moreover, the fact that its employees in a given country very often include both nationals of that country and non-nationals presents it with additional social security problems. As a rule, national social security legislation applies to foreign and domestic companies alike. Hence, as regards compulsory social security schemes of a national character, the multinational corporation has neither advantages (exemptions) nor disadvantages (higher charges) as compared with a local employer.

However, in addition to the basic social security protection provided for in national legislation, there are often non-statutory complementary benefits, which employees enjoy by virtue either of collective agreements or of arrangements made by the employer for the benefit of his staff (occupational pensions, supplements to basic sick pay, and so on). The employees of a multinational corporation very often enjoy such additional social security coverage through company schemes, although these are not necessarily comprehensive, in the sense that membership is often limited to certain categories of employees and may exclude local staff or employees with less than a certain length of service in the company or, again, staff whose employment relationship with the corporation is only temporary.

In industrialised countries most large companies—not only the multinational corporations—guarantee supplementary social security protection to

---

[1] Geiger, op. cit., pp. 65 and 66.

[2] Subbiah Kannappan and Eugene W. Burgess: *Aluminium Limited in India*, Eleventh case study in an NPA series on business performance abroad (Washington, DC, National Planning Association, 1961), pp. 48 and 49.

[3] W. Paul Strassmann: *Technological change and economic development: The manufacturing experience of Mexico and Puerto Rico* (Ithaca (New York), Cornell University Press, 1968), p. 134.

their employees, in addition to that offered by the basic state schemes, so that the multinational corporations and the large local companies are in similar positions. On the whole, the employees of large companies enjoy comparable social security rights irrespective of whether the employer is a local or a foreign company.

In a number of developing countries the situation is different. Firstly, the scope of compulsory state schemes (pensions, medical care, family allowances, and so on) is, as a rule, limited and the benefits provided by them tend to be modest. Secondly, local companies are less inclined or less able to operate company schemes. Exceptions do, of course, exist, but they are few. Consequently, in developing countries the employees of affiliates of multinational corporations tend to be better off than other workers as far as social security is concerned.

Information concerning conditions of work other than wages in the subsidiaries of multinationals has been gathered in the case of a few firms in certain host countries. However, much more systematic research is necessary before an assessment can be made of the practices of subsidiaries in this field as compared with those of indigenous firms.

THE QUESTION OF FAIR LABOUR STANDARDS [1]

There is no agreed definition of what is meant by "fair labour standards". The problem of what constitutes fair standards in wages and working conditions is an important aspect of the current controversy in the United States surrounding off-shore operations, that is the assembly, manufacture or processing of goods of US origin outside the United States (notably in Mexico, the Caribbean, Hong Kong, the Republic of Korea and Singapore) by US companies for re-export to the United States. US trade unions have strongly complained that this amounts to unfair competition made possible by low wages and fringe benefits together with tariff concessions on certain articles granted by the United States, and that it results in the loss of jobs and the depression of standards for workers in the United States. Briefly, the argument

---

[1] Reference to fair labour standards was made during the Governing Body's discussion of the ILO policy statement for the Third Session of the United Nations Conference on Trade and Development (UNCTAD), which dealt with trade, development co-operation, employment and labour in the Second Development Decade. In the ILO's communication to the Third Session of UNCTAD, to which the policy statement was attached, it was stated that the Governing Body had decided to consider at its November 1972 Session the establishment of a new procedure designed to promote the universal observance of fair labour standards, on the basis of ILO Conventions and Recommendations, with a view to ensuring that the benefits of trade liberalisation would find adequate reflection in improved living and working conditions.

is that hand-assembling and other labour-intensive operations are being transferred out of the United States, that wages and fringe benefits in the countries to which they are being transferred are a fraction of those in the United States, that—owing in part to the transfer of technology—productivity is not correspondingly lower than in the United States, and that the consequent difference in unit labour costs makes it difficult or impossible for US workers to compete. These workers, it is argued, are therefore losing jobs and employment opportunities, and their wages and conditions of work are being undermined by the threat of transfers of production; the benefits to workers in the developing countries are minimal, since such operations are unstable sources of employment, offering poor wages and conditions; the companies, it is said, are interested primarily in low labour costs and exert pressure to keep them low by threatening to "shop around" among different countries for the most advantageous terms. It has sometimes been alleged that certain governments deliberately maintain wages and conditions at low levels in order to attract investment.[1]

This argument immediately leads to two basic issues. First, are wages in the host country so significantly below those in the home country that they serve as a primary motive for firms to go abroad, and second, what would constitute fair standards in wages and working conditions? There are some indications that, in certain lines of industry, lower labour costs make enough difference to influence firms in their decision to go abroad. A report to the Ninth Session of the ILO Metal Trades Committee quoted two studies dealing with this question.[2] In the first study, undertaken in 1960, labour costs were mentioned by only 6 per cent of the respondents as a major factor in deciding to invest abroad; repeated in 1963, this survey gave the same results. In the second study, published in 1961, lower labour costs ranked eighth out of a total of twenty factors motivating investment abroad. More recent studies, however, have shown that, if broken down by lines of industry, labour costs can play an important role in some cases. In a study made by the Emergency Committee for American Trade, out of the ten lines of industry investigated, companies in two—electrical machinery and other machinery—mentioned labour costs as an important factor in their investment decisions; with regard

---

[1] Examples of trade union statements on off-shore operations may be found in United States Tariff Commission: *Economic factors affecting the use of items 807.00 and 806.30 of the Tariff Schedules of the United States*, Report to the President on Investigation No. 332–61 under section 332 of the Tariff Act of 1930 (Washington, DC, TC Publication No. 339, Sep. 1970), Appendix C, and in United States Congress: *A foreign economic policy for the 1970s*, Hearings before the Subcommittee on Foreign Economic Policy of the Joint Economic Committee, Congress of the United States, Ninety-first Congress, Second Session, Part 4: *The multinational corporation and international investment* (Washington, DC, US Government Printing Office, 1970).

[2] ILO: *General report*, op. cit., p. 148.

to electrical machinery, it was stated that "labour costs played major roles in Far Eastern investment decisions".[1] In the machinery sector the study noted that "in Western Europe, where the bulk of plant and equipment expenditures have occurred, respondents were equally divided as to whether or not trade restrictions, market demands, or labour cost advantages were the most important factor in their investment decisions".[2] The US Tariff Commission estimated that, in the case of wearing apparel, unit labour costs in the Caribbean averaged 24 per cent of those in the United States, and in Mexico, 32 per cent; for certain electrical and electronic goods they averaged 8 per cent in the Far East (excluding Japan) and 20 per cent in Mexico; as regards various other articles, they ranged from 7 per cent for baseballs to 46 per cent for scientific instruments.[3]

Lower labour cost as a factor motivating investment abroad appears not to be restricted to the United States. For example, it has been maintained that Rollei finally chose to transfer production from the Federal Republic of Germany to Singapore "mainly because labour costs are a sixth of those in Germany—a vital consideration, since labour accounts for 50 per cent to 60 per cent of SLR [a Rollei camera model] production costs in Germany. However, since current productivity in Singapore is much lower than that in Germany, the effective saving in labour costs per unit will be only about 50 per cent."[4]

It has often been said that lower productivity in developing host countries tends to even out wage differentials between the industrialised home country and the developing host country. However, such an assumption can certainly not be generalised. The US Tariff Commission study, for instance, contains the following statement:

Productivity of workers in foreign establishments assembling or processing products of US origin generally approximates that of workers in the same job classifications in the United States. However, even for those few instances in which foreign labour productivity was significantly less than that of United States workers, the hourly earnings abroad were such that, save for Canada, labour costs per unit of output were substantially lower in the foreign than in the domestic establishment.[5]

---

[1] Emergency Committee for American Trade: *The role of the multinational corporation (MNC) in the United States and world economies: Individual industry analyses* (Washington, DC, Feb. 1972), p. A–77.

[2] Ibid., p. A–61.

[3] United States Tariff Commission: *Economic factors affecting the use of items 807.00 and 806.30 . . .*, op. cit., pp. 172–173.

[4] Charles Levinson: *Capital, inflation and the multinationals* (London, George Allen and Unwin, 1971), p. 99.

[5] United States Tariff Commission: *Economic factors affecting the use of items 807.00 and 806.30 . . .*, op. cit., p. 171.

It will be recalled that corporations, even when agreeing that labour costs are lower in some foreign operations, argue that they have no other choice than to produce abroad with the same cost advantages as those enjoyed by competing foreign firms. Faced with the alternative of closing production or producing abroad, they prefer to remain in business through foreign operations. They reject the charge that there is anything "unfair" in such a decision, since the workers employed in these operations are granted wages and conditions of work at least equal to those for comparable work in the domestic firms and industries of the host countries concerned. The notion of "fair labour standards" raises once again the practical problem of international wage comparisons and the conceptual problem of determining what wage practices would be both fair to the workers in a multinational company and consistent with the promotion of social justice for all workers.

CULTURAL DIFFERENCES AND THEIR IMPACT ON CONDITIONS OF WORK

Apart from relative wage levels and conditions of work, the most frequently discussed aspect of the problem of the multinational corporation as an employer is the potential conflict between the cultures of the home country and the host country and the effect of any such conflict on industrial relations. John C. Shearer has suggested that "American firms which operate in foreign countries usually premise their industrial relations policies on the base of the values, assumptions and habits they have developed in the United States. They then may or may not modify them in response to the different circumstances abroad." [1] Examples of conflicts arising or apparently arising out of a failure to adapt to the environment are not difficult to find. While the most serious ones are undoubtedly those that concern job security, trade union recognition, grievance procedures and collective bargaining, intense conflicts also take place over practices relating to wage systems and conditions of work. A number of examples are cited here by way of illustration. The attempt by Chrysler to change from a payment-by-results system to a measured day-work system shortly after having taken over Rootes in the United Kingdom and, according to the trade unions, without adequate consultation or prior agreement on the manning and pace of the assembly line led to a strike [2] and

---

[1] Shearer, op. cit., p. 117.

[2] Trades Union Congress: *Report of a Conference on International Companies, Congress House, London, 21 October 1970* (London, n.d.), p. 7.

to lasting resentment—even though General Motors and Ford already applied a measured day-work system in their United Kingdom plants; it was eventually accepted only as part of a very high settlement. General Motors experienced a long strike in Canada when it attempted to replace the traditional fixed rest period, requiring a full shutdown, by a rotating rest period, and eventually it had to abandon the attempt.[1] A strike took place at a John Deere-Lanz AG plant in the Federal Republic of Germany when the company reduced the length of the breakfast break.[2]

Such conflicts may bring to the surface the latent distrust and frustration of both sides in the face of attitudes alien to them. The Trades Union Congress in the United Kingdom has noted that when Brititsh firms are taken over by foreign ones there is "a suspicion that foreign managements or foreign control will lead to proposals for new methods of work and a new basis for determining wages and conditions. As a result of this, there is often a negative attitude to management proposals on the one hand and an insensitivity on the part of management on the other." [3] For example, according to one writer, the replacement of British by US managers and the appointment of a US managing director at General Motors/Vauxhall led to "an outburst of anti-American feeling and an aggressive, militant opposition to some of the changes introduced".[4] A regional personnel director at Chrysler has said that certain one-day walkouts at various Rootes plants following the Chrysler takeover were due to hostility to the rapidity with which certain changes were instituted by local US managers.[5]

Short of outright conflict, there is sometimes a frustration on the part of foreign managements deriving from failure to understand or to accept local customs and practices. Examples of this include unsuccessful attempts in Japan to introduce wage systems based on job evaluation and merit rating as opposed to the traditional criteria of education and seniority (though such attempts may simply have been premature, since the traditional system is now showing signs of change), complaints by US managers about long tea-breaks and other alleged obstacles to efficiency in the United Kingdom, and

---

[1] Kujawa, op. cit., p. 198.

[2] Shearer, op. cit., p. 117.

[3] Trades Union Congress: *Report of a Conference on International Companies . . .*, op. cit., p. 7. On the other hand, the General Secretary of the Trades Union Congress has written: "Multinational companies may be giants, but they do not therefore have to be ogres. They have much to offer in terms of increased employment, greater productivity and higher efficiency on a global scale. Their growth creates the chance of great economic benefits. It is the job of trade unions and governments everywhere to make sure that these benefits are shared by everyone." (Victor Feather: "Multinational companies: The British experience", in *Free Labour World*, May 1972, p. 5.)

[4] Roberts, op. cit., p. 120.

[5] Kujawa, op. cit., p. 233.

difficulties in adjusting to such European practices as rigid holiday seasons and restrictions on overtime.[1]

A further source of tension largely, though not wholly, peculiar to multi-national companies is the privileged position of expatriate staff. Normally this affects technical, supervisory, executive and perhaps clerical staff, but there have been situations in which large numbers of manual workers have been recruited from abroad. To give an example, disparities in wages and benefits between expatriate and indigenous miners were a constant and severe social problem in Zambia during the years immediately following independence. Wide disparities in compensation and limited opportunities for advancement for nationals of the host country are a frequent grievance, especially in developing countries, where the disparities may be dramatic and where there may be undertones of racial distinctions.[2] A last point worth considering is the suggestion of underlying cultural conflict in a more subtle sense contained in the following statement by an Indian businessman and sometime public servant: "An Indian enterprise is responsive to local social needs: there is a certain flexibility, for example, in employment and in meeting employees' needs among Indian employers which is absent—because of their impersonality— among foreign units."[3]

Yet, while many examples may be cited and while their individual significance should not be minimised, it would be dangerous to generalise from them or to exaggerate their extent. There is nothing to suggest that multi-national corporations as a category are especially prone to suffer from conflicts over conditions of work as a result of cultural differences. What does seem true is that their foreign character may make them more vulnerable to attack in case of conflict, that conflicts over working conditions may be aggravated by the cultural gap and that labour conflicts not originating in cultural differences may eventually take on a cultural aspect.

It should also be stressed that the application of practices and ideas developed abroad has enabled multinational companies to make various innovations in respect of working conditions in different countries. Perhaps the best-known recent example is the growth of productivity bargaining in the United Kingdom, a trend in which Esso/Fawley was a pioneer and other foreign companies were among the leaders. Several companies, including General Motors, Chrysler and Massey-Ferguson, have broken away—though

---

[1] Shearer, op. cit., pp. 119–120; Roberts, op. cit., p. 127; and Roger Blanpain: "American involvement in Belgium", in Kamin, op. cit., p. 459.

[2] An indication of the depth of feeling aroused by this problem may be found in *Esso Eastern Review*, July-Aug. 1971, a special issue containing the opinions on foreign investment given by a number of Asians from business, government and academic circles.

[3] Gaganvihari L. Mehta, ibid., p. 12.

sometimes at considerable immediate cost—from what they regarded as loosely administered payment-by-results systems responsible for, in the words of a vice-president of Massey-Ferguson, "an endemic UK problem, incentive wage drift".[1] Job evaluation, work measurement and the refinement of wage structures and systems are among the areas in which US firms have often been leaders. A recent example was a negotiation of a thorough reform of the wage structure at Ford in the United Kingdom, after an extremely elaborate job evaluation effort carried out in close consultation with the trade unions, shop stewards and the workers themselves.[2]

WELFARE FACILITIES AND LIVING CONDITIONS

Finally, mention should be made of measures taken by multinational corporations to improve living conditions in the developing countries where they operate, through the establishment of welfare facilities at the plant or the community level and through contributions to workers' housing. Enough information is not available to permit comparisons between their efforts and those of domestic companies; in any case, even the conditions for comparison do not always exist, since the subsidiaries of multinational corporations are often unique in nature or scale in the areas where they are located. It is clear, however, that many have built up extensive networks of welfare facilities, social services and housing.

This is especially true in the petroleum and mining industries, which are generally carried on in isolated and sometimes topographically difficult areas. The provision of housing and other services in such circumstances not only is an important element in contracting and retaining labour but also can be essential for meeting the companies' own needs. An illustration of this is the Aramco operation in Saudi Arabia, which over the years has played an important role as a provider or promoter of housing, medical care, recreation, education, training and agricultural, industrial and commercial development in its region. While the company has encouraged the growth of a strong and diversified local economy, its activities have obviously been the direct determinant of living conditions not only for its own employees but for the general population.[3] This is an extreme case, but the provision of fairly comprehensive services is quite common among multinational corporations in petroleum and mining. Here again cultural factors may need to be taken

---

[1] John A. Belford: "The supranational corporation and labor relations", in Kamin, op. cit., p. 9.

[2] Robert Copp: "Negotiating a new wage structure at Ford of Britain", ibid., pp. 109–114.

[3] Arabian American Oil Company: *Aramco handbook: Oil and the Middle East* (Dhahran, revised edition, 1968), pp. 154–170.

into account: for example, in a number of developing countries it is customary for one worker to support a large "extended" family, which may even accompany him to the area in which his workplace is located; this clearly has implications in cases where the company assumes responsibility for the housing of its employees and other community facilities. According to the study of resource industries cited earlier, the companies have drawn substantial benefits from the services provided by them, in the form of a much stabler, healthier, more assiduous, better-trained and more highly motivated workforce. The study also claims that "while a trained and experienced labour force undoubtedly has greater bargaining power in negotiations with the company through their union representatives, such a labour force is easier for management to deal with on a business basis and less likely to engage in strikes for political or ideological reasons".[1]

On a rather smaller scale plantations also provide extensive housing, medical care and other facilities. The labour force is in many cases resident and heavily dependent on the plantation for essential services. Such services are often prescribed by law, but many companies, especially the larger ones, go well beyond legal requirements. In manufacturing the position is less clear. Many examples of measures exceeding the legal minima, applied by virtue of collective agreements or on the company's own initiative, have been cited in ILO studies on employers' contributions to workers' housing in Latin America and on employment-connected welfare facilities in the same region, but no real comparisons between foreign and domestic firms are possible.[2]

It may nevertheless be useful to raise certain questions which, like the problem of income disparities, are not exclusively relevant to multinational corporations but are often brought into focus by their activities. Is the provision by companies of comprehensive social services, going beyond welfare facilities connected with work, the most effective way in which they can contribute directly to the improvement of living conditions? Does it create a danger of excessive dependence on the company by the workers and their families? What methods could be used to extend the benefits of such services to workers employed by small undertakings or by companies without the capacity to provide many services on their own? Again, the basic problem is the extent to which available resources can be used to benefit the community as a whole.

---

[1] Church, op. cit., p. 97.

[2] ILO: *La contribution des employeurs à l'amélioration des conditions de logement des travailleurs dans les pays d'Amérique latine*, Informations sur les conditions générales de travail, n° 18 (Geneva, doc. D.10/1972, 1971; mimeographed). The study on welfare facilities has not yet been issued.

4. INDUSTRIAL RELATIONS IN A MULTINATIONAL FRAMEWORK

TRADE UNION VIEWS

The trade union movement is increasingly concerned at what it considers to be the actual and possible problems raised by the multinational corporation, not only as an employer but also as an economic and political force. Thus a large part of the trade union movement not only advocates measures on the part of the public authorities to control multinational corporations on a national and international basis but is also concerned with organising itself better to deal with these corporations on a bilateral basis.

Trade union views are expressed by their national and, more emphatically, by their international organisations in various policy pronouncements, some of which are reported below.

However, it may first be useful to review briefly the components of the existing international trade union structure. Of great significance in connection with multinationals are the specialised international trade union bodies covering a particular industry or group of more or less related industries. Certain of the International Trade Secretariats (ITSs)—bodies composed of national trade unions of given industries, which are associated with the International Confederation of Free Trade Unions (ICFTU)—have been particularly active, especially those covering industries where multinational corporations are most in evidence. The other two major international trade union organisations, the World Confederation of Labour (WCL) and the World Federation of Trade Unions (WFTU), have equally close relationships with their respective international industrial groupings, namely the Trade Internationals and the Trade Unions Internationals. There are also regional groups of all these international confederations and federations as well as trade union bodies within regional economic organisations.

Multinational enterprises and social policy

At its Ninth World Congress in Brussels in July 1969 the ICFTU adopted, after discussions with various of the ITSs, a resolution [1] which, while recognising that the international organisation of production can play an important role in spreading new technical know-how and in giving an impetus to economic growth and social progress, provided that trade union action is brought to bear upon multinational corporations so as to safeguard the interests of the workers and the public, nevertheless calls attention to a number of possible dangers and points out, in particular, that by concentrating vital economic and financial decisions at their international headquarters and establishing world-wide employment and industrial relations policies, multinational corporations may undermine established industrial relations systems, restrict the right of the workers to organise in defence of their interests (a right which, the resolution affirms, has often been denied them as part of a systematic anti-trade union policy), limit their right to enter into co-ordinated collective bargaining at whatever level is appropriate, and exploit international labour cost differentials in order to increase profits. The ICFTU resolution calls for international solidarity of the workers and co-ordination of trade union efforts to take up the multinational challenge, and it demands the recognition of the right to organise and bargain collectively. It urges the multinational corporations to negotiate wages, working conditions and fringe benefits with the trade unions, in keeping with their high corporate profit levels and the need for social progress, and to abide by all ILO Conventions and comply with existing social legislation, collective agreements and established conditions and rights; it draws attention to the need to ensure that the priorities of national economic and social planning are respected, in particular that company mergers be subject to the approval of public authorities, and that all measures are taken in good time to avoid social hardships caused by structural change and plant closure; it insists that any new laws governing the international, regional or national operations of multinational corporations must include the principles set forth in the resolution; and it emphasises the need for adequate measures to establish democratic control at each level of decision in multinational corporations.

In December 1970, the ICFTU Executive Board, meeting in Brussels, adopted a resolution on freedom of association and multinational companies.[2] This resolution refers, among other things, to the concern felt by trade union organisations, especially in developing countries, at the activities of multinational companies, particularly in so far as these engender government

---

[1] "Resolution on multinational corporations and conglomerates", in *ICFTU Economic and Social Bulletin* (Brussels, International Confederation of Free Trade Unions), July-Aug. 1969, pp. 16–17.

[2] *ICFTU Economic and Social Bulletin*, Jan.-Feb. 1971, pp. 21–22.

restrictions on trade union rights and objectives, and to the alleged practice, on the part of some governments, of offering anti-trade union measures, among other inducements, in efforts to attract foreign investments. The resolution calls attention to the moral responsibility of governments of capital-exporting countries to ensure that multinational companies offer satisfactory conditions of employment, including recognition of trade union activities, in their overseas subsidiaries. It emphasises that restrictions on trade union freedom in developing countries may lead to increased pressure in industrialised countries for protectionist measures. Finally, it calls for a United Nations conference to lay down a code of conduct for multinational corporations. Many of these points are included in a statement adopted by the ICFTU World Economic Conference of the Free Trade Unions held in Geneva in June 1971.[1]

At its Tenth World Congress, held in London in July 1972, the ICFTU adopted another resolution on multinational companies [2], in which it reiterated its appeal, made the year before through the World Economic Conference of the Free Trade Unions, for closer co-operation within the whole international free trade union movement in order to meet the challenge of these companies. The resolution proposes a more vigorous effort through the establishment of a joint ICFTU-ITS working party, which should work out guidelines for a common research programme concerning: *(a)* the position and development trends in the process of multinational concentrations; *(b)* the publication of information on the decision-making structures of multinational concerns, their internal organisation, their accounting system and the basic features of their investment policy; and *(c)* the effects of the spread of multinational concerns on national economic policy and the carrying out of democratic reforms.

The WCL, in a resolution adopted in October 1971 by the Trade Internationals affiliated to its European Organisation, voices many of the same fears.[3] The resolution proposes an extensive information campaign among workers as well as international trade union action to ensure that the technical progress achieved through multinational corporations is of benefit to the whole of society. It recommends all the organisations affiliated to the European Organisation of the WCL to equip themselves with the necessary structures and means of action to mobilise workers and their representatives at the

---

[1] "Free trade unions and multinational companies", in *ICFTU Economic and Social Bulletin*, July 1971, pp. 38–42.

[2] Ibid., July-Aug. 1972, pp. 16–17.

[3] *Résolution concernant les entreprises multinationales*, Conférence sur les fusions et concentrations et les entreprises multinationales, Strasbourg, 25–26 October 1971 (Brussels, Commission de coordination et d'information professionnelles, June 1972; mimeographed).

enterprise and industry levels, and affirms that it is for the trade union organisations to see to the effective defence of the interests of workers employed in multinational corporations. The resolution calls upon the international organisations to make every effort to promote effective democratic control of multinational corporations and direct worker influence on the policies of these corporations. It urges the co-operation of all democratic trade union movements at the European level, as well as the study, by the Trade Internationals, of the problem of multinational corporations.

The WFTU, in the May-June 1971 issue of its review [1], also stresses the need for exchanges of information and co-ordinated action among trade unions in respect of given multinational corporations to meet the threat of "capitalist concentrations", which is growing because of the increased internationalisation of capital in the search for a maximisation of profits. The review also contends that the mobility of the multinational corporation leads to lessened job security and mass redundancies. References are made to activities against "international monopolies" undertaken by the Trade Unions Internationals of the WFTU.

More recently, the WFTU Bureau adopted a resolution [2] calling for co-ordinated action by the workers, on an international scale, in response to the level of organisation achieved by the managements of multinational corporations. It states that such co-ordination is an urgent necessity for the WFTU, the ICFTU and the WCL as well as for independent national and regional trade union centres, and it suggests that as regards Europe, it would be desirable to establish between all trade union organisations flexible forms of consultation, co-operation and co-ordination, ranging from more or less regular ordinary meetings to flexible co-ordination structures in which each trade union body would maintain its independence, particular outlook and freedom to act.

A resolution of the Oil Workers' Anti-monopolist World Conference [3], which was organised at Leuna (Halle) in May 1971 at the initiative of the Trade Unions International of Chemical, Oil and Allied Workers (WFTU) and certain other organisations, after enumerating the claims of workers in the oil industry, refers to the power of the "international oil cartel", which is harmful to the workers' aspirations, and calls for the full nationalisation of every aspect of the industry. The resolution proposes a world co-operation committee of all interested trade unions, regardless of their affiliation.

---

[1] "The trade unions against multinational companies", in *World Trade Union Movement* (London, World Federation of Trade Unions), May-June 1971, pp. i–xii.

[2] Ibid., Apr. 1972, pp. 1–2.

[3] For a description of the Conference see Charles Salducci: "From IG Farben to the struggle against the oil cartel", ibid., July 1971, pp. 26–27 and 32.

The International Metalworkers' Federation (IMF), at its 22nd Congress (Lausanne, October 1971), adopted a resolution [1] which states that the growth of multinational corporations, concentrating enormous economic and political power in a dwindling number of such corporations, presents the world's workers and governments with unprecedented problems and dangers. In addition to calling upon IMF affiliates to review, inter alia, their policies and bargaining procedures and to determine which, if any, of them may have to be reconsidered in order to facilitate effective international joint action, the resolution envisages a number of measures, including international company laws to regulate the activities of corporations that operate across national frontiers and to afford protection of the workers' interests. It urges the ILO to establish and publish a black list of multinational corporations found to be violating the provisions of international company law relating to matters of particular concern to workers.

The International Federation of Chemical and General Workers' Unions (ICF), at its 14th Statutory Congress (Copenhagen, October 1970), adopted two resolutions concerning multinational corporations.[2] The first, which deals with international collective bargaining policies, stresses the need for co-ordination of trade union claims and action and calls for the convening of an ICF conference and the subsequent election of a committee for these purposes. The second, which concerns the strengthening of international trade union action, notes, inter alia, that multinational corporations are not only growing in size but also consistently improving a strategy based on the division of the workers in the various countries; it calls for an international trade union strategy and the promotion of trade union action to counter the favourable conditions enjoyed—at national and international levels—by these corporations.

EMPLOYER VIEWS

It is clear from the statements and resolutions referred to in the preceding section that the growth of multinational corporations has given rise to great concern and hence wide discussion within the international trade union movement. There are fewer resolutions and declarations on this subject on the part of organised employers. Employers generally do not share the trade unions' convictions as to the adverse social and economic effects of the growth

---

[1] "Resolution on multinational corporations", in *IMF News* (Geneva, International Metalworkers' Federation), Nov. 1971, pp. 6–9.

[2] *ICF Bulletin* (Geneva, International Federation of Chemical and General Workers' Unions), Jan.-Feb. 1971, pp. 67 and 74.

of multinationalism. There are, in any case, fewer international employers' organisations than trade union organisations. Nevertheless, many employers recognise that the relationship between multinationals and social policy is an important question, and have made policy statements on the issues raised.

The subject of international corporations was the central theme of the 22nd Congress of the International Chamber of Commerce (Istanbul, May-June 1969).[1] The statement of conclusions adopted by the Congress makes no direct reference to matters connected with industrial relations. It does, however, reflect and, in a sense, respond to some of the trade unions' more general economic and social preoccupations described earlier. While stressing the positive effect of the international corporations in fostering balanced economic growth and the transfer of experience and skill, the statement expresses the view that these corporations must recognise the economic and social objectives of the countries in which they operate and also integrate themselves in the host country's life and contribute to its progress. It reminds host countries that the adoption of measures affecting the operation of companies subject to their jurisdiction invariably affects the investment climate, either adversely or favourably, and that rising living standards will be facilitated by liberal laws, regulations and policies applicable to foreign and national companies alike. The creation of regional markets of sufficient capacity is advocated, since market size is important in the development and application of technology. Governments are called upon to seek to remove barriers to free capital movement. Finally, the statement mentions that the International Chamber of Commerce intends to give continuing consideration to a possible formulation of agreed principles governing the conduct both of international corporations and of governments.[2]

The Council of the Organisation of Employers' Federations and Employers in Developing Countries discussed problems relating to multinational corporations and international trade unionism at its meeting held in Geneva in June 1971. The discussion paper on this subject contained the following statement:

The companies by and large accept that above all they must be "good citizens" of the countries in which they operate. This is usually taken to mean a respect for the host country's laws and regulations. Apart from showing respect for the host country's laws and providing good conditions of work, which are essential, it is

---

[1] International Chamber of Commerce: *World economic growth: The role, rights and responsibilities of the international corporation*, Statements and conclusions on the Congress theme, 22nd Congress of the International Chamber of Commerce, Istanbul, 31 May-7 June 1969 (Paris, brochure dw3, July 1969), p. 31.

[2] Since the Meeting, the International Chamber of Commerce has published *Guidelines for international investment*, Text adopted unanimously by the Council of the ICC, 120th Session, 29 November 1972 (Paris, brochure 272, Dec. 1972).

necessary that they are seen to be benefiting the country in other ways. . . . With this in mind many companies have adopted a structure in which the national organisations (i.e. the local subsidiaries) are themselves responsible for framing and implementing their own policies.

This view implies that there does not exist any major difference between the subsidiary of a multinational corporation and a domestic company of the host country and that, consequently, the multinational corporation does not require special consideration in the field of industrial relations.

The last-mentioned point is also made by the Deputy Managing Director of the Confederation of German Employers' Associations. Examining the various aspects of labour law in international corporations, he arrives at the conclusion that the subsidiaries of such companies necessarily operate in the economic and legal conditions of the host country, that both in law and in practice the position of their workers does not differ from that of workers in domestic firms and that there is no justification for instituting a dual system of industrial relations.[1]

In its annual report for 1971 the Confederation of German Employers' Associations took note of the international trade unions' discussions and activities concerning multinational corporations and asserted that it would devote special attention to, and oppose, trade union activity seeking the imposition of a network of controls and discriminatory, restrictive and anti-economic measures on such corporations, which would limit the investment activity of employers in home and host countries and result in loss of employment.[2]

In a recent issue of its bulletin the International Organisation of Employers reports the views expressed by the Deputy President of the Confederation of British Industry in the Confederation's review[3], where he points out that many of the problems alleged to be associated with multinational corporations are not very real; moreover, multinational corporations cannot be expected to locate their plants where the costs would be above those of competitors from other areas, and hence collective bargaining with trade unions on wages or discussions with government on taxes and investment must be seen in the context of the need to remain competitive and to survive, even if it is necessary to move in order to do so; the writer also doubts that transfer pricing, varying dividend payments and other practices to avoid taxes can escape the rigorous control nowadays exercised by governments.

---

[1] E.-G. Erdmann: "Arbeitsrechtliche Aspekte im internationalen Unternehmensverband", in *Recht und Steuer der internationalen Unternehmensverbindungen* (Düsseldorf, 1972).

[2] *Jahresbericht der Bundesvereinigung der Deutschen Arbeitgeberverbände, 1. Dezember 1970-30. November 1971*, vorgelegt der Mitgliederversammlung in Bonn-Bad Godesberg am 7. Dezember 1971, pp. 174–175.

[3] *IOE Information Bulletin* (Geneva, International Organisation of Employers), 31 Jan. 1972, pp. 3–4.

PARTICULAR INDUSTRIAL RELATIONS QUESTIONS

Transfer of operations and power relationships

A key problem as seen by trade unions is the power of a multinational corporation to shift production or operations, provisionally or permanently, from one country to another. In the absence of concerted resistance on the part of trade unions, this possibility can constitute a significant power factor in union-company relations. In collective bargaining the threat of a transfer of production, spoken or implicit, can seriously weaken the union's position and reduce the effectiveness of strike action.

A related factor which the trade unions see as weighing against them in the balance of bargaining power is the financial ability of the multinational corporation to withstand a strike. Where production at the plant affected by a strike is not necessary for continued operations in plants of the corporation in other countries, the actual loss of revenue resulting from the strike may be relatively insignificant in terms of the total turnover of the corporation.

While trade unions maintain that transfers of production have occurred in practice, certain commentators have pointed to the obstacles to such transfers. In the case of temporary transfers, for example during a strike, there would have to be other plant facilities capable of producing the same goods for the market in question. Doubts have been expressed whether transfers are possible at short notice, since investments are subject to long-term production plans; further, the plant to which production might be transferred may not, in fact, be near enough and may not have sufficient excess capacity to take on the production. The question of whether the production of the multinational corporation is organised vertically or horizontally is also significant. Indeed, the bargaining power of a national trade union may be greater vis-à-vis a multinational corporation than vis-à-vis a domestic enterprise if a stoppage of production in one country deprives plants of the corporation in other countries of the components necessary for their production or assembly work.

The shutdown of a plant in one country and the transfer of its production to another can, moreover, be problematical quite apart from considerations of loss of the company's fixed investment and the liability of the employer in certain countries for extensive severance payments and other financial charges in the event of plant closures. When considering a transfer of production, a multinational corporation will certainly take into account not only labour relations and labour costs in the new location but also such factors as the degree of inflation in the country, its political stability, the possibilities of capital repatriation, tariff regulations, the amount of government intervention, and so forth.[1]

In some cases, particularly in certain developing countries, the existence of industrial courts and similar tribunals to which disputes may be referred, with or without the consent of the parties concerned, can make the relative power of each party a somewhat academic issue. The ultimate decision on a dispute may be made by a court or in the course of some other arbitration procedure.

Locus of management decisions

Trade unions are concerned that, in the case of a multinational's subsidiary, the locus of managerial decision making, particularly as regards matters arising in collective bargaining, is not always where the confrontations between management and trade unions take place. Rather, it is contended, the relevant decisions are made at the headquarters of the multinational, beyond the reach of the trade union concerned.[2] It is argued that not infrequently, when demands, claims or grievances are submitted to local management, the reply is that such a matter can only be decided at headquarters. This means that trade union negotiators do not have the opportunity of personally presenting their case to those who ultimately take the decisions. Trade unions feel that it is of the highest importance to them to have access to the source of decisions on industrial relations and related issues.

It is obvious that practices vary among different multinational corporations, depending, for example, upon the type of economic activity in which they are engaged and upon the question at issue. Managements in multinational corporations affirm that on many issues, and in any event on those related to collective bargaining, the greatest decentralisation in decision making prevails, mainly because collective bargaining policy cannot be isolated from the legal and social environment of the locus of operation, and this, of course, differs greatly from one country to another. It has been asserted, however, that, owing to the very nature of the bargaining process, it may not make very much difference where the decisions are made: the business interests of the multinational corporation will result in the same response to a trade union, whether the response originates at headquarters or at the subsidiary.

[1] See Christopher Tugendhat: *The multinationals* (London, Eyre and Spottiswoode, 1971), p. 169.

[2] *Trade union strategies on multinational companies*, Notes on report of Daniel Benedict, Assistant General Secretary of the International Metalworkers' Federation, to the Conference on Multinational Corporations of the Queen's University of Belfast, Newcastle, Northern Ireland, 31 May-2 June 1971 (Geneva, IMF), p. 3.

In studies on the foreign operations of US automobile companies certain general findings suggest a relatively high degree of decentralisation in decision making on most bargaining issues and, in any event, a careful consideration by the central management of the views of local managements when decisions are taken.[1]

Adjustment of industrial relations and personnel policies and practices

A further problem raised in certain trade union circles and elsewhere is that multinational corporations frequently seek to transfer the industrial relations and personnel policies and practices of the home country to the other countries in which they operate, or fail to conform to the practices of the host countries. Indeed, there are documented cases of this kind, some of which have had adverse business effects on the corporation concerned. Moreover, a foreign company that breaches locally accepted standards is much more subject to criticism than is a local company acting in the same way.[2]

Employers' circles, whilst agreeing that some errors may have been made in the earlier days of international operations, argue that such examples belong to the past and that the importance of respecting the law and practices of the host country is now generally recognised by multinational corporations.

As regards the aspects of industrial relations that are regulated by law in the host country—including questions of trade union recognition and collective bargaining—the subsidiary of a multinational corporation has, of course, the same obligations as an indigenous company and is likewise subject to the host country's labour administration system, including, for example, factory inspection. Trade unionists [3] agree that cases of refusal by subsidiaries of multinational corporations to recognise trade unions are not very numerous

---

[1] Duane Kujawa: *International labor relations management in the automotive industry: A comparative study of Chrysler, Ford and General Motors*, Praeger special studies in international economics and development (New York, Praeger, 1971).

[2] The Trades Union Congress in the United Kingdom has found that "most international companies pursue industrial relations policies acceptable to the trade union movement, and at least no worse than those of many British-owned companies" but goes on to cite particular problems with regard to certain multinationals (Trades Union Congress: *Economic review, 1971* (London, Mar. 1971), p. 57). See also John Gennard and M. D. Steuer: "The industrial relations of foreign-owned subsidiaries in the United Kingdom", in *British Journal of Industrial Relations* (London), July 1971, pp. 143 ff.

[3] See, for example, International Confederation of Free Trade Unions: *The multinational challenge*, ICFTU World Economic Conference reports, No. 2 (Brussels, Sep. 1971), p. 19. On the other hand, trade union organisations have expressed apprehension "at the growing

in the industrialised countries of Europe. Mention may be made here of the Swedish Government's scheme for guaranteeing the overseas investments of Swedish companies, under which protected companies must undertake, with due regard for the legislation of the host country as well as national and international practices, to respect trade union rights, bargain collectively and disclose wage information for purposes of bargaining.

It should also be noted that multinational corporations have sometimes been responsible for innovations in industrial relations practices that have generally been recognised as constructive, both in developing and in industrialised countries. The development of collective bargaining itself in some countries is an example.[1]

As regards the more specific question of personnel policies and practices, there is increasing evidence—for example in the personnel manuals and guides of multinational corporations—that these corporations seek to adapt their policies and practices to national customs and patterns or at least not to do violence to them. It is not unusual for the internal directives of the corporation to specify that within the framework of central guidance—to the extent that it may be applicable—personnel and industrial relations policies can only be decided by local managements in the light of the local situation.[2] Some studies indicate, for instance, that even where most members of the management of a multinational's subsidiary are drawn from the home country, the person in charge of personnel matters is nearly always a national of the host country.

It has been observed that the managerial staff of multinational corporations are becoming increasingly international in outlook. This is a result of their own training policies as well as the programmes and curricula of business schools. Such an evolution can serve to diminish cultural tensions in industrial relations and personnel management, since internationally minded managers

---

practice of governments to indulge in an auction of incentives offering anti-trade union measures among other inducements in efforts to attract foreign investments instead of promoting regionally co-ordinated investment attraction schemes" (Resolution on freedom of association and multinational companies adopted by the ICFTU Executive Board in December 1970. See *ICFTU Economic and Social Bulletin*, Jan.-Feb. 1971, p. 21).

[1] John Gennard: *Multinational corporations and British labour: A review of attitudes and responses* (London, British-North American Committee, Jan. 1972), pp. 27–28; and L. Turner: *Invisible empires* (London, Hamish Hamilton, 1970), pp. 44–45.

[2] It has also been suggested that problems can arise from foreign management assuming differences of a national or cultural kind which do not really exist. It has been asserted that in many areas workers' expectations, goals and so on are similar, regardless of cultural background. See David Sirota and J. Michael Greenwood: "Understanding your overseas workforce", in *Harvard Business Review* (Boston (Massachusetts)), Jan.-Feb. 1971, pp. 53 ff.

can appreciate the dangers inherent in seeking blindly to impose alien practices on a local operation.[1]

There has also been discussion of participation by subsidiaries of multinational corporations in employers' organisations in host countries as an indication of their integration in the local industrial relations system. Here, however, it is necessary to consider the nature and purpose of the particular employers' organisation: whether it is consultative and concerned only with general policy or whether it is a vehicle for centralised collective bargaining. It is in the latter case that certain questions have arisen. At all events, it is evident that more and more subsidiaries of multinational corporations are becoming active members of the employers' organisations in host countries. In developing countries multinational corporations have sometimes even been largely instrumental in the founding of employers' organisations.

Financial practices and company data

The size and often far-flung operations of the multinational can make it difficult for the national trade union representing its workers in a given country to obtain what the union deems sufficient information for purposes of its relations with the local subsidiary, and in particular for collective bargaining purposes. Certain aspects of this question are discussed later in this chapter, but two may be mentioned here. The first concerns transfer pricing, that is pricing practices in regard to sales, transfers and other transactions within the corporation itself. While this practice is usually discussed in terms of tax avoidance, trade unionists point out that it can also have an effect on collective bargaining.[2] Transfer pricing, for instance, can give a misleading picture of non-profitability, which can be used by the management of a subsidiary to argue against wage claims and other demands made by the trade unions in local negotiations. However, the possibility of showing low profits as an argument against meeting trade union demands may become less attractive to the subsidiary if, in the same host country, tax rates are so low that it is advantageous, for tax purposes, to show relatively high profits.

A second aspect of the relationship of financial information to collective bargaining is the availability of detailed financial data on the multinational corporation as a whole and on its various subsidiaries. The argument of non-profitability used by a subsidiary might then be countered by a reference to the over-all profitability of the multinational corporation (as in the case of

---

[1] See Frederick A. Teague: "International management selection and development", in *California Management Review* (Berkeley (California)), Spring 1970, pp. 1–6.

[2] See, for example, Stephen Hugh-Jones: "The multinational strike", in *Vision: The European Business Magazine* (Geneva), Nov. 1970, p. 34.

St. Gobain, mentioned later in this chapter). Conversely, however, management would be in a position to counter claims of the local trade union based on the subsidiary's profitability by citing the poor over-all financial position of the corporation.

THE TRADE UNIONS' STRUCTURAL AND ORGANISATIONAL RESPONSE

As may be seen from the various resolutions and pronouncements of trade union bodies cited earlier, great stress has been laid on the need for co-ordinated trade union action as a counterforce to the multinational corporations. Such action, capable of reaching to the very centre of the multinational's decision-making apparatus, is regarded as essential to redress the balance of power between the corporations and the unions. But progress in this field is not easy. Effective co-ordination presupposes an identity or similarity of views on a number of issues and a willingness to co-operate.

The division of the world labour movement along ideological, political and other lines has resulted in largely separate efforts by the various international trade union organisations concerned with the same industry or multinational corporation. Even within these organisations the national constituents do not necessarily have the same preoccupations. There are sometimes differences concerning priorities as between trade unions in the developing countries, which may be interested in an influx of capital in order to promote economic development and employment, and trade unions in industrialised countries, which are, precisely, concerned about job losses in their own countries caused by the export of capital and the relocation of production facilities.

However, this does not mean that there is not agreement on many basic issues, such as the need for international solidarity in seeking to ensure that the best possible conditions are provided by a multinational corporation for its workers in all the countries where it operates. While activities in this area of international trade union co-operation are increasing at a rapid pace, they have hitherto gone little beyond expressions of mutual support.[1]

The International Trade Secretariats (ICFTU) are playing a major role in co-ordinating trade union activity in connection with multinational corporations. Mention may be made of the organisation by the International Metal-

---

[1] See, for example, Abe Morgenstern, International Union of Electrical, Radio and Machine Workers (AFL-CIO-CLC): *Bargaining with General Electric Company*, Paper presented to the International Conference on Trends in Industrial and Labour Relations, Tel-Aviv, 1972.

workers' Federation (IMF) of permanent councils for major multinational companies or groups of companies in the automobile industry. These councils are composed of representatives of national trade unions covering workers of the company in the various countries concerned. The councils meet regularly to exchange information and agree on bargaining tactics. The activities of the councils have been supplemented by the holding of world automotive conferences. Similar groupings have been organised by the IMF for multinational corporations in the electrical and electronics industries.

The International Federation of Chemical and General Workers' Unions (ICF) has also taken steps to establish permanent world councils for certain major multinational corporations in the rubber, plastics, chemical and paper industries, which meet as and when necessary. All trade unions having members employed by the corporation concerned may become members of the council, the chairman and vice-chairman being leaders of the trade unions responsible for bargaining with the corporation in its home country.

Other International Trade Secretariats, such as the International Union of Food and Allied Workers' Associations (IUF), the International Transport Workers' Federation, the International Federation of Commercial, Clerical and Technical Employees (IFCCTE) and the International Federation of Petroleum and Chemical Workers, although apparently not yet establishing special structures to deal with multinationals, have nevertheless been moving in this direction through the convening of special meetings of trade sections and other activities. The IFCCTE appears to have made a start in organising a council in respect of at least one corporation.

An example of co-operation between International Trade Secretariats is the decision of the ICF and the IUF in 1972 to set up a joint company council for a multinational conglomerate employing workers covered by both Secretariats. The task of the council will be to co-ordinate international solidarity action in support of bargaining demands and strikes by employees of the corporation in its various activities and locations.

Meetings largely devoted to formulating policy on multinational corporations have also been sponsored by the Trade Unions International of Chemical, Oil and Allied Workers (WFTU).

TRADE UNION RESEARCH, INFORMATION AND ADVISORY ACTIVITIES

It is generally considered that, both in their own right and as a prerequisite of further action, research and information activities by international trade union organisations are of capital importance. In one form or another such activities have long been undertaken by the International Trade Secretariats in support of the bargaining activities of their national affiliates, but the importance of research in respect of multinational corporations has provided the impetus for increased and more sustained efforts, perhaps of a somewhat different type.

It is hard enough to compile information on national enterprises. The difficulty is compounded in the case of the multinational corporation both by the sheer dimensions of the task and the complexities of analysing and correlating international information on a particular company, as well as by the lack of uniformity in national provisions relating to public disclosure and the greater or lesser propensity of the company for secrecy. Only the biggest national trade unions are in a position to engage effectively in the collection and analysis of the information necessary for bargaining purposes. It is, in fact, considered a task with which only International Trade Secretariats and similar bodies can cope. Indeed, one of the items on the list of points that trade unions would like to see incorporated in possible future international provisions governing multinational corporations relates to the obligatory disclosure of pertinent information; this would enable the trade unions to engage in bargaining, with a firmer knowledge of the real position, financial and otherwise, of the corporation concerned and of its subsidiaries in the various countries.

A number of International Trade Secretariats have been devoting much energy to research designed to produce full profiles of selected multinationals, including the terms of collective agreements applicable to their subsidiaries throughout the world. Work has been done by the International Metalworkers' Federation and the International Federation of Chemical and General Workers' Unions, in which computers have been used to assist in the compilation, analysis, storage, updating and retrieval of information and statistics on selected corporations. Items of interest include structure, location of plants, joint ventures, finances, applicable collective agreement provisions, trade union organisation, and working conditions.[1]

Direct assistance by the International Trade Secretariats to their national affiliates has similarly taken on new dimensions with the growth of multi-national corporations. For example the trade unions cite a number of cases in which it has been possible for an International Trade Secretariat itself, or one of its members in the home country of the multinational corporation, to intervene at the headquarters of the corporation in order to find a solution to a problem arising in a host country.

---

[1] See, for example, *ICF Bulletin*, Jan.-Feb. 1971, p. 19; and Norris Willatt: "The multi-national unions", in *Management Today* (London), Feb. 1971, p. 72.

MULTINATIONAL EMPLOYER-TRADE UNION CONSULTATIONS

Consultation on a transnational scale between multinational corporations and international trade union organisations is conceptually different from international collective bargaining. Although certain trade unionists see such consultation as a possible forerunner of collective bargaining, and although in practice consultation within countries sometimes leads to negotiations and may in certain situations overlap with, or be indistinguishable from, collective bargaining, the limited experience of multinational employer-trade union consultations to date does not indicate any such development. Nevertheless, this experience is regarded by trade unions as quite significant in itself.

A number of meetings are reported to have taken place between the senior management of the multinational Philips company, based in the Netherlands, and the European Metalworkers' Committee, which consists of trade unionists both from ICFTU-affiliated unions and from unions affiliated with the World Confederation of Labour. Consultations at the first meeting dealt with production problems, European production shifts and job security questions. Items brought up for discussion at subsequent meetings related to workers' retraining needs resulting from production shifts, the effects of financial operations between subsidiaries and the parent company on profit-sharing plans, the relative responsibilities of parent and subsidiary company managers, the company's policies on wages and working conditions for manual and non-manual workers and the possibility of holding regular consultations and setting up a special committee for the purpose of bringing about wage parity in the company's various European subsidiaries. The company has agreed to give advance notice to national trade unions of production changes in their respective countries and to notify the European Metalworkers' Committee where such changes would have effects in plants in other European countries.[1]

Starting at the end of 1969 consultative meetings have also taken place between the central management of Brown Boveri (Switzerland) and a delegation from the International Metalworkers' Federation including trade unionists connected with the company's operations in various countries of Europe.

---

[1] I. A. Litvak and C. J. Maule: "The union response to international corporations", in *Industrial Relations* (Berkeley (California)), Feb. 1972, pp. 67–68; Willatt, op. cit., p. 122; and Karl Casserini: "The challenge of multinational corporations and regional economic integration to the trade unions, their structure and their international activities", in Hans Günter (ed.): *Transnational industrial relations: The impact of multinational corporations and economic regionalism on industrial relations*, A symposium held at Geneva by the International Institute for Labour Studies (London, Macmillan, St. Martin's Press, 1972,) pp. 79–80.

The first meeting took place when the company was putting into effect a far-reaching international restructuring programme. The items discussed included the company's production programme for the various countries in which it operates, employment ramifications and possible effects of the structural changes on the company's employment policy.[1] Subsequent subjects of consultation included social security, questions of transferred workers, and improvement in communications. The parties have accepted the principle of annual meetings and the possibility of additional meetings if necessary.

On the occasion of the 1966 Detroit world company council meetings for the automotive industry, delegates from Ford plants all over the world met senior Ford labour relations staff, and similar meetings were held in the case of General Motors. The World Auto Company Councils have subsequently called for "meetings of representatives of each of the IMF World Auto Company Councils with the top policy makers of their respective international corporations. Among the priority items to be discussed at such meetings are information concerning investment and production plans and job security." [2]

Mention may also be made of the contacts which have taken place between IBM and the International Federation of Commercial, Clerical and Technical Employees, and between Nestlé and the International Union of Food and Allied Workers' Associations.

Employers' circles emphasise the informal character of such contacts.

INTERNATIONAL ASPECTS OF COLLECTIVE BARGAINING AND BARGAINING DISPUTES

Collective bargaining in the context of a multinational corporation can take on an international character in various ways, ranging from a situation in which a trade union bargaining with the corporation at the national level is given support of various kinds by the trade unions covering the employees of the corporation in other countries, to a situation in which direct bargaining takes place between the central management of the corporation and a trade union body representing the workers of all the corporation's subsidiaries. The different international aspects of collective bargaining in a multinational corporation are set out schematically in this chapter, but it should be noted that in practice more than one aspect may be evident in a given set of circumstances.

---

[1] *La Lutte syndicale* (Berne, Fédération des ouvriers sur métaux et horlogers), 10 Dec. 1969.

[2] Declaration of London IMF World Auto Company Councils, 23–25 March 1971, in *IMF Sector News* (Geneva, International Metalworkers' Federation), Apr. 1971, p. 13.

Supporting activities

Supporting action in the case of national bargaining situations, either by trade unions representing the workers in other subsidiaries of the same multi-national corporation or by bodies such as the International Trade Secretariats, is far from new. Such action can take the form of moral or material support for workers on strike, refusal to work on transferred production or to handle goods affected by the strike, sympathy strikes, and so on.

The declaration of the joint meeting of the IMF World Auto Company Councils in London in 1971 calls upon national affiliates representing workers of a corporation against which another national affiliate is striking to commit themselves to use all practicable means, including financial assistance, to help the striking union and to do nothing which would lessen the possibility of victory.

Mention may also be made of the not infrequent internationalisation of disputes in developing countries, where relatively weak unions have been assisted through the exercise of pressure at the headquarters of multinational corporations in Europe or North America by International Trade Secretariats or by the powerful corresponding union in the home country.

The issue of sympathy strikes or other types of sympathy action, such as boycotts, can raise serious legal and social questions in certain countries, where they may be illegal or provide a ground for dismissal. In addition, in many countries, including Canada, the Federal Republic of Germany, Sweden, Switzerland and the United States, the peace obligation during the term of a collective agreement, as dictated by the agreement itself (in the United States) or by national legislation (in Canada) or by jurisprudence (in the Federal Republic of Germany), could limit the possibility of resorting to sympathy action.

Apart from the question of the peace obligation, it would seem that there is a dearth of law or jurisprudence on sympathy strikes having international aspects. An important question can arise in countries where such strikes would be legal if the primary strike were legal: by the law of which of the two countries involved is the legality of the primary strike to be tested? It would seem that, as a general principle, the refusal to handle work affected by a strike is rather widely accepted in most Western European countries.[1]

Trade unions are seeking to secure legislative modifications in these areas, where necessary, to allow them greater freedom to co-ordinate their actions.

---

[1] However, a recent analysis of this whole question under present British law has led Professor Wedderburn to conclude that "sympathetic industrial action in Britain as part of an internationally co-ordinated campaign against a multinational group would run . . . grave risks of liability . . ." (K. W. Wedderburn: "Multinational enterprise and national labour law", in *Industrial Law Journal* (London), Mar. 1972, p. 18).

They argue that this is necessary to match a multinational corporation's freedom to co-ordinate its action internationally. However, irrespective of legal considerations, questions have been raised as to the general feasibility or desirability of the sympathy strike as an economic weapon, since it can involve substantial loss to workers who may not feel very strongly about the issues involved in the primary strike or may even have divergent interests.[1] It is considered by some unionists that the less painful refusal of overtime, either as a general measure or to avoid making up the production lost at the plant affected by the strike, might offer greater possibilities of effective economic pressure.

Corresponding action on the part of employers can, of course, be envisaged in the form of sympathy lockouts and other kinds of support.

Co-ordinated bargaining

There has been some limited experience with international co-ordinated or coalition bargaining of varying types. In its most discussed form, this implies simultaneous bargaining with all or most subsidiaries of a multinational corporation, either throughout the world or in a given region, which would be facilitated if trade unions were to work for common termination dates of existing and future collective agreements in the subsidiaries concerned.[2] The demands made in co-ordinated bargaining need not be the same, a principal object being the reinforcement of each national union's position through co-ordinated action, not the least element of which might be the threat of a strike affecting all of the subsidiaries concerned in the negotiations. In this sense, although the rules and principles are not hard and fast, one possibility would be for none of the national trade unions to finalise a settlement until all were ready to do so. In effect, co-ordinated bargaining is perceived by the trade unions as one means of marshalling their resources to match those of the multinational corporation.

A significant example of this trade union approach to bargaining with multinationals is the case of the simultaneous negotiations in 1969 between St. Gobain and trade unions in four countries (the termination dates of the

---

[1] For example, the question has been posed whether workers in developing countries should be expected to use their organised power to support wage increases for workers in industrialised countries and thereby widen the income gap and perhaps endanger their own employment prospects. See Hans Günter: "The future of transnational industrial relations: A tentative framework for analysis", in Günter, op. cit., p. 436.

[2] The establishment of common termination dates was recommended as an objective for the IMF company councils by the IMF-sponsored World Automotive Conference held in Turin in 1968 and again at the London joint meeting of IMF World Auto Company Councils in 1971.

various collective agreements happened to be reasonably close). The International Federation of Chemical and General Workers' Unions organised co-ordinated support for its four affiliates involved in the negotiations. Affiliates of this International Trade Secretariat in a total of 12 countries co-operated directly or through pledges of support. A permanent committee was established, and it was agreed not to conclude negotiations in any country without general concurrence. Other decisions involved the provision of material support for strikes, the prevention of any transfer of production, refusal to increase overtime, and a possible world-wide cessation of overtime in all St. Gobain plants in the event of a prolonged strike at any of the subsidiaries.[1]

Centralised multinational collective bargaining

Direct international collective bargaining between the central management of a multinational corporation and a trade union body representing its employees in several countries—a form of centralised bargaining—is sought by many leaders of trade union organisations; they feel that it is a means of access to the real locus of decision making in the multinational corporation and of arriving at an upward harmonisation, at the world-wide or regional level, of the employment conditions of workers of the corporation. The view has also been expressed that international collective bargaining will give the trade unions greater leverage in connection with decisions affecting certain of the corporation's operations having social implications, for example decisions to transfer production facilities or to relocate plants.

Employers have expressed the view that the idea of international collective bargaining is not realistic. They are of the opinion that the conditions in the various countries in which a multinational corporation may be operating are likely to be so disparate as to preclude any attempt to establish common world-wide or even regional norms through bargaining. Moreover, labour relations and labour law practices and systems, based as they are on distinct historical, political and social factors, vary widely between countries. It is further pointed out that, depending upon the country, the conditions of work or other items upon which international negotiation is sought may be subject to regulation through national legislation. One example cited in this regard is the difficulty of defining "wage parity" when in certain countries statutory fringe benefits can amount to more than 50 per cent of wages, while in others legislation plays a minor role. It has also been suggested

---

[1] See *ICF Bulletin*, Jan.-Feb. 1971, pp. 25–26; and ICFTU: *The multinational challenge*, op. cit., p. 25.

that centralised multinational collective bargaining would not be of great importance, since only minima could be set, which would not bring about any significant upward harmonisation of conditions or lessening of disparities. Moreover, certain employers note that since wages and working conditions may not or cannot be the key bargaining issues—and indeed even where they are—the trade unions will be likely to turn to issues that employers have traditionally considered to be exclusive management prerogatives and which can affect a main objective of multinational operations, the optimum allocation of resources on an international scale. Indeed, trade unionists, although they are not necessarily in agreement on the degrees of priority to be attributed to various issues, have indicated that they would expect to bargain on such issues as those related to investments, resource allocation, plant location and transfer, and the introduction of technological change.[1]

As there are no international rules for multinational collective bargaining, it would appear that such bargaining can take place only where both parties agree to bargain. It is, however, questioned in employers' circles whether, even if such agreement between the parties exists, there can be multinational collective bargaining in the absence of any international legal basis for it, particularly since multinational corporations are subject to national laws and regulations governing collective bargaining.

In spite of the varying viewpoints of employers and trade unionists[2], it is worth considering a number of questions which have been raised in discussions on the possible development of centralised international collective bargaining involving multinational corporations.

Industry-wide bargaining is a dominant pattern in a number of countries today, particularly in Europe and certain parts in Africa. On the other hand, bargaining with a multinational corporation on a world-wide or regional scale would constitute bargaining at the enterprise level. If bargaining were to take place at both levels in the same country, difficulties could arise. These difficulties might be more pronounced where, through the legal procedures for extending collective agreements, which exist in certain countries, the multinational corporation might be bound by the industry or association agreement, whether it was a party to the agreement or not. However, it is conceivable that possible difficulties could be mitigated where centralised multinational collective bargaining dealt with issues quite distinct from those dealt with in industry or association bargaining in a given country; or accommodation could come about where an agreement reached at one level

---

[1] See, for example, Günter, op. cit., p. 431; and Casserini, op. cit., p. 89.

[2] The Canadian-US agreement between the Chrysler Corporation and the United Automobile Workers of America, which is described in Chapter 3, is generally held by trade unionists to be an example of real centralised international collective bargaining.

improved on the provisions of the agreement reached at another level. In the latter case, however, difficulties might arise from the possible impact on the local employers and their associations, if the multinational enterprise agreement provided for an improvement in benefits and conditions beyond those negotiated for the industry at the national level.

The question of the subject-matter of centralised collective bargaining with multinational corporations suggests the related question of the level of such bargaining and the possible co-ordination of bargaining at different levels of the corporation (world, regional, plant).

Account would also have to be taken of the impact of centralised multi-national collective bargaining on national incomes (wages and prices) policies, such as exist or are being considered in a number of countries, both industrialised and developing, particularly where wages and related economic benefits were a subject of such bargaining.

Deadlocks arising in multinational collective bargaining might also create problems. Mandatory national settlement procedures might be applicable. Strikes or lockouts might not be legal in a host country in cases where the international bargaining was taking place elsewhere, if the legislation of the host country required that bargaining and conciliation procedures be exhausted before resort could be had to direct action. In certain countries statutory compulsory arbitration procedures might have to be applied. If a strike or lockout arose in one or more countries from an impasse in multinational bargaining, it might be regarded as illegal in countries where sympathy action is prohibited.

In discussing international collective bargaining, it is relevant to refer to the provisions of the draft European company statute (now being discussed within the European Communities) which deal with European collective agreements in respect of enterprises incorporated under the statute. According to these provisions, the agreements are to be negotiated with trade unions represented in the company, but little further guidance is given on the determination of the competent unions. Employers have expressed the view that such European collective agreements would be neither feasible nor desirable in tha absence of unified European labour legislation, particularly as regards collective bargaining.

Workers' participation in decision making in multinational enterprises

There has been some discussion of instituting workers' participation in management in multinational enterprises through workers' representation on the management boards of the parent company.[1] It is the view of some trade unionists that international collective bargaining in any of its forms is not sufficient: only by being on the spot when policy is framed—through membership of the boards of multinational corporations—can the trade unions concerned adequately defend the workers' interests and those of the public.

At present such representation exists only in the framework of national laws and regulations in certain countries, without distinction between local and foreign enterprises. Reference should again be made to the draft European company statute. This draft, in one of its more debated parts, would generally require the future European company seeking incorporation under the statute to provide for workers' representation on its supervisory board, which oversees the board of management. The draft provides for a minimum one-third worker representation (the corporate statutes may provide for a higher percentage), and for workers' representatives to include trade unionists from outside the enterprise.

Provision is also made in the draft statute for company-wide works councils, the agreement of which would be required for certain decisions concerning recruitment, promotion, dismissal, training, remuneration principles, health and safety, work schedules, vacations and the administration of welfare schemes.

Employers have strongly criticised the section of the draft statute concerning workers' representatives on supervisory boards.[2] Even among trade unionists unanimity is not complete on all aspects of this question, which is one of the most delicate issues in the field of industrial relations.

* * *

The foregoing chapter illustrates the unsettled nature of most issues involving industrial relations in a multinational framework. The phenomenon of the multinational corporation is too recent for firm opinions and inflexible positions to have developed among the many parties concerned.

---

[1] See, for example, "The multinational corporation", Secretary-General Charles Levinson's activities report to the 14th Statutory Congress of the International Federation of Chemical and General Workers' Unions (Copenhagen, October 1970), in *ICF Bulletin*, Jan.-Feb. 1971, pp. 28–33.

[2] Erdmann, op. cit., and the declaration by the Union of Industries of the European Community, dated 12 March 1971 (Union des Industries de la Communauté Européenne: *Avis de l'UNICE relatif à la proposition d'un statut des sociétés anonymes européennes* (Brussels, 12 Mar. 1971; mimeographed).

5. INTERNATIONAL LABOUR STANDARDS AND SOCIAL PRINCIPLES DEVELOPED BY THE ILO

When deciding on the scope of the Meeting, the Governing Body, after lengthy examination of the subject, defined the final item for discussion as follows: "The measures appropriate for the application by national legislation of ILO standards on working conditions, trade union rights and free collective bargaining."

The operations of a multinational corporation in a host country are affected by the application of international instruments by the government of that country in exactly the same way as are those of corporations of an indigenous character. However, the International Labour Conference, in its resolution concerning the social problems raised by multinational undertakings, adopted in 1971, recognised that the increasingly rapid development of multinational undertakings raised new social problems. This chapter is therefore devoted to an examination of the relevance of international standards and social principles to the settlement, on tripartite lines, of some of these new social problems.

It may be useful to begin with a brief outline of the special character of ILO instruments and how they are applied.[1]

ILO CONVENTIONS AND RECOMMENDATIONS

The ILO Constitution lays down specific procedures for framing international instruments. Year by year, as part of its regular business, the tripartite International Labour Conference considers major social problems and seeks to crystallise national experience in a series of instruments taking the form

---

[1] For a fuller description of the ILO standard-setting system, see Nicolas Valticos: "Fifty years of standard-setting activities by the International Labour Organisation", in *International Labour Review* (Geneva, ILO), Sep. 1969, pp. 201–237 (available in off-print).

of Conventions and Recommendations. Both Conventions and Recommendations have to be adopted by a two-thirds majority vote of the Conference, following careful technical preparation, consultation and discussion, generally at two successive sessions. Conventions are open to ratification by member States and, upon ratification, create binding obligations to make their provisions effective through legislative and other action. Recommendations are not intended for ratification, but—as their name indicates—are meant to provide guidance for national law, practice and policy. However, ILO standards should not be thought of merely in terms of whether or not they may lead to ratification. Conventions, even in the absence of formal ratification, can serve as guidelines for the development of national laws and policies, and set objectives for social advance. It is the current practice of governments, when they wish to prepare new labour laws or develop new social institutions, to draw upon the relevant ILO instruments, whether or not these instruments are binding in their countries.

To date, the Conference has adopted 136 Conventions and 144 Recommendations. Together, these instruments have come to be referred to as the "International Labour Code". There are instruments relating to human resources development (including employment policy, employment services and vocational guidance and training), general conditions of employment (including employment security, wages, hours of work, weekly rest and holidays with pay), industrial safety, health and welfare, social security and labour administration. A number of instruments deal with the special problems relating to the employment of specific groups, such as children and young persons, women, migrant workers, seafarers, indigenous and tribal populations and plantation workers. Some instruments contain special provisions regarding developing countries, while others deal specifically with social policy in such countries. Among the most widely accepted ILO standards are the Conventions on such basic human rights as freedom of association and the right to organise, freedom of labour and freedom from discrimination. In the field of industrial relations, in addition to the instruments on freedom of association, there are Recommendations dealing with collective agreements, voluntary conciliation and arbitration, co-operation at the level of the undertaking, consultation at the industrial and national levels, communications within the undertaking, termination of employment, the examination of grievances, and the recently adopted Convention and Recommendation on workers' representatives. A number of instruments revise earlier standards in order to meet changing needs, thus maintaining the dynamic character of international labour standards.

With regard to the 136 Conventions so far adopted, a total of 3,880 ratifications was registered on 11 July 1972, an average of 31 for each of the

123 States which are at present Members of the ILO. Thus an extensive network of international obligations to respect these minimum standards has been created.

If an ILO Convention is formally accepted through ratification, two forms of international supervision may come into play. On the one hand, reports indicating the measures taken at the national level must be sent to the ILO at regular yearly or two-yearly intervals. Copies of these reports must be communicated to representative employers' and workers' organisations, which thus have an opportunity to submit comments. The reports are examined in turn by a committee of independent experts and a standing committee of the International Labour Conference, where Government, Employers' and Workers' members are able to discuss and determine what difficulties stand in the way of the implementation of ILO standards and how these difficulties can be overcome. Besides this normal procedure for noting problems and progress, there are contentious procedures under which, inter alia, employers' or workers' organisations may submit representations concerning non-observance of a ratified Convention for investigation by the Governing Body.

It should be noted that the status of an unratified Convention and that of a Recommendation are broadly similar. The Constitution of the ILO states that in both cases, apart from the undertaking to bring the instrument before the competent authority or authorities, no further obligation shall rest upon a Member, except that it shall report to the Director-General of the International Labour Office, at appropriate intervals as requested by the Governing Body, the position of its law and practice in regard to the matters dealt with in the Convention or Recommendation. From time to time, the Governing Body has exercised its right to request such information. For example the Conference in 1964 adopted the Employment Policy Convention and Recommendation. Subsequent to the framing of these instruments the ILO initiated a World Employment Programme, which was conceived as a contribution to the Second United Nations Development Decade launched in 1970. Because of the decisive role played by employment promotion in such a programme, the Governing Body decided to ask for reports on the Convention and Recommendation, the evaluation of which by the ILO's committee of independent experts was submitted to the 1972 Session of the Conference.

This succinct description may suffice to illustrate the working of the system of ILO standards and in particular the unique way in which representatives of employers and workers participate, together with governments, both in framing the international instruments and in supervising their implementation.

In an examination of how international labour standards are applied it must be borne in mind that the primary responsibility for the implementation of ILO Conventions and Recommendations rests with States and, consequently, national governments. Two situations may be distinguished. In so far as Conventions ratified by the host country are concerned, the position regarding multinational corporations would be similar, as regards observance of national legislation, to that discussed in the preceding chapter: operations taking place within a particular national context would be governed by the pertinent national legislation. The implementation of international instruments may, however, transcend the field of legislative action. Thus there are promotional instruments, such as the Employment Policy Convention, 1964, mentioned above, the implementation of which in relation to all enterprises, including multinational corporations, involves measures of employment promotion, including training requirements, adapted to the mobility of employers operating even beyond the limits of the national employment market.

Another factor to be kept in mind in considering the application of ratified Conventions is the increasing frequency with which ILO instruments call for collaboration or consultation with employers and workers or their organisations: approximately half of the Conventions now in force or likely soon to enter into force (and 90 per cent of the Conventions adopted since 1947) contain provisions of this kind. Under their terms, governments may be required to consult employers and workers or their organisations prior to the adoption of legislative measures, or the competent authorities may have to collaborate with employers and workers in the application of relevant legislation or other measures; in a number of cases, equal participation of employers' and workers' representatives in special bodies or machinery is mandatory.[1]

OTHER PRINCIPLES OF SOCIAL POLICY

As explained earlier in this chapter, the International Labour Code consists of the body of Conventions and Recommendations adopted by the Interna-

---

[1] In the resolution concerning the strengthening of tripartism adopted at its 56th Session, in 1971, the International Labour Conference, inter alia, noted with approval the establishment in many States of advisory or other tripartite bodies on which employers and workers were equally represented, and referred to the development of the International Labour Code as an example of the solid foundation provided by the tripartite element in the ILO. See also ILO: *Report of the Committee of Experts on the Application of Conventions and Recommendations*, Report III (Part 4A), International Labour Conference, 57th Session, Geneva, 1972, Part One: "General report", section III: "Role of employers and workers and their organisations in the implementation of ILO standards", pp. 10–25.

It should be noted that the Conference adopts, by a simple majority, resolutions in respect of which Members are not bound by any obligations such as those pertaining to Conventions and Recommendations. The majority of these resolutions consist of suggestions for the current or future work of the ILO, but some of them formulate conclusions on social and economic policy which are of permanent interest.

tional Labour Conference. These, however, must be read in conjunction with a whole series of other principles of social policy which have been evolved by the International Labour Organisation by a variety of procedures. The policy-defining function of the Organisation tended from the beginning to outgrow the limitations of the Convention and Recommendation procedure provided for by the Constitution of the Organisation. Less formal procedures have been developed to supplement them by guidelines adopted, in the form of resolutions, conclusions, reports and memoranda, by ILO bodies representing the views and interests of particular regions of the world, industries, sectors of the economy or types of worker. The conclusions on social policy expressed in this manner do not have the same authority as the Conventions and Recommendations; they involve no obligations such as those provided for by the Constitution in respect of Conventions and Recommendations; they have to be seen as agreed guidelines designed to promote the development of a progressive social policy and concerning matters for joint negotiation rather than for legislative action.

The various bodies established within the ILO for this purpose vary widely in their terms of reference and structure. Some are ad hoc meetings dealing with a particular problem. Others are permanent bodies and meet periodically. The most important in this connection are the Industrial and analogous Committees, because, as has been seen, there is a concentration of multinational operations in a limited number of industries: petroleum, mining, chemicals, motor vehicles, electronics and food processing. For almost all these sectors there exist Industrial Committees, each of which brings together persons with practical experience in the sector concerned and provides a forum for a free exchange of views on new problems of common concern.

Perhaps the most important characteristic shared by all these bodies is the high degree of voluntarism involved in the implementation of the principles of social policy they enunciate. The conclusions and resolutions they adopt constitute a body of recommendations and suggestions, on which action should be taken, according to their nature, separately or jointly by governments and national organisations of employers and workers in the sector concerned. At the request of the Governing Body the Director-General of the ILO communicates them officially to governments, with the request that they transmit them to the employers' and workers' organisations concerned, together with any observations of the Governing Body. However, it is for the governments and employers' and workers' organisations concerned to consider the effect to be given to conclusions and resolutions containing suggestions the application of which is within their competence.

SOME TRADE UNION AND EMPLOYER VIEWS ON THE RELEVANCE OF INTERNATIONAL LABOUR STANDARDS TO MULTINATIONAL ENTERPRISES

Up to this point consideration has only been given to the traditional working of international labour standards (Conventions and Recommendations) and of the other, less formal, principles of social policy which have been developed within the ILO. Both the legal and promotional aspects of Conventions, Recommendations, and other principles of social policy have been explained. No distinction was made between multinational enterprises and enterprises of an indigenous character.

It may, however, be useful, at this stage, to give a brief account of some new thoughts expressed outside the ILO on the particular relevance of ILO standards to some of the problems raised by multinational enterprise operations.

The possibility of international standards, regulations or codes for multinational enterprises has received some attention from international organisations, business organisations and individual persons.[1] The most recent examples of such attention from international organisations are provided by resolutions adopted at the Third Session (April-May 1972) of the United Nations Conference on Trade and Development (UNCTAD) and the 53rd Session (July 1972) of the Economic and Social Council of the United Nations. In the first case, it was decided to establish an ad hoc group of experts to study and make a report on restrictive business practices, including those resulting from activities of multinational corporations, and to examine the possibility of drawing up guidelines for the consideration of governments of developed and developing countries regarding restrictive business practices

---

[1] For example, in the United States the Assistant to the President for International Economic Affairs (subsequently Secretary of Commerce) stated: "It would be desirable for developing countries to subscribe to and honour such a code [i.e. an international code to govern national treatment of foreign investments]. ... At the same time, such a code... might well be supplemented by a code of good behaviour for corporations." (Peter G. Peterson: *The United States in the changing world economy*, Vol. I: *A foreign economic perspective* (Washington, DC, US Government Printing Office, Dec. 1971), p. 46).

The International Chamber of Commerce, at its 22nd Congress, discussed the desirability of an international convention on restrictive business practices in international trade and the possibility of the various countries promulgating uniform anti-trust legislation. See International Chamber of Commerce: *World economic growth: The role, rights and responsibilities of the international corporation*, Statements and conclusions on the Congress theme, 22nd Congress of the International Chamber of Commerce, Istanbul, 31 May-7 June 1969 (Paris, brochure dw3, July 1969), p. 17.

The International Bank for Reconstruction and Development opened for signature in 1965 a Convention on the Settlement of Investment Disputes between States and Nationals of Other States, administered by an autonomous international institution, the International Centre for the Settlement of Investment Disputes.

adversely affecting developing countries.[1] The resolution of the Economic and Social Council requests the appointment of a group of eminent persons intimately acquainted with economic, social and international policy to study the role of multinational corporations and their impact on the process of development, especially of the developing countries, and to formulate conclusions which may possibly be used by governments in making their sovereign decisions regarding national policy in this respect. The resolution further recommends that the above-mentioned study group take advantage of, and take into account, the research being carried out in this field by other international organisations and, in particular, that carried out in the ILO as a result of the Meeting on the Relationship between Multinational Corporations and Social Policy.[2] However, the discussion in this context centred on economic and political questions, such as the harmonisation of international business law, development policies, anti-trust legislation, expropriation of property and investment disputes.

The question of international standards in the context of multinational corporations and social policy, however, has, with very few exceptions, only been discussed in trade union circles. The subject has received a great deal of attention from the international trade union movement and, to a lesser degree, from national trade union bodies.

The measures most commonly called for by the trade unions are a "code of conduct", a "code of behaviour", or "international fair labour standards", and in this connection reference is often made to the international labour standards developed by the ILO, especially those relating to trade union rights, collective bargaining and freedom of association. One international trade union view was spelled out in detail in hearings before the Subcommittee on Foreign Economic Policy of the Joint Economic Committee of the United States Congress in July 1970.[3] It was said on this occasion that an international instrument was needed outlining the obligations of multinational companies toward governments and trade unions; the instrument should

---

[1] *Resolution on restrictive business practices*, adopted at the Third Session of the United Nations Conference on Trade and Development, Santiago, Chile, 13 April-21 May 1972 (Geneva, doc. TD/III/RES/73, June 1972; mimeographed).

[2] United Nations, Economic and Social Council, 53rd Session: *Resolution on the impact of multinational corporations on the development process and on international relations*, adopted at the 1836th meeting on 28 July 1972 (Geneva, doc. E/RES/1721; mimeographed).

[3] "Statement of Heribert Maier, Director, Economic, Social and Political Department, International Confederation of Free Trade Unions", in *A foreign economic policy for the 1970s*, Hearings before the Subcommittee on Foreign Economic Policy of the Joint Economic Committee, Congress of the United States, 91st Congress, Second Session, Part 4: *The multinational corporation and international investment* (Washington, DC, US Government Printing Office, 1970), pp. 824–825. Mr. Maier is now Assistant General Secretary of the ICFTU.

include clauses making it compulsory for the companies to abide by ILO principles and, in particular, international Conventions guaranteeing freedom of association and the right of workers to organise and engage in collective bargaining; it should also call for compliance with all other ILO Conventions, whether or not they had been ratified by the governments of the countries in which the company might be operating.

In December 1970 the Executive Board of the International Confederation of Free Trade Unions (ICFTU) adopted a resolution on freedom of association and multinational companies in which an appeal was addressed to governments for measures to compel multinational companies [1] to produce global accounts and for action to secure respect for trade union rights by these companies in accordance with the relevant ILO Conventions, and to the United Nations to convene a conference in order to lay down a code of conduct for such companies.[2] The World Economic Conference of the Free Trade Unions, organised by the ICFTU in June 1971, adopted a statement on the same subject [3] in which it called for intensified activity in international and regional organisations, in particular UN bodies, the General Agreement on Tariffs and Trade (GATT), the ILO and the Organisation for Economic Co-operation and Development (OECD), to secure the adoption of an international agreement laying down a code of conduct for multinational companies and making institutional provisions with trade union participation for its enforcement, including a complaints procedure. Finally, at its Tenth World Congress, in July 1972, the ICFTU adopted a resolution on multinational companies in which it insisted that such companies operating in the developing countries should not impinge on the political sovereignty and integrity of the countries concerned and should strictly observe ILO Conventions in their industrial relations.[4]

At the level of the International Trade Secretariats, the International Metalworkers' Federation (IMF) and the Miners' International Federation have both made references to codes of conduct. As early as 1968 the IMF, at its 21st Congress (Zurich, May 1968), adopted a resolution stating that in the event that treaties are negotiated providing for international corporate law or the issuance of international charters, such treaties should require as

---

[1] A highly complex question concerning the extra-territorial application of national law arises in this context.

[2] "Resolution on freedom of association and multinational companies", in *ICFTU Economic and Social Bulletin* (Brussels, International Confederation of Free Trade Unions), Jan.-Feb. 1971, pp. 21–22.

[3] "Free trade unions and multinational companies", ibid., July 1971, pp. 38–42.

[4] Ibid., July-Aug. 1972, pp. 16–17.

a minimum that the companies subject to them honour the rights of employees, in whatever the national political entity, to organise, to bargain collectively over all matters affecting wages, hours, working conditions, and employment and income security, and to abide by all provisions of all ILO Conventions, whether or not ratified by the country in which the multinational corporation may be operating.[1] At its 22nd Congress (Lausanne, October 1971) the IMF reaffirmed the substance of the resolution adopted at its 21st Congress and stated, in addition, that national laws for the regulation of corporations must be supplemented by international corporate laws to regulate the activities of corporations that operate across national boundaries and that such international laws should include the provisions requested by the 21st Congress.[2]

The Executive Committee of the Miners' International Federation adopted in May 1972 a resolution concerning an international code of conduct for multinational companies in which it asserted that such a code should have the effect of obliging these companies to guarantee to their workers everywhere complete freedom of association and full trade union rights, as laid down in the pertinent ILO Conventions [3], and called on the pertinent UN bodies, the European Economic Community, GATT, the ILO and OECD to give priority to the speedy establishment of an international code of conduct for multinational companies.

With regard to "international fair labour standards", the IMF has been particularly active in promoting this concept at the international trade union level. At its World Conference of Electrical and Electronic Workers (The Hague, September-October 1970) it was stated: "Trade union action for fair labour standards has included support for ILO Conventions and Recommendations and for greater ILO attention to these problems. Efforts should be made on the national and international level to require multinational companies to comply fully with such standards in every country in which they operate."[4]

Trade unions in a number of countries have also shown an active interest in the concept of international fair labour standards. The Executive Committee of the AFL-CIO in February 1971 called upon the Government of the United States to press for the establishment of international fair labour standards in world trade; speakers at a conference convened by the Industrial Union

[1] "Resolution on multinational corporations", in *Bulletin of the International Metalworkers' Federation* (Geneva), Oct. 1968, p. 18.
[2] "Resolution on multinational corporations", in *IMF News* (Geneva), Nov. 1971, pp. 6–9.
[3] The Freedom of Association and Protection of the Right to Organise Convention, 1948, and the Right to Organise and Collective Bargaining Convention, 1949.
[4] *IMF News*, Oct. 1970, p. 2.

Department of the AFL-CIO in March 1970 also called for the establishment of such standards.[1]

While many employers recognise that the development of multinational corporations raises new social problems, their suggestions as to how to solve these problems differ in many respects from those of the trade unions quoted above.

As was mentioned in Chapter 4, the 22nd Congress of the International Chamber of Commerce stated in its conclusions that international corporations must recognise the economic and social objectives of the countries in which they operate and also integrate themselves in the host country's life and contribute to its progress. The conclusions reminded host countries that, among other things, " the achievement of rising living standards will be facilitated by liberal laws, regulations and policies that affect business operations of foreign or national companies alike".[2]

In a similar manner, in a discussion paper for its Council Meeting in Geneva in 1971, the Organisation of Employers' Federations and Employers in Developing Countries stated, as was also mentioned in Chapter 4, that the companies by and large accept that, above all, they must be "good citizens" of the countries in which they operate.

It is therefore quite clear that the employers look upon the integration of a multinational corporation in the country in which it operates as the main way of solving such new social problems as may arise. Such integration would mean that the multinational corporation should respect the national laws, policies and economic and social objectives of the host country in the same way as would a good national company.

As to the relevance of ILO standards, a statement on this subject was made by an Employers' member when the agenda for the Meeting on the Relationship between Multinational Corporations and Social Policy was discussed in the Governing Body of the ILO. He said that multinational companies, which in actual fact always take the form, in the various countries, of entities answerable to certain national authorities, cannot be subordinated directly to the application of ILO standards without running the risk of ignoring the national authorities. They may be subordinated to these standards only through national law.[3]

---

[1] *Statement by the AFL-CIO Executive Council on international trade and investment, Bal Harbour, Florida, 19 February 1971* (mimeographed); and William C. Shelton: "The changing attitude of US labor unions toward world trade", in *Monthly Labor Review* (Washington, DC), May 1970, pp. 51–54.

[2] International Chamber of Commerce: *World economic growth: The role, rights and responsibilities of the international corporation*, op. cit., p. 31.

[3] Statement made by Mr. Verschueren, Employers' substitute member of the Governing Body of the International Labour Office, at the 185th Session of the Governing Body, Geneva, February-March 1972.

A further problem has been raised by the International Organisation of Employers in a discussion paper on multinational corporations. In examining the demand of the trade unions for a "code of behaviour" or for "fair labour standards", to be drawn up by the ILO, the discussion paper stated that quite apart from the fact that the situation did not seem to warrant it, and the many problems of a juridical nature it would pose, one effect of adopting such a suggestion would be to discriminate clearly between multinational subsidiaries and other firms within a country as well as to create two separate sets of ILO standards.

On the other hand, it is often pointed out by employers that modern and successful companies, whether they are subsidiaries of multinational corporations or national companies, frequently apply unratified ILO Conventions on a voluntary basis, as well as Recommendations and many of the guidelines adopted, in the form of resolutions, conclusions, reports and memoranda, by other ILO bodies, such as the Industrial Committees, the provisions of which often go beyond the requirements of national legislation and collective agreements.

*   *   *

The foregoing chapter has reviewed some aspects of international labour standards and other general principles developed by the ILO, with a view to promoting an open discussion on the possible role and relevance of such standards and principles within the particular context of the relationship between multinational corporations and social policy.

PART II

REPORT OF THE MEETING

REPORT OF THE ILO MEETING ON THE RELATIONSHIP BETWEEN MULTINATIONAL CORPORATIONS AND SOCIAL POLICY

INTRODUCTION

1. In accordance with a decision taken by the Governing Body of the International Labour Office at its 185th Session (Geneva, February-March 1972), a Meeting on the Relationship between Multinational Corporations and Social Policy was held in Geneva from 26 October to 4 November 1972.

2. Twenty-four experts, drawn from government, employer and worker circles, took part in the Meeting, which was also attended by substitutes and advisers nominated by the Governing Body and by a number of observers. A list of participants is attached to this report as Appendix III.

3. Mr. N. P. Dube, Additional Secretary to the Government of India, Ministry of Labour and Rehabilitation, was unanimously elected Chairman of the Meeting.

4. The Meeting held 11 sittings.

5. On behalf of the Director-General of the International Labour Office, Dr. Abbas Ammar, Deputy Director-General, welcomed the participants. He noted that over the past few years the problems associated with multinational corporations had aroused ever-increasing interest and concern. Amongst these problems were those relating to the social aspects of the multinational corporation; such problems constituted only one band in a broad and complex spectrum of considerations, but it was an extremely important one. That was why the Governing Body of the International Labour Office had decided to convene the Meeting, with a view to exploring the specific problems of social policy that might result from the operations of multinational corporations.

6. The essential purpose of the Office's consultations with the experts was to clarify the extent to which, and the manner in which, the ILO, within its particular field of competence and with its tripartite structure, could contribute to the solution of these problems of social policy. The findings and advice of the Meeting would be reported to the Governing Body of the ILO for its consideration. The task before the Meeting was not an easy one. Firstly, too little was known about the problems in question to enable anyone to speak with full assurance. The working document that had been prepared by the Office to serve as a basis of discussion admitted this freely; it was submitted in the hope that it would help the experts in reaching their own conclusions. Secondly, the subject-matter was controversial and emotional. Some considered multinational corporations to be invaluable instruments for the wider distribution of capital, technology and employment. Others regarded them as huge business concentrations which existing institutions, national and international, were not able to control adequately and the activities of which tended to disregard the public interest and to ignore or undermine established social and labour standards. In these circumstances it was natural that the experts, representing different segments of society in different countries, would have conflicting views on many aspects of the matter. It was to be hoped, however, that, with good will and with objectivity, they would be able to overcome any difficulties encountered and to concentrate on policies and points of common interest rather than on issues that would separate them. It was important for the experts to consider the problems with an open mind and to use the Meeting as a forum where some of the uncertainties that had grown up around the operations of multinational corporations might be dispelled and where conjecture would be replaced with more rational analysis.

7. Multinational corporations were currently a part of the institutional framework within which everyone lived and worked, and their validity, like that of any other institution, should be judged in terms of their responsiveness to the purposes that were had in mind. The ILO was concerned with the social aspects of their operations, and the Meeting's assignment was to examine these as carefully as possible. Its deliberations might help the ILO to work out any constructive adjustments that might be necessary to achieve the social objectives pursued by all. Dr. Ammar expressed the hope that they would help to promote these adjustments not only within the United Nations system but also within the various States.

8. Mr. B. Bolin, Assistant Director-General, representative of the Director-General at the Meeting, recalled the terms of reference of the Meeting and the scope of its discussions, as established by the Governing Body of the ILO.

9. Although the subject of multinational corporations had received a great deal of attention in recent years, very little objective analysis had been undertaken to clarify the potential or real impact of this new form of international business on the various aspects of social policy. Introducing the working paper prepared by the Office for the Meeting's use, Mr. Bolin explained the various chapters of this document. Many of the aspects connected with multinational undertakings were outside the scope of the ILO's competence and were therefore not of direct concern to the Meeting. He hoped that the limited time available would be devoted to aspects having a direct bearing on social policy. The experts had a difficult task before them. Granted the usual good will on the part of all concerned, the Meeting would be able to make an important contribution towards a greater understanding of the complex issues it was to deal with.

GENERAL DISCUSSION

10. In the opinion of Mr. Allen, the subject of multinational corporations was not a new one, but in the period since the Second World War it had taken on larger dimensions. His country, the United States, not only was the home country of many such corporations but also served as a host country, which had received foreign investment in excess of US$13,000 million. This investment was increasing at a rate of US$1,000 million per year. Offices of both the Federal Government and individual states had been established abroad to encourage such investment. There was a readiness to help the ILO in its study of multinational corporations. In this matter, the ILO had its own expertise, while other international organisations also had expertise in specific areas; overlapping between the investigations of the various organisations should be avoided. The Meeting was called upon not to judge whether multinational corporations were good or bad but to establish the terms of the inquiries which the ILO could usefully undertake.

11. Mr. Smith noted that many myths had grown up around the multinational corporation. It was necessary now to separate fact from fiction and to eliminate the emotional charges based on misunderstandings and even misrepresentation rather than on the true situation. The resolution adopted by the International Labour Conference in 1971 referred to "multinational undertakings"—a term which he preferred. The term "multinational corporation" was misleading, as it implied a legal entity which simply did not exist. What could be termed a "multinational corporation" was, in fact, a family of corporations, which were tied together, to some extent, by common ownership but each of which was a separate legal entity subject to the laws

and the restrictions of the country in which it operated. Thus the multinational corporation could not be distinguished from the national firm, either legally or in terms of the problems and responsibilities it faced. The working paper of the ILO had drawn heavily on statistics from the United States. This was not surprising in view of the lack of meaningful statistics from other countries. However, whilst it was true that many multinational firms were based in the United States, almost as many such firms had headquarters in other countries, including Eastern European countries. The Meeting could count upon his constructive co-operation in objectively analysing the difficult subject before it, but the discussions should keep within the terms of reference laid down by the Governing Body. By 1990, an estimated 595 million jobs had to be created in developing countries alone. There was also a vast need to improve the supply of goods and services so badly needed, such as food, housing and clothing. The multinational corporation had demonstrated that it was the best and most effective device for solving these problems and for increasing the welfare of the two-thirds of the world's population that now had inadequate conditions of life and work. Social progress was the ultimate object of social policy, and this required material progress, including more and better jobs. It would be a disservice to put any obstacles in the way of the most efficient instrument for achieving these ends.

12. Mr. Weinberg stated that it was beside the point to say there were no such legal entities as multinational corporations. The fact was, they existed. While it was true that they were subject to the laws of both home and host countries, it was also true that they had a great influence on the nature of those laws. The problem was that there were no international regulations governing these corporations comparable to the regulations every country had found necessary to impose on national corporations. Consequently, international corporations were able to escape from the regulations that would bind them if their operations were restricted to one country. They were in a position to play off one country against another in such areas as labour legislation and labour practices. There was a need for the international regulation of these corporations, and here ILO standards could play a part. Some aspects of the operations of multinational corporations fell outside the ILO's competence but could nevertheless have a social impact. In these cases, it was for the ILO to draw the attention of other international organisations to the matter. It was questionable whether international corporations contributed positively to development and whether they created employment. For example, the technology brought into a country by an international corporation was often of a type that did not maximise employment. Moreover, the operations of such a corporation often led to balance-of-payments deficits.

13. Mr. Ivey noted that for hundreds of years United Kingdom companies had been developing links abroad. In the same way companies based in other countries operated in the United Kingdom. This trend had increased over the past few decades, and multinational corporations today had to be considered in the context of the growing economic inter-relationship between countries. Depending on their circumstances, countries saw multinational corporations from a different viewpoint: for some, they represented growing foreign ownership; for others, they implied increasing operations overseas, with consequences for the economy of the home country. The United Kingdom was in the unusual position of having both major overseas investments and a substantial element of foreign ownership in its home industry. The United Kingdom also attached great importance to private investment in developing countries; its experience was that multinational corporations could play an important role in creating new and better employment opportunities and that they offered good wages, training and other conditions of employment. Foreign firms operating in the United Kingdom were subject to the same legal requirements and the same tax laws as British firms. Experience had shown that multinational companies, particularly those with a large investment in the United Kingdom, were naturally keen to safeguard their investment and therefore acted as good corporate citizens. Although there was already a substantial amount of literature on multinational corporations, there was apparently a need to improve the scope and quality of the information available, particularly in view of the increasing share of these corporations in general economic activity and in the utilisation of manpower.

14. Mr. Yelnik stated that, difficult as it might be to define multinational corporations, they were easily recognisable. Most commonly they consisted of a parent company in one country, with branches or subsidiaries in other countries. However, what might start as a simple structure often became exceedingly complex; subsidiary groups set up their own subsidiaries, and the relation between the latter and the main parent company might be in the second or even third degree. The size of multinational corporations also varied greatly; some of them were a good deal smaller than certain national companies. The decision to establish a subsidiary, in the home country or abroad, was not determined by the character of the firm but by such factors as the need to diversify activities, the location of raw materials, power requirements, markets, and the need to integrate various activities. The problems encountered by a company differed according to the stage of development of the country it was entering. The diversity of national circumstances and the need to adapt to them constituted a challenge to the company and required dynamic management; the experience could be enriching both to the firm

and to the host country. However, successful adaptation could be achieved only if management was decentralised enough to ensure that the subsidiary was in harmony with its environment and that it operated from the outset on a par with the local companies in the country concerned.

15. Mr. Zaidi emphasised that there was no lack of appreciation for the potential role of multinational corporations. There was no doubt that in some places they were doing good work; elsewhere, however, their operations were not so beneficial. Multinational corporations were growing in number, and the new problems arising from their operations could not be tackled within the boundaries of individual countries. These problems were being discussed not with a view to attacking the corporations but with the aim of identifying the problems generated by their growth. Multinational corporations did not all come from the United States and the United Kingdom; some of them were based in Japan and Hong Kong, for example. It was therefore regrettable that the experts attending the Meeting did not include persons from employer circles in these countries. An examination of their problems would have shown the need for a code of conduct to regulate business dealings in these countries.

16. Mrs. Ljubimova stressed the importance of studying multinational corporations in order to make recommendations concerning ILO action in this field. Although it might be difficult to define these corporations in legal terms, their general characteristics were known. They exhibited a concentration of capital, and each one operated in a number of different countries. However, they did not have multinational managements and their operations were controlled in each case by the parent company. Most of their profits were repatriated to the home country or transferred elsewhere instead of being reinvested in the host country. They raised problems regarding national sovereignty and did not always take into account the economic development plans and policies of the host country's government. Furthermore, the workers' organisations in the host country encountered great difficulties because managerial decisions were taken far away from the place where the company was operating. Multinational corporations employed cheap unskilled labour, and this was why they transferred their operations to developing countries; however, they reserved the skilled jobs for staff imported from the home country. The question should be asked: to what extent did multinational corporations raise the skills of the population in developing countries? In a developed host country a different problem arose: here the multinational corporation made use of skilled local manpower, the cost of whose training had been borne by the host country. USSR companies engaged in technical co-operation

or other overseas activities were in no way analogous to multinational corporations. They trained local staff and equipped them with the skills needed, and there should be no confusion between the two types of undertakings.

17. Mr. Bouillon drew attention to the fact that there were many different types of multinational corporation, and they were far from constituting a homogeneous group. There were differences in: historical development; degree of internationalisation (some firms had 60 to 65 per cent of their staff in the home country and only 35 to 40 per cent abroad, while in others it was the reverse); size; financial structure (joint ventures, wholly-owned subsidiaries, and so forth); degree of centralisation or decentralisation of management; and techical structure (according to whether the company was engaged in service activities, manufacturing or mining). Other differences concerned: the type of processes used (ranging from labour-intensive to highly automated); the proportion of research activities; the type of production (a single isolated type or a series of vertically integrated technical processes, such as was found in the chemical industry), which affected the location of investments; the structure of the staff; the internationality of the shareholders; and the economic and political system of the host country. All these differences made it impossible to speak of "the multinational company" as a standard type of undertaking.

18. Mr. Maier stated that the purpose of the Meeting was not to discuss whether multinational corporations were good or bad or to go into the question of the philosophy behind their development. The objective of the Meeting was to find out what the ILO could do to help establish international industrial relations, as mentioned in several resolutions submitted to the International Labour Conference in the past. The Meeting should advise the Governing Body on further action by the ILO, in the form of research and fact finding, dissemination of information, or the holding of small meetings. In his view, the ILO could be particularly useful in undertaking research with a view to establishing new standards or applying existing ones. It would be difficult to divide economic and social issues and, in fact, according to the Declaration of Philadelphia the ILO was competent to deal with problems of an economic and financial nature. The ILO was tripartite, and the purpose of the Meeting was to discuss problems of a tripartite nature, regardless of whether they arose at the national or international level. He had often heard the argument that multinational corporations were subject to national legislation. However, it should be recognised that there was an international problem. In the context of multinational operations, the Secretary of Commerce of the United States had made a statement in which he recommended the establishment of a code of foreign investment, which could usefully be supplemented by a code of

good behaviour for corporations. Such a code fell within the competence of the ILO and was the code the elaboration of which the trade unions considered to be of the utmost urgency.

19. Mr. Okogwu pointed out that no purpose was served in going over the general information contained in Chapter 1 of the Office working paper. The question of whether or not the multinational corporation was a legal entity was not important. ILO standards had, of course, influenced national legislation. If, for example, a particular country had ratified the ILO Guarding of Machinery Convention, 1963, which sought to prevent the purchase and hire of inadequately guarded machinery, a multinational corporation operating in that country was bound by the legislation implementing the Convention. What was of importance was the economic impact of multinational corporations, since they tended to operate in sensitive areas of a country's economy, often by remote control. The Meeting should consider this essential issue of remote control: to what extent did it affect the human aspects of the company's operations, and in what way could the ILO help the States Members of the Organisation to oblige multinational corporations to conform to the social standards applicable in the countries concerned? Some multinational corporations might attempt to circumvent the intent of the national laws. For instance, to escape paying for social insurance and other schemes, some of these firms contracted out their labour recruitment, and the question then was: who was the employer and who should pay the social insurance contributions?

20. Mr. Mehta referred to the important role to be played by the multinational corporation in the coming decade in aiding the development process. In discussions on this subject, confusion was often caused by a failure to distinguish the various motives for investment abroad. Three main reasons were often given: the need to surmount tariff and other barriers; the need to go where the raw materials were; and finally the need to go where cheap labour was available. The growth and aspirations of the developing countries themselves had accelerated the investments of multinational corporations. There was a need to define clearly what was meant by social policy, for what was social policy in one country might not be social policy in another. Often a particular country would play one multinational corporation off against another in seeking to maximise gains, and even states within a particular country, such as in Australia, the United States or India, did this. At times the multinational corporation was accused of distorting an economy if it brought in the latest technology; yet if it did not apply the most modern technology it was accused of foisting second-hand machines and techniques onto the developing country.

21. In the opinion of Mr. Esponda, the discussions should not be limited to the issues brought up in the Office working paper or in the points suggested for discussion. Apart from their legal structures, multinational or transnational companies could be defined by certain common denominators; regardless of whether they were in developed or developing countries, their repercussions were the same. There was no doubt that regulations could bring about equity in the operations of multinational corporations. Such regulations adopted under ILO auspices should be an effective tool for helping trade union organisations when bargaining with these corporations. The Meeting should consider such things as the limitation of the outflow of profits from developing countries, which should not weaken the economy of these countries. There should not be a depletion of a country's non-renewable resources, and even if benefits did accrue to developing countries from the operations of multinational corporations, there was a need to ensure that the entry of such corporations took place in a rational manner. Multinational corporations should pay full taxes and respect the host countries' laws; this was not always the case. The ILO, like other international organisations, should find ways and means and methods of ensuring social justice and equity.

22. Mr. Nakatani noted the lack of information on the social impact of multinational corporations. It would be useful if the ILO collected such information from its member States by means of questionnaires sent not only to governments but also to employers and trade unions. The Organisation for Economic Co-operation and Development had done this successfully in other areas. Although the views held by management and labour on the subject differed greatly, there was some common ground. Thus some trade unions recognised that the multinational corporation contributed to social progress and employment creation, while most employers agreed that these undertakings should observe and respect the laws and customs of host countries. There was, therefore, a basis for dialogue and agreement.

23. Mr. Benedict pointed out that although some multinational corporations made high capital outlays in their overseas investments, there were some cases where this was not true, as, for example, in the electronics industries. Investment had a direct bearing on the basic problems of employment, and "fast in, fast out" movements of capital caused real resentment in many countries, all the more so as such capital was sometimes drawn from local and national resources and public funds. Many countries were now adopting or considering legal and other controls of the multinational corporation; they wanted to share in the decisions concerning the use of their human and natural resources and their scarce monetary resources. However, often the key to national economic progress rested in hands located in the home country,

which was both geographically and socially distant. There was a problem of remote control, regardless of the nationality of ownership and regardless of location. Not all multinational corporations were the same and they did not act identically, but, even so, their actions were important. Some companies did not respect the laws of host countries and even—at the cost of causing problems to the economic and labour situation in other countries—carried on economic warfare against countries like Chile, as in the current case of the Kennecott Copper Company. Workers had had problems with management in both government and privately owned firms, even with the management of firms based in Eastern European countries. Progress should be made in solving these problems through collective bargaining, national legislation and the international application of fair standards (including ILO standards), for which there was a growing demand.

24. Mr. Stavenhagen emphasised that the main concern of the Meeting was social policy, conceived in the broad sense. For national governments responsible for formulating development strategy and for defining and implementing social policy, it was not enough to point to indices of growth per head or indices of education and housing. It would be a serious mistake to consider only the personnel policies of multinational corporations in certain countries. Some of these corporations applied good policies in this field and offered high wages and other benefits, but social policy was a much more comprehensive concept. It meant social development consistent with a national development strategy. Some of the basic problems facing developing countries were: the distribution of wealth between regions, sectors of the economy and social classes; the active participation of the people in decisions on economic and social policy; and the safeguarding of national sovereignty and autonomy. All three were directly linked to the operations of multinational corporations in developing countries. Studies by the Economic Commission for Latin America and other bodies showed that with the establishment and expansion of multinational corporations, there was a progressive denationalisation of industrialisation, a process of decapitalisation, and a growing inequality in the distribution of income and employment. The objectives should be: a wider distribution of wealth; participation by the masses in decision making; and respect for national sovereignty. The question was: to what extent did multinational corporations respect these objectives in their operations?

25. Referring to Mrs. Ljubimova's statement that there were no multinational companies based in socialist countries, Mr. Smith read quotations from certain journals to show that enterprises based in Hungary, the German Democratic Republic, Poland, Yugoslavia, Romania and the USSR were

engaged in the manufacture of miniaturised batteries, the assembly of tractors, the operation of restaurant chains, the building of hotels, oil exploration, the retail sale of petroleum products and other activities in such countries as the United Kingdom, the Netherlands, Canada, the Federal Republic of Germany, Finland and Belgium, and the Middle East. He also referred to a sales subsidiary of an automotive firm with headquarters located in the USSR which, in 1971, had been engaged in a labour dispute in Sweden.

26. Mr. Allen stated that it was increasingly clear that the USSR was investing in market economies, hiring foreign labour and distributing and marketing its products widely. The United States welcomed such investment. It was to be hoped that any definition of the multinational enterprise would not be so narrow as to exclude those enterprises from Eastern Europe which exhibited multinational characteristics.

27. Mr. Ferrero (observer, International Confederation of Executive Staffs) recalled that for many years his organisation had made an effort to draw attention to the serious consequences arising from mergers and concentrations of enterprises, for managers, engineers and higher supervisory personnel, and especially for older staff. The expansion of multinational corporations led to results that were sometimes more serious for managerial personnel than others. Future studies, resolutions and ILO instruments should take into account the interests of these persons. There was a need for life-long training and retraining to facilitate job changes, and allowances should be provided not only for changes in occupational qualifications but also for changes in family conditions, climate, housing, dependants' status and other matters which were particularly important if a loss of employment occurred.

28. Mr. Vittori (observer, World Confederation of Labour) expressed his organisation's concern over what it felt was a minimisation of the role of the ILO's activities, when it was asserted that questions relating to the growth of multinational corporations were outside the ILO's competence. If this was accepted, it would constitute a denial of the Declaration of Philadelphia, which stated that the ILO had a responsibility to examine and consider all national and international economic and financial policies and measures in the light of its fundamental objective. The Meeting should not merely seek means of improving social policies within multinational corporations as they now were. It was also essential to know to what extent multinational investment took into account development plans, especially in the developing countries, and to what degree such firms took advantage of exemptions from taxes and other concessions in choosing their locations, to learn about the

use of fictitious prices in dealings between subsidiaries and parent companies, and to find out as precisely as possible where the supreme power was located in such corporations. Corporations should be required to provide at least a minimum of information on their internal accounts, and the Meeting should stress the need for supranational legislation on this matter. The ILO should promote the establishment of a working party together with other agencies within the United Nations family, such as the Economic and Social Council, UNCTAD and FAO, to look into these problems. The speaker referred to a statement made by the spokesman of the Worker members of the Governing Body at its 186th Session, in which it was suggested that the ILO should be an essential element in the struggle against inequality and exploitation among nations and in the defence of human rights and social justice.

29. Mr. Magniadas noted that the social effects of the multinationality of capital were substantial and were becoming intolerable. Limiting the scope of the Meeting, as proposed by certain experts, would lead to negation of the hardships and social difficulties resulting from the development of multinational corporations. The pseudo-typology of multinational firms, brought into the discussion by some speakers, focused attention on secondary aspects. The multinational development of monopolies or oligopolies had imposed constraints on the life and wages of workers in their own countries and at the same time reinforced foreign domination over certain parts of the world. It was essential that the Meeting consider violations of national sovereignty and the deterioration of the development process. All of these factors had severe consequences for employment and the further development of the developing countries. He did not understand why such points as the connection between multinationals and monetary speculation, the role of firms in the erratic movement of capital, the relations between multinationals and national and international inflation, and the price increases due to restrictive policies should not be discussed at the Meeting, having regard to their considerable effects on income and employment security and the living standards of workers. The most marked characteristic of multinational growth was the effort to seek any form of relative advantage with a view to gaining the greatest possible profits. This had a marked effect on employment structures and extensive social consequences for both employees of the corporations themselves and the whole labour force of the countries concerned. The multinational development of capital raised new problems, now being discussed in a number of international bodies. With regard to the control of national economic development in the face of the domination of some economies by multinational corporations, it should be recalled that the expropriation and subsequent nationalisation of natural resources were acts of national sovereignty, which concerned only the States in question. Similar problems

had arisen in developed countries, for example in France. The ILO should direct its activities toward adequate measures designed to limit the consequences of such a development.

30. Mr. Lewis (observer, International Federation of Commercial, Clerical and Technical Employees) drew attention to the increasing internationalisation of commerce and to the possibility of commercial employees becoming the "poor relations" of the International Labour Organisation. His organisation intended studying the implications of internationalisation for the labour market situation and for employees in the commercial sector. The Advisory Committee on Salaried Employees and Professional Workers, which dealt with commercial employees in the ILO context, had not met since 1967, and no date had been set for its next session. This appeared to mean that current problems of commercial employees were not being examined, and yet 13 to 16 per cent of the labour force in Western Europe were employed in commerce, banks, insurance and real estate. Mr. Lewis gave several examples of multinationality in enterprises in the retail trade and noted that workers in the commercial sector were faced with the same problems as production workers, particularly with regard to the standardisation of working conditions. The International Labour Office had ignored these important sectors of economic activity, but it was to be hoped that the Meeting would pay attention to the workers in commerce, whose exploitation was no secret.

31. Mr. de Angeli (observer, World Federation of Trade Unions) believed that multinational corporations not only raised obstacles to the ratification of ILO Conventions but also restricted the exercise of trade union rights. It was essential to strengthen these rights, to increase the workers' participation in the economy, and to safeguard national freedom in social and economic development. The effect of the ILO's technical co-operation programmes was sometimes nullified by the activities of multinational corporations. For example, nationals of developing countries who had participated in management development courses were subsequently recruited by multinational corporations, and the country in question thus lost the benefit of the technical co-operation programme. The main problem arising from the operations of multinational corporations was their undermining of national sovereignty. In particular, they obstructed the implementation of economic development plans. The Meeting should emphasise the right of a country freely to select the most appropriate means to development. The problems arising in connection with training and the brain drain were by no means balanced by the benefits resulting from the transfer of technological know-how. Finally, it must never be forgotten that the solution of all development problems was basically a question of enabling workers to enjoy their right to participate

in decision making. The activities of multinational corporations tended to obstruct the full enjoyment of this right.

32. Mrs. Ljubimova, replying to Mr. Smith, pointed out that it was correct to say that the USSR gave assistance to certain countries as regards petroleum prospecting and that it marketed petroleum products in several countries. However, these activities could not be regarded as coming under the category of multinational corporations. The USSR's trading relations with other countries had always been based on mutual benefit, especially in the case of developing countries. Private enterprises would never agree to the conditions offered by Soviet enterprises, which generally provided greater advantages to the developing countries than those offered by United States firms, for example.

33. Mr. Preziosi said that the ILO working paper contained elements that would facilitate the search for a satisfactory way of improving international relations between workers and employers and also the implementation of a social policy designed to strengthen the application of ILO Conventions and Recommendations. It had been suggested that there was a need to conduct an exhaustive examination of all the economic aspects of the multinational corporation, but if such a course were followed there would be a risk of missing the real problem, which was the social consequences of the growth of these corporations. Perhaps it was necessary to know the economic motivations behind multinational growth in order to understand social problems, but it was more important to catalogue the action to be taken within the framework of the ILO with a view to influencing the relations between employers and workers at the international level through ILO Conventions dealing with collective bargaining, trade union rights and the protection of workers. The States Members of the European Economic Community had studied these matters in connection with the elaboration of a European company statute and with the merging and concentration of national companies. The French Government had insisted on the need for machinery to ensure that workers would be informed of and consulted in economic matters. It was also necessary to guarantee the maintenance of the social rights which the worker had acquired before any amalgamations of firms took place. The future did not exclude the possibility of European collective agreements which would permit a harmonisation of the social systems in force in the countries of the Community.

34. Mr. Terver (observer, Food and Agriculture Organisation of the United Nations) gave a detailed account of the co-operation programme established by the FAO with the agro-allied industries. It had been initiated

as a means of opening a dialogue between the FAO and the companies in these industries in order to benefit from their experience and expertise as well as using them as a source of much-needed capital in the development process of the developing countries. Companies in this programme came from developed market economies, socialist countries and even some of the developing countries themselves. Their activities ranged from food processing to the production of fertilisers, pesticides and agricultural equipment. The success of this programme showed that these companies, many of them multinational, could make a great contribution to the progress of the developing countries concerned without losing sight of their own legitimate aspirations.

THE IMPACT OF MULTINATIONAL ENTERPRISES ON MANPOWER

35. At the outset of the discussion of this aspect of the subject a worker expert, referring to a passage in the working paper, maintained that the doctrine of comparative advantage could not be invoked to justify the decisions of the corporations to allocate production among the countries, as none of the conditions (full employment, price competition, immobility of factors of production and, implicitly, international equality of wage rates) prevailed in which this doctrine would be effective. In practice both the consumer and the worker were deprived of the benefits of comparative advantage. The corporations often located their production not for reasons of factor endowment but according to the incentives offered by governments, and these sometimes included tolerance of lower labour standards.

36. An employer expert agreed that it was an oversimplification to say that the corporations were primarily motivated by comparative advantage. A study in the United States had shown that the two dominant motives for opening foreign subsidiaries were to service local markets better and to overcome trade and tariff barriers. The possibilities of tax avoidance through transfer pricing had been grossly exaggerated; in the United States, the Bureau of Internal Revenue was very strict on these points. Experts also referred to the many double taxation agreements concluded by the Federal Republic of Germany and the United Kingdom, for example, and to the fact that tax inspectors in these two countries were alive to this issue and closely checked the reasonableness of prices charged between affiliates.

37. A government expert suggested that the doctrine of comparative advantage, in its more sophisticated present-day form, still had relevance; certain locations for production were more rational than others, and in the

international division of labour there had to be some consideration for the optimum allocation of resources.

38. An employer expert said that in the Federal Republic of Germany the transfer overseas of production in certain industries, as had been described in the working paper, was in many cases a rational move; there was a great shortage of national workers, and many essential jobs could be filled only by attracting foreign workers. In the circumstances it was surely better to transfer production to a developing country which had large manpower surpluses and was badly in need of jobs. The workers becoming redundant in the home country suffered no hardship, as they were eagerly snapped up by other employers and received generous income maintenance during any interval between jobs.

Effects in the home country

39. A worker expert observed that not all countries had full employment. In the United States the United Automobile Workers (UAW) was not as opposed to capital transfer as the AFL-CIO, whose statements had been quoted in the working paper, but the Meeting must understand that, in a situation of high unemployment with limited compensation for job loss, it was inevitable that workers threatened with losing their jobs should give some thought to import restrictions as a solution. The UAW was prepared to accept capital exports subject to safeguards regarding conditions in the host country and satisfactory fulfilment of obligations to displaced workers in the home country. The fact that in the United States a corporation's foreign profits were not taxed until they were repatriated positively encouraged it to reinvest abroad. An employer expert suggested that reinvestment in a developing country in which profits had been made was in the interest of that country, but it was objected by a worker expert that the bulk of these foreign investments was not made in the developing countries but in developed countries. Another worker expert remarked that in other countries too workers' attitudes to transfer of production abroad were likely to be negative so long as there were no adequate labour market policies and adjustment measures.

40. Several experts regretted that there was a shortage of reliable factual information on the practical effects of the activities of multinational corporations. In this connection a government expert reported that in the United States two fairly exhaustive studies—one by the Department of Commerce and the other by the Tariff Commission—on the job effects in the United States as a whole would shortly appear. He hoped other governments would carry out similar studies.

41. Several experts felt that it was unfortunate that the working paper had had to rely to so great an extent on data about United States-based companies. Corporations based in many other countries had similar world-wide activities. Sweden was mentioned as a country whose foreign investment per head was higher than that of the United States and where corporations had expanded employment in their foreign subsidiaries while reducing it in their home establishments. Yet the attitude of the unions was not negative; one expert suggested that this might be due in part to the fact that the Swedish Government would not give financial guarantees unless it was satisfied that certain standards would be applied in the foreign subsidiary.

42. A government expert mentioned that the United Kingdom Government had commissioned a study of the effects of direct inward investment in the United Kingdom and that this would shortly be published.

43. Several worker and government experts considered that systematic collection of information on the social effects of multinational corporations' activities in the different countries would be an appropriate task for the ILO. The most effective way of doing this might be for teams to visit countries, to contact employers and workers as well as governments and to prepare case studies; it was recognised however that this would be costly and might well be beyond the resources available to the ILO. Several worker experts appealed to the multinational corporations to provide information more freely. One employer expert said that much information was in fact already freely published; it was just a matter of getting it into the hands of the ILO.

Manpower adjustment

44. One worker expert supported the suggestion in the working paper that a study should be made of actual cases of plant closure by multinational corporations in the home country and of the extent to which ILO instruments, such as those on employment policy, employment services, vocational guidance and social security, could be of use to protect the workers against the adverse effects of dislocation. The employer experts had no objection to case studies being made of closures and of adjustment measures in general but rejected the implication that there were many cases in which redundancies were due to the multinationality of the undertakings concerned. The proportion of such redundancies as compared with total redundancy was surely very small, and the study, if it were undertaken, should indicate how small it was.

45. One government expert suggested that the study should be directed to finding out whether there was anything peculiar about redundancies due

to multinational corporations' activities which justified special treatment. A worker expert considered in this connection that it was desirable that these corporations should be required to bear the social cost of redundancies, since that might influence them to prevent their occurrence. Another worker expert considered that multinational companies should not impose manpower adjustment programmes for their own interests alone. The training of manpower, the further training of supervisory personnel and of higher and subordinate technicians, and manpower adjustment must be envisaged in the framework of concerted planning between the government, the employers and the workers.

Effects in the developed host countries

46. A worker expert considered that some multinational corporations, by not reinvesting their profits in the host country or by insisting that they obtain their supplies from the home country, created less employment than might otherwise be possible. He thought that the working paper had overstated the benefits which they gave in regard to transfer of technology. In some cases research work in the acquired subsidiaries was stopped and all research centralised in the home country, and this resulted in a brain drain. Even where research was not centralised in the home country, the transfer of technology operated within the closed circuit of the multinational corporation and was not available to the economy of the host countries.

47. Another worker expert referred to cases in the United Kingdom where multinational corporations had bought up national companies, had given assurances to the Government that they would maintain certain levels of employment and had failed to abide by these assurances, in some cases closing down their British plants and transferring production elsewhere. In other countries also there had been cases of multinational corporations buying up national concerns and then closing them down. Takeovers were by no means the only cause of employment problems, but he considered that in recent years they had accounted for a significant proportion of them. He regarded it as essential for the conditions attached to an international takeover to be negotiated on a tripartite basis and for them to be strictly enforced.

48. In regard to the examples referred to, an employer expert suggested that, if the employers concerned had been present, they might have had another version of the events to recount and that without this second version the Meeting could not judge the actions of the multinational corporations concerned.

Effects in the developing host countries

49. A worker expert regretted that no reference had been made in the working paper to foreign mining and plantation companies, which had a great influence in Malaysia, for example. Some were excellent employers but others pulled out after having made quick profits and left behind not only derelict areas but large numbers of workers without any possibility of earning their living; in some cases the responsible employer could not even be traced. The developing countries required two things: a better international division of labour, with the simpler industries being relinquished to the developing countries, and better prices for their raw materials. The two were linked, and if Malaysia could get a good price for its rubber, it would have less need to set up a tyre industry. Another worker expert stressed the negative effects that the instability in the world prices of raw materials had on the economic, social and cultural development of developing countries. Furthermore, the activities of multinational corporations should fit in with national and regional development policies and plans.

50. Several government and worker experts from the developing countries considered that the working paper had concentrated too narrowly on the number of jobs created directly by the activities of subsidiaries of multinational corporations. It was also necessary to know how many jobs had been eliminated and what had happened to the redundant workers. In many countries it was the indirect effects of the multinationals which had the greatest influence on the social situation. For instance it was said that they sometimes failed to comply with the social development strategies laid down in the development plan and had a distorting effect on the economic and social milieu. Sometimes they created new demands which could only be met by increased imports, and in certain countries the economic growth which they had introduced has resulted, in practice, in greater inequalities in income and wealth distribution. Their products were geared to the high-income market and their marketing techniques were addressed to this social stratum.

51. On the other hand, the employer experts pointed out that the positive indirect effects could not be overemphasised. The entry of a multinational corporation, manufacturing a particular product, had far-reaching multiplier effects on the employment situation in the economy as a whole. Moreover, it was stated that in India the multinational corporations had introduced more professionalism in business and a much better understanding of marketing and management methods, which had had an effect on the methods used by the national industry and therefore on employment. Local companies were also stimulated to adopt the superior advertising techniques of the

multinational firms, since they realised that they had to follow the same methods if they were to overcome consumer prejudices in favour of foreign brand-names.

52. While it was true that the corporations brought in capital, a government expert observed that capital was not always lacking, as for instance in Latin America, where there was plenty of national capital which was not being properly used because of a social, political and economic atmosphere unfavourable to national investment; yet, at least in the past, it had been favourable to foreign investment. In many cases the interests of the multinationals did not coincide with the interests of the country. Latin American countries faced an enormous problem of surplus manpower from the rural areas, which was not being absorbed in urban employment. Industrial employment was stagnant or even receding, and the multinationals were not helping to solve this problem.

53. A worker expert observed that in many cases investment was no longer directed to greater production but to wider profit margins and the strengthening of a corporation's future position. Except in the construction phase, new investment did not result in much new employment. Investments and transfers of technology should not only increase the number of jobs but also raise skill levels and diversify employment. In general, they should contribute effectively to the economic, social and cultural development of the home and host countries.

54. A government expert stated that sometimes governments were so keen to attract foreign capital that they did not question the appropriateness of the technology which the foreign investor would introduce. Multinational companies had pressed the sale of computers although such equipment often did not make sense in countries with many unemployed office workers.

55. An employer expert reported that in Kenya the multinationals' investments were welcomed but were subject to very strict control so that the Government could ensure that their activities coincided with the national interest. This control was reinforced by the fact that the Government contributed in some cases 20–25 per cent of the capital. Moreover, the conditions were such as to oblige the different companies to compete among themselves. The multinationals exercised no political influence, while contributing to the economic development of the country by processing primary produce, by saving on imports and by raising export earnings.

56. A worker expert commented that an equal measure of control was desirable in all developing countries.

57. There was considerable discussion of the margin of choice of technology in fact open to multinational corporations. Several experts insisted that in certain industries—such as steel and chemicals—there was no alternative to the most up-to-date technology. Moreover, in certain circumstances there were considerations other than those of employment which imposed the use of modern technology. In India, despite an enormous problem of under-employment among rural workers, there were agricultural operations in which tractors were increasingly being used, and not merely for prestige reasons. Much had been written about intermediate technology but little had been achieved, since solutions which appeared obvious in economic theory were very complex when it came to practical realisation. It was also suggested that the introduction of modern technology was a means of raising the workers' earning power. On the other hand, some experts remarked that raising an individual worker's earning power had a lower priority than spreading average earnings over a larger number of workers.

Vocational training

58. A government expert stated that training needs were directly related to the technology employed. Changes in skill structures would occur, both in multinational and national corporations. While many multinational corporations had excellent training schemes, there was a need to integrate these with over-all national training schemes, particularly as they affected national standards.

59. A worker expert suggested that the levy systems established in some countries to finance vocational training generally might be useful for developing countries, where they should be applied equally to national companies and multinational corporations. There was also a need for increasing use of the various training facilities, including those of multinational corporations, to train people at the supervisory level.

60. A worker expert considered that insufficient effort was being applied at the present time to providing long-term training possibilities which would enable nationals to play their full role in economic development.

CONDITIONS OF WORK AND LIFE IN MULTINATIONAL ENTERPRISES

61. Much of the discussion concerning conditions of work and life focused on the question of wage parity and harmonisation of conditions of work.

62. An employer expert criticised what he termed the facile presumption that harmonisation was desirable in itself. It was not clear what was to be harmonised. If this referred to a harmonisation of living standards, it was for governments and not industry to take initiatives to that end, having regard to such problems as currency values, taxation and the threat of inflation. The argument for harmonisation was generally a tactical move, a peg on which to hang a wage claim. Even within a country, an industry or a single company, harmonisation was a complex matter which could involve great difficulties for all companies, national no less than multinational. Another presumption in the working paper was that so-called cultural differences created problems for multinational companies different from those faced by national companies. While it was undeniable that true cultural differences must be respected, such matters as systems of payment and tea-breaks were not cultural; efforts to improve efficiency in regard to them were made by national companies as well as multinational ones. In general, all that multinational companies could be expected to do was to live within the systems, laws and procedures of the host country.

63. Several other employer experts also stressed the importance of operating within the framework of national institutions, using national collective bargaining or wage-fixing machinery, observing the guidelines set by national incomes policies and adjusting to the provisions of national development plans, including programmes to attract investment. Any imposition of conditions from outside the country in the name of harmonisation would be a breach of national sovereignty which no State could allow. It was pointed out by one employer expert that wages could not be abstracted from the social, economic and cultural environment of the host country. The conditions and constraints imposed by that environment affected not only national companies but also companies which were, in fact, the national entities of multinational undertakings, and there was no basis for differentiating between the two. There might, however, be some possibility for harmonisation at the regional level. Where economic integration was taking place, as in the European Economic Community, social integration might be expected to follow.

64. Additional points made by employer experts in support of the argument that harmonisation was not practicable or necessarily desirable were that conditions were often governed, within a given country, by national or regional collective agreements to which both domestic and multinational companies were parties, that there were important differences between countries in social charges, currency values, cost-of-living and government policies; that there were variations in national productivity; and that even if harmonisation were attempted, the result would be a distortion of the labour market to the detri-

ment of local firms. Finally, another employer expert drew attention to the contradiction between the demand for upward harmonisation of wages and conditions of work and a desire for the use of labour-intensive technology to promote employment in developing countries.

65. A worker expert noted that the fact that parity within countries had not yet been achieved did not mean that parity between countries was not a problem. He welcomed the recognition by an employer expert of the possibility of progress towards harmonisation at the regional level. Other worker experts suggested that international comparisons and demands for harmonisation formed only one element of a continuing drive for the satisfaction of basic needs of workers in both national and multinational companies, that pressure for harmonisation in the sense of the correction of anomalies was inescapable, and that demands were based on such considerations as productivity, skill levels, profits, and claims for a more equitable distribution of income. One worker expert urged that there should be a fair distribution of the multinational corporations' profits among the workers and the rural masses.

66. Several worker experts stressed that the question of harmonisation was essentially that of fair labour standards. It could be considered, one expert suggested, under three subheadings: working conditions, trade union rights, and wages and fringe benefits. As regards working conditions, such as safety measures and relief time on assembly-line jobs, there was no reason why all workers should not benefit from high standards. Similarly, there was no reason why all workers should not enjoy trade union rights. The third item was more complex, and no one was proposing that wages should be the same everywhere regardless of productivity. The important point was that all workers should get a fair share of the wealth they helped to create. The principle of fair labour standards linked to productivity had been included in the Havana Charter, which had been signed in 1948 but had never come into force, and a similar idea had recently been put forward in the United States Government by two national commissions in connection with international trade. This was an area in which the ILO could make an important contribution. An employer expert pointed out that this problem was not specific to multinational enterprises.

67. A government expert observed that the nature of such standards required further precision. Harmonisation would only be possible once a certain level of development had been reached. He agreed that there might be scope for it in Europe.

68. A major concern expressed by several worker experts was that multinational corporations could exert a downward pressure on wages and conditions of work by shopping around among countries for the lowest labour

costs or threatening to move away if costs went up and thus influencing governments to maintain wages and conditions at low levels in order to attract or retain foreign investment. Several employer experts, on the other hand, argued that among the reasons for which companies invested abroad, the following were more important than the reduction of labour costs: to service existing markets better, to overcome tariff barriers, to make a countermove aimed at preventing competitors from pre-empting foreign markets, to reduce transport costs and to meet situations in which home products were unacceptable to foreign markets. Where labour costs were the main reason, the partial transfer of production abroad was most often a last resort against the alternative of bankruptcy and the consequential loss of jobs in the home country. A worker expert commented that surveys of motivation tended to be based on self-serving declarations and that more objective studies were needed. He emphasised that wage levels should be judged in relation to personnel policies and the pace of work, which was generally greater in multinational corporations.

69. An extended discussion centred around one country in which, according to some worker experts, the activities of multinational corporations had led to a depression of wages and the government's search for foreign capital had led to restrictive labour legislation. A neighbouring country had followed the same course shortly thereafter. A government expert and several employer experts, recalling that the country in question had been faced with exceptional problems at independence, maintained that the government had formulated a development plan based on the need to attract foreign investment and thus expand job opportunities, that it had, in fact, converted a labour surplus into a labour shortage and that the formulation and implementation of the development plan had represented the legitimate exercise of national sovereignty and as such should be respected.

70. Throughout the discussion, the level of wages, fringe benefits and conditions of work in multinational companies received considerable attention. In the view of several employer experts, that level tended to be above the local average. While there might be occasional exceptions, multinational companies in general were among the leaders in wages and other conditions. With regard to the problems of safety measures, working conditions and trade union rights mentioned by a worker expert, the effect of multinational companies had generally been beneficial, but these were in any case matters for national regulation, which affected domestic and multinational firms alike. Several worker experts challenged the assertion that wages and conditions in multinational corporations tended to be above average. They maintained that the available data were far from conclusive, that many examples

to the contrary could be cited and that more refined comparisons were needed before any generalisations could be made.

71. A government expert suggested that conditions of work and life should be examined not only in relation to multinational corporations themselves but also in relation to the impact of such corporations on the development patterns of developing countries. In his own region, Latin America, industrial output was growing faster than the economy as a whole, but employment in the manufacturing sector was stagnating or even declining. The large numbers of people who were leaving the primary or traditional sector were not being absorbed by the industrial sector. The result was mass unemployment. This was not imputable to multinational corporations, but it might be the consequence of a kind of development strategy in which multinational corporations played an important role. This kind of development strategy, based on a rapidly expanding modern sector, tended to foster the creation of the relatively high income markets which multinational corporations serviced and to reinforce the existing unbalanced patterns of income distribution. The structure of the market tended to be an obstacle not to economic efficiency but to social efficiency. When considering the relationship between multinational corporations and social policy, such possible indirect effects of their operations should also be studied. Social policy should be interpreted as covering not only the workers employed by multinational corporations but also the mass of marginal labour which did not benefit from the type of development multinational corporations tended to promote. When national governments did attempt to alter such development strategies, they often incurred not only the wrath of their own privileged minorities but also the economic aggression of the multinational corporations whose interests were affected by such changes of strategy. It was because of this situation and similar problems that the Government of Mexico had recently proposed to the United Nations the formulation of a Declaration of Economic Rights and Obligations of the States, in which these matters would be covered.

72. Some worker experts supported the idea of examining multinational corporations in relation to the social efficiency of development strategies and agreed that the problem of incomes and living standards in society as a whole should not be overlooked. Another government expert, however, argued that the process of modernisation and urbanisation was going on all over the world as a result of many different factors. It did not have much to do with multinational corporations. While agreeing that income distribution was a problem deserving examination, he did not think this should be done within the framework of a study on multinational corporations.

INDUSTRIAL RELATIONS

Transfer of operations and power relationships

73. The worker experts considered that the possibility or threat, as well as the fact, of the temporary or permanent transfer of operations by multinational corporations in general or as a pressure tactic was a most significant factor, pointing out the special nature of industrial relations problems with multinational corporations. Instances were referred to by these experts in which transfers were reported to have been made during a strike situation, and in which multinational employers had warned of the permanent transfer of operations out of a particular country or the curtailment of expansion in that country if certain industrial relations practices did not change.

74. An employer expert questioned the real relevance of arguments concerning possible effects on the power relationships between unions and the multinational companies resulting from the latter's ability to transfer production or other operations, either temporarily or permanently. It was pointed out by this expert that in a number of industries, such as chemicals, temporary transfers were completely impossible because of the manner in which the industry was integrated and that in other cases cost factors made such a move prohibitive. Factors cited as militating against more permanent transfers of operations included: the resultant loss of skilled manpower; the high costs of termination indemnities payable in the case of closures in some countries; the costs of planning, preparing and implementing such transfers; loss resulting from the sacrifice of non-movable equipment that was not saleable; the possible adverse effects on units continuing to operate in the country concerned; the high cost and over-all difficulties of starting up and "breaking in" a new plant; and the fact that the services provided by the operations might not be transferable, the need for proximity to raw materials, etc. He wondered whether such transfers—on the assumption that it was at all feasible to transfer operations—might not, in certain cases, indeed be an appropriate counter-measure to a strike by the trade unions concerned; the internationalisation of disputes by trade unions with increasing power on the international level could engender and justify corresponding protective measures by multinational enterprises. A government expert also stressed that transfers of operations could not be lightly undertaken.

Locus of decision making

75. In the view of several of the worker experts, while there were variations in practice, and the management of subsidiaries sometimes had great

autonomy, particularly as regards decision making on matters of detail, there were nevertheless frequent cases in which the delegation of authority by the central headquarters of multinational corporations was so limited that even relatively simple decisions could not be made by the local management of the subsidiary; in respect of many collective bargaining issues, the locus of management decisions was, in an even greater number of cases, not to be found at the level of the subsidiary where collective bargaining was supposed to be taking place. Among other things this situation had led to disputes and strikes and made for a real obstacle to healthy labour-management relations. A government expert also cited cases in his country where local negotiators in multinational enterprises (and sometimes in national enterprises) lacked authority to bargain with the unions concerned and thus made illusory any real collective bargaining. Moreover, perhaps of more importance in the view of the worker experts, decisions affecting the international strategy and finances of the multinational corporations were made in any event at headquarters.

76. Several employer experts, while recognising that certain corporation-wide and other important policy decisions had ultimately to be made at the headquarters of the multinational corporation, nevertheless emphasised that in fact there was in general a very high degree of decentralisation of decision making. In their view, this was indeed an essential aspect of good management, for decisions in respect of conditions of employment and labour-management relations had to reflect an understanding and appreciation of the local and national conditions, requirements and realities. One employer expert pointed out that in certain countries legal regulations required that, in the case of certain local operations of multinational enterprises, local managers have sufficient power in respect of social matters.

77. A worker expert saw an inconsistency in the statements of the employer experts. On the one hand, they asserted that decision making in industrial relations matters was decentralised; on the other hand, one employer expert had felt that in certain circumstances transfers of operations might be justified in a strike situation. It was, however, obvious that such transfers could only be decided upon at a level above that of the subsidiary, which indicated that decisions relevant to industrial relations were taken at headquarters.

78. A government expert suggested that further study was warranted on the practices of multinational corporations regarding the delegation of decision-making power and the consequences which flowed from varying degrees of such delegation.

Adjustment of industrial relations and personnel policies and practices

79. A number of worker experts as well as a government expert referred to instances in which it was reported that multinational corporations failed to adapt their personnel and industrial relations policies to conform with the national and local customs, practices and requirements of the host country in which they were operating. Aggravating this situation, in the view of a worker expert, was the presence, in management positions in host country operations of multinational enterprises, of foreign nationals who were not always sensitive to or knowledgeable about national practices and conditions. Certain of the worker experts pointed to instances where foreign enterprises refused to affiliate with the national and local employers' organisations, thereby seeking to avoid the obligations of industry-wide collective agreements covering industry members of the organisation; further instances were cited of refusal to recognise bona fide representative trade unions or to bargain collectively with such unions or in respect of certain workers, contrary to national practice, or of acts of anti-union discrimination by multinational corporations. In the opinion of one worker expert, the denial of trade union rights by multinational corporations was not an occasional phenomenon but a flagrant and widespread practice; he referred to the reports of the ILO Governing Body's Committee on Freedom of Association, in which one might find interesting examples involving multinational corporations.

80. Various employer experts stressed that abuses in the areas cited, if they existed at all—and this had by no means been established—were not usual practice. It was pointed out by a number of the employer experts that subsidiaries of multinational corporations had to and did fully conform with national obligations and practices and generally integrated themselves into the industrial life of the host country, affiliating where appropriate with national employers' organisations and dealing with local trade unions. According to one of the employer experts, it was common practice to train and use national managers and to rely, for instance, on the local personnel manager's knowledge of the local situation.

81. With regard to allegations of non-respect of freedom of association and trade union rights on the part of multinational corporations, it was further asserted by an employer expert that such corporations were certainly no less respectful of trade union rights than national enterprises and, indeed, recognised the need for dialogue with workers' representatives; if anything, multinational corporations were particularly susceptible to criticism as foreigners in a host country and thus were particularly careful to act in a proper manner.

82. A government expert referred to a systematic inquiry made by his country's embassies abroad. This inquiry had shown that multinational corporations based in his country but operating abroad, with few exceptions, could not be held to have committed abuses of the type alluded to by some of the experts and that in general these corporations were considered to have industrial relations and personnel policies and practices at least as good as, and sometimes considerably better than, national enterprises.

83. The suggestion was made by a government expert that multinational corporations, when or before beginning operations in a new host country, should make contact with the local employers' organisation and the labour department in order to be briefed on the national and local industrial relations situation; that they should review their employee handbooks with the labour department to verify their conformity with national law and practice; and that they should make use of labour department personnel management advisory services where these existed. He believed that the ILO could play a role in encouraging multinational corporations to act in this manner. Finally, he stressed the need for more effective national labour inspection in order to avoid, prevent, and remedy possible abuses by multinational corporations in the labour-management relations field; here again the ILO could contribute.

84. Another government expert explained that in his country, which was the home country for some multinational corporations, the Labour Ministry was planning to establish an international labour information centre, which would offer advice and information on the national laws and practices of various other countries where corporations based in his own country were intending to commence operations, in order to alleviate possible conflicts. He suggested that the subjects of study by the ILO might include the measures and information services of this type undertaken by national governments.

Availability of information and data

85. Many worker experts referred to the difficulty, which they considered very real, of securing information and data on and from the multinational corporations—information and data, financial and otherwise, for purposes of collective bargaining, and general information on the future plans of the corporation. Although, as explained by certain of the worker experts, some of the international trade union organisations had been making progress in this important area of gathering and using information, regulations on full disclosure, particularly of financial information, were to be desired; moreover, the ILO could play a useful role, on an international level, in the gathering of certain types of information from the companies.

86. In recognition of this situation, it was pointed out by a government expert that in Nigeria new legislation provided for disclosure by multinational corporations of certain financial data. In his view, provision of information on multinational corporations was an area in which the ILO could render assistance. In addition, he thought that the ILO might undertake a comparative study of national company laws with particular reference to the manner in which they called for the disclosure of company information.

87. It was also pointed out by a worker expert that in consultations between certain multinational corporations and international trade union committees an understanding had been reached regarding the provision of advance information by the corporations in respect of certain matters such as aspects of production changes and expansion plans and location of new plants as well as plans for partial or complete closure of plants.

Collective bargaining in a multinational context

88. The possibility of collective bargaining on a multinational scale was both undesirable and unrealisable, in the view of those employer experts who addressed themselves to this question. In their opinion the great differences in industrial relations and collective bargaining systems, in law and in practice, militated against such a possibility. Among other problems posed, certain employer experts cited a number of difficulties, such as: the problem, which they considered insoluble, of reconciling bargaining at the international and national levels in those situations, which were widespread, where employers' associations bargained for their members on an industry basis; the lack of a necessary international legal framework for collective bargaining; the impossibility of international legal enforceability of collective agreements; the fact that the "peace obligation" during the term of a collective agreement, which existed as a legal matter in a number of countries, could lead to problems of international application, etc. Moreover, it was pointed out by some employer experts that, as had been mentioned earlier in the Meeting's discussions, to the extent that international collective bargaining implied a harmonisation of wages and conditions of work, this would in their view be entirely inappropriate.

89. It was argued by a number of worker experts that it was necessary to negotiate at an international level with the responsible headquarters management officials of multinational corporations, since meaningful bargaining on a variety of important issues could not be achieved at the level of the subsidiary in a given country. In their view, presumed problems of a legal or other nature were not entirely relevant or they could be surmounted if the

parties agreed to engage in international collective bargaining. Moreover, certain worker experts emphasised that it was obviously not the aim of international collective bargaining to bring about absolute identity of wages and conditions for workers in all countries.

90. There was some discussion among the experts concerning the problem of determining the representative character of trade union groupings for purposes of international collective bargaining, certain employer experts considering that this raised an additional substantial problem in this area. It was, however, argued by worker experts that established international trade union groupings of known representative character already existed. One employer expert noted that trade unions representing workers of multinational corporations in certain host countries had no international affiliation and hence could not participate in international collective bargaining.

Workers' participation and co-determination

91. There was little discussion on the question of workers' participation in management decisions in multinational corporations through co-determination and other methods. However, an employer expert expressed the view that, to the extent that trade unions advocated such participation, it might represent an attempt to obtain in respect of multinational corporations what could not be had, except in very few cases, in respect of national enterprises under national legislation. He further emphasised that, in addition to raising innumerable technical and institutional difficulties, such participation would be impracticable and undesirable, particularly if it were to involve the participation of trade unionists from outside the enterprise.

92. A worker expert recalled, on the other hand, that under the proposed European company statute, which was under discussion in the European Economic Community, provision was made for such participation. An employer expert noted that the proposal was strongly contested in the discussions that were currently taking place.

Further considerations

93. An employer expert raised the question whether the increasing international concentration of trade union power did not represent a threat as great as the multinational corporations; yet there had been no reference to international regulation or supervision of their activities. In reply, a worker expert commented that it was an illusion to think that trade unions had countervailing power compared with the big multinational corporations; as opposed to the demonstrated existence of abuses commited by such corporations, trade

unions had not commited international abuses; had they done so on the scale of the corporations, regulation would be warranted in their case also.

94. It was added by a number of employer experts that for the most part the types of alleged abuses cited during the discussions were in no way unique to multinational corporations in particular; they were, if anything, national problems involving national enterprises, which could be dealt with by national measures, to which multinational corporations, as well as national enterprises, were subject in a given host country.

95. The worker experts insisted that the existence of abuses in industrial relations and other areas on the part of multinational corporations, which were very real and not of insignificant incidence—even if limited, as suggested by employer experts—called for some international pronouncement, such as a code of good conduct, which would aim at a harmonisation of national law and practice to meet international standards. They realised that some length of time and further study might be required before the necessary provisions of such a code could be effectively worked out, but it was now necessary to make a beginning. It was added by a worker expert that the chief executive of a leading multinational corporation had called for the adoption of international safeguards in relation to fair labour practices to be followed by multinational corporations. A worker expert considered that the basic principles concerning the protection of workers in the undertaking should be applied by multinational corporations, in particular the ILO Workers' Representatives Recommendation, 1971, and the resolution concerning trade union rights and their relation to civil liberties. The workers' right to take part in trade union activities, not only at the national but also at the international level, should be assured.

96. Two government experts, without discounting the possibility of the future preparation of some sort of international code, emphasised that the information at present available did not conclusively demonstrate the need for such a code, Further study could determine whether there were possible areas that warranted international attention in this form.

97. The employer experts maintained that a code of behaviour, at least of the kind proposed by the workers, had not been shown to be necessary and would result in an unwarranted discrimination against multinational corporations as compared with national enterprises.

98. A worker expert suggested that the Governing Body of the ILO should be invited to consider the amendment of the ILO Constitution so that the international standards contained in Conventions and Recommendations could apply to multinational corporations, in the spirit of articles 24–26 and 35 of the Constitution.

99. It was stressed by a worker expert that workers' education activities by the ILO and on the national level should include programmes which would lead to a better understanding of multinational corporations on the part of workers.

INTERNATIONAL LABOUR STANDARDS AND SOCIAL PRINCIPLES DEVELOPED BY THE ILO

100. The question of whether or not there is a need for a code of conduct for multinational undertakings in the social field was the main subject of discussion. The exchange of views on this issue followed a number of references made to it in connection with some of the other matters discussed by the Meeting, as indicated earlier in this report.

101. In an opening statement from the employers' side, an expert questioned the assumption that multinational corporations did not observe ILO standards in the countries in which they operated or interfered in their political and social life. On the contrary, it was in the interest of such corporations to act as good citizens, and neither host nor home countries would allow such behaviour. The demand of the workers' organisations for an international instrument outlining the obligations of multinational corporations towards governments and trade unions involved compliance with all ILO Conventions, whether ratified or not, and this might run counter to the law of the land, might create a double standard as between multinational and national firms and might well hinder development efforts. Ultimately only the workers in the capital-exporting countries would benefit. The same employer expert questioned the need for an international code of fair labour standards applicable to multinational corporations: host countries were quite free to establish any necessary rules and might in any case not accept such a code to any larger degree than they had ILO Conventions. Moreover, the working of an international body set up to administer it would meet with practical difficulties. The operation of such a code would be discriminatory, and thus contrary to ILO practice, and would in fact be looked upon as violating national sovereignty. In his opinion, the only workable solution was for governments to abide by the ILO instruments in force in their country and for workers to draw attention to cases of non-enforcement. The present Meeting should support the call of the International Chamber of Commerce that multinational corporations help to realise the economic and social objectives of their host countries. The Meeting should also recommend the Governing Body to appeal to the governments of the home countries to supervise the activities and practices of their multinational corporations abroad. A worker expert

stressed that the ILO and the national, regional and world trade union organisations should combine their efforts to induce governments which had not already done so to ratify and apply the international Conventions on conditions of work, hours of work, wages, occupational safety and health, occupational accidents and diseases, women's and children's work, etc.

102. A worker expert reiterated the necessity for a code of behaviour for multinational corporations. However, in view of the strong opposition of certain employers, the Meeting would not be in a position to reach a consensus on the contents of such a code; this issue should therefore be submitted to the Governing Body for further study. International labour standards and social principles developed by the ILO, as well as future action thereon, were the most important item on the agenda of the Meeting. The ILO should also support the creation of national tripartite bodies to obtain information on the activities of multinational corporations. In the workers' view, companies should commit themselves on a voluntary basis to respect Conventions chosen by a working party. This world-wide commitment might be made to the ILO and would not interfere with the sovereignty of States, which alone could ratify and enforce Conventions. The claim by employers that multinational companies behaved as good citizens wherever they operated had to be considered with reservations. In fact, they were "super-citizens". For these reasons, multinational corporations could be requested to make a special effort and instruct all their subsidiaries to respect Conventions on their own, without interfering with national sovereignty. The social clauses attached in Sweden to the state guarantee scheme for investments abroad were an example of how governments should act and how multinational companies should cooperate in applying social clauses in their subsidiaries wherever they operated. The code of behaviour should lay down the obligations of companies towards governments and employees. Referring to statements by national and international authorities concerning the need for an international code to guarantee investments, the worker expert considered that any such code should be supplemented, as mentioned, for instance, by the US Secretary of Commerce, by a code outlining the obligations of the companies to their workers, and it was at the level of the ILO that initiatives for establishing such a code would be most appropriate.

103. An employer expert stated that multinational corporations could only be requested to respect international labour standards where these were not in contradiction with national legislation. It was out of the question to elaborate international regulations more stringent than existing ILO standards. Where companies wanted to do more, they should do it of their own free will. Referring to the resolution adopted by the International Labour Conference in

1971 dealing with the new social problems raised by the development of multi-national undertakings, the same employer expert maintained that any study pursued by the ILO should ascertain which problems were new and created specifically by multinational corporations. A list of any new problems involving multinational companies should be submitted to all parties concerned for discussion and approval. There were obligations not only for companies but also for workers and for governments, arising, for example, out of contracts concluded between governments and companies. Only on the basis of thorough study could any proposals be submitted to the Governing Body.

104. A government expert, referring to the social and political aspects involved, stressed the fact that ever since the Second World War relations between States and people on various matters had been increasingly influenced by international organisation and that this had been a positive factor in maintaining world peace. New social and economic phenomena such as the importance, growth and spread of multinational corporations on the international scene obviously called for some sort of international response to deal with and regulate them. The revision of ILO instruments to meet changing needs and the tendency of the policy-defining function of the ILO to outgrow the limitations of the Convention and Recommendation procedure had been referred to in the working paper. The purpose of this Meeting was precisely to explore the possibility of new means and instruments. Quoting from an address of the President of the World Bank to its Board of Governors, the expert stressed the necessity of reorientating development policy. While responsibility basically rested with national governments, the availability of international instruments to refer to was an aid to development in the wider sense.

105. A worker expert recalled that the International Labour Conference resolution concerning the social problems raised by multinational undertakings had been adopted unanimously in 1971. There was an international patent code, under which inventions were protected; human beings could also be protected by an international code. There was no question of double standards, because national and multinational companies were not the same. Progress had to be made and standards should be levelled up, not down.

106. An employer expert doubted the necessity, possibility and desirability of approving an international code of behaviour for multinational companies. The working paper did not establish that the behaviour of multinational companies gave rise to more criticism than that of national companies, and it had not been shown that national legislation was not sufficient to deal with any abuses. The possibility of imposing an international code in all countries where multinational companies operated was doubtful in view of the legal structure of nations, and further difficulties related to the definition

of the persons or entities which would be subject to this code, the nature of the standards included therein and the effect of the rules adopted. Even if these legal and factual difficulties might be overcome, he doubted the desirability of adopting a code.

107. A worker expert referred to the economic weight of multinational corporations. As high an authority as Pope Paul VI had recently drawn attention to their concentration of power and their flexibility, to the possibility of abuses and to the absence of supervision. The expert added that these corporations had themselves asked for special treatment and investment guarantees at the international and regional levels, for example protective measures within the framework of the Latin American Free Trade Area and the European Common Market. Particular progress had been made toward a code of conduct in the Andes Pact sub-region in Latin America. More sensitive reactions to violations of trade union rights and other socially backward actions were understandably aroused when foreign concerns committed them than when even equally reprehensible actions involved only local concerns.

108. A government expert stressed the need to respect political integrity and national sovereignty, especially in calling for the application of unratified Conventions. The working paper had indicated that such Conventions provided a good basis for social policy; it had also pointed to the existence of certain promotional instruments. Within this general context there might well be room for a code of conduct.

109. An employer expert stated as his individual opinion that while the idea of a code of conduct was not wholly inconceivable, neither would it represent a panacea. It would not help developing countries unless they wanted to be helped. The matter depended on the governments rather than on the multinational corporations, and if ratified Conventions could not be properly applied, there would be even less respect for a code. If the main purpose of a code was upward harmonisation, this would conflict with employment objectives in developing countries. Governments would not tolerate infringements of their sovereignty either by international companies or by international trade union organisations.

110. A worker expert referred to the Convention on the Settlement of Investment Disputes drawn up under the auspices of the World Bank. What had been done in the case of money should also be done in the case of human beings. To enforce a code of conduct, reliance should be placed on strong governments, such as that of the United States, which had found it possible to take forceful action in the past. Thus anti-trust legislation was applied to foreign subsidiaries of US corporations abroad. The ILO Discrimination (Employment and Occupation) Convention, 1958, through its application as

part of a code of good behaviour enforced by the home countries of international corporations, could help to prevent racial discrimination against workers of multinational companies in South Africa.

111. In reply to the statement by a worker expert that multinational corporations were something more than plain citizens, an employer expert drew attention to the many restrictions imposed on foreign companies in certain countries. Multinational enterprises could not make commitments to the ILO, because they were not subjects of international law and they had no special status with the ILO. The employers considered that there were no objective differences between multinational and national companies. For these reasons, the ILO could not adopt a code of behaviour specifically for multinational corporations. The code of the International Chamber of Commerce which had been referred to was a free commitment drawn up by an employers' organisation itself.

112. A government expert stated that before discussing the precise form that such a code of good behaviour might take it would be necessary to establish whether or not a need clearly existed for such a code. This whole question should not be prejudged, and that was why further study was necessary. It also was, of course, up to individual national authorities to determine their own policies and national interests. Therefore the magnitude of the problems raised needed to be quantified first, before discussing the desirability or otherwise of such a code, let alone the precise nature that such a code might take, should the desirability of such a code be established.

113. Another government expert stated that many new social problems had arisen out of the activity of multinational corporations. The Meeting should study the possibility of recommending standards to be followed by governments with a view to the control of the activities of multinational companies. These standards might also be used by trade unions and International Trade Secretariats with a view to drawing up programmes of unified activity. Within the specific context of multinational companies, the preparation of instruments should be pursued in such spheres as conditions of work, hours of work, leisure, safety and health protection and vocational training.

Opinion of the Legal Adviser

114. In reply to a question raised previously by an employer expert, the Legal Adviser gave his opinion on the possibility for the legislation of States Members of the ILO to permit the application of a code of good behaviour to multinational companies but not to other companies. The question was whether undertakings belonging to what had come to be called multinational

companies could be submitted to certain special legal rules. At the international level, a variety of solutions could be conceived for what were, in fact, new legal phenomena. At the national level, national legislation was the determining factor. It was relevant to ask whether there were any objective distinctions between national and multinational companies which might justify different treatment. Legislation and case law did not as yet provide clear indications; the subject was very new. However, some evidence of differentiated treatment in particular cases could be found in isolated court decisions.

CLOSING PROCEEDINGS

Address by the Director-General

115. At the commencement of its final sitting, the Meeting was addressed by the Director-General of the International Labour Office, Mr. Wilfred Jenks. The Director-General said—

I have come here this morning for one simple purpose: to thank you all for the work which has been done in the course of a very full ten days. I should have liked to be here at the outset of your proceedings to welcome you. If I had been here at that time, what I should have had to say would have been equally simple. It would have been to express the hope that this Meeting would provide the elements of an agreed beginning in dealing with a difficult problem which by its nature cannot be solved overnight. I should have repeated what is said in the document which was the basis of your discussions, and what I have ventured to say whenever I have had occasion to make any public statement on this subject: that the whole question which you have had under discussion is by its nature and by its importance highly controversial, and that the role of the ILO in these matters is not to espouse any side of such a controversy but to provide a forum within which all of the conflicting views can progressively lead to agreed conclusions, which may serve as a basis for effective common action.

It is clear that there has been throughout the Meeting an instinctive response to that kind of plea. I do not mean that you have not had your disagreements. I do not mean that you have not had your moments of frustration and almost of despair. Although I have not been able to be present during your proceedings, I have been kept informed of what was going on. I should like to place in relief what I believe to be the significance of what was agreed in your Drafting Committee yesterday. I, of course, have no knowledge of the inner secrets of what may have transpired this morning, and I have no idea at all how far what was agreed in your Drafting Committee yesterday is likely to be agreed to by the Meeting this morning. I will therefore not in any way foreclose that issue. But I should like to say what I believe would be the significance of your reaching agreement in the Meeting as a whole on the measure of agreement which was reached yesterday.

You will have made a beginning in developing an agreed approach to a most difficult problem. That, in my judgment, is something quite invaluable. You have laid down the elements of approach not to the solution of substantive problems, perhaps—that comes later—but to a procedure through which we can progressively come to grips with substantive problems. That procedure consists of certain stages.

Firstly, of assembling all the necessary basic information and presenting it not as statements of *ex parte* views but as the most objective information possible.

I am very happy to hear that there has been a number of tributes to the manner in which we at least attempted—and in the judgment, I think, of most people, with some success—to approach the task in that spirit in the document which was submitted as the basis of your work. On my part, I am grateful. Naturally the document has imperfections, and there may have been some critical observations in the course of your discussions. It was because we did not wish to issue that document for wider circulation until we had been able to take into account such observations that it was issued as a reserved document for your use alone at this stage.

We will now be able, in the light of your discussions, to reconsider the contents of that document and to make it available for wider distribution. That will provide a framework of a general nature within which we can proceed to undertake some of the more detailed studies which have been suggested by participants in this Meeting and which are listed in papers which have, as I understand it, as yet been only partly distributed.

I cannot, of course, promise that all these studies will be completed or even initiated next week. They represent a very considerable programme of work, but I should like you to feel that we shall put in hand vigorously the preparation of —may I call it a balanced sample of—the studies which have been suggested or requested by different participants in this Meeting. We will try and put that work in hand vigorously within a reasonably limited period of time.

I am happy also to see the suggestion that all of you would willingly remain available for further consultation as the work proceeds.

I do not think, Mr. Chairman, that there is really much more I ought to say at this stage of your deliberations. It will not, I think, be helpful now for me to enter into the substance of any of the questions which you have reviewed, and more particularly any of the questions which you have debated, and some of which you have debated rather intensively. That does not mean that at some later stage it might not be appropriate for us to see whether or not we can evolve suggestions which would bring closer together the views that have been expressed by different participants in the Meeting. But we should do that, I think, only on the basis of fuller studies, wider consultations and very careful reflection on all the various points of view which have been expressed.

I should, therefore, like to lay emphasis on just one final point. I trust that no one inside or outside this room will underestimate the value of what you have achieved during these past ten days. There is nothing more difficult than to make a beginning towards seeking agreed action in a field in which initial points of view are widely divergent from each other and in which much of the information available is information representing divergent views on the subject rather than an agreed basis of objective fact.

The mere fact that for the first time all of the parties in interest are sitting together in an international body, seeking to develop a basis of agreed fact from which they can ultimately evolve agreed policy and conclusions is, in my judgment, a major step forward. And for that step I should, on behalf of the International Labour Organisation, like to thank you and to say how much we look forward to continued co-operation with you in the future.

Work of the Drafting Committee

116. The Meeting set up a Drafting Committee to work out a text of Draft Conclusions for consideration by the Meeting. The Drafting Committee was composed of Mr. Allen and Mr. Stavenhagen, government experts, Mr. Smith and Mr. Yelnik, employer experts, and Mr. Weinberg and Mr. Zaidi, worker experts. It was presided over by Mr. Dube, Chairman of the Meeting.

117. The Drafting Committee considered a draft text of conclusions submitted by the employer experts, a draft text of conclusions submitted by the worker experts and a compromise text worked out by the two government experts that were members of the Drafting Committee.

118. The Drafting Committee, after full consideration of all these drafts, agreed to submit a revised text of Draft Conclusions for consideration by the Meeting.

Consideration of the Draft Conclusions

119. The text of Draft Conclusions prepared by the Drafting Committee was examined by the Meeting at its final sitting, on Saturday, 4 November.

120. Several experts paid tribute to the work which had been accomplished by the Drafting Committee. The employer experts and some government experts felt that the Draft Conclusions represented an acceptable compromise. The employer experts welcomed the suggestion that studies be carried out, as there was a need for fuller information with regard to the relationship between multinational enterprises and social policy—even if only to show that the criticism of multinational enterprises was erroneous.

121. Several worker experts expressed regret that the Draft Conclusions did not more fully reflect the proposals made in the text which had been submitted by them. Serious attention should be given to one of their proposals which had not been retained by the Drafting Committee, to the effect that the Governing Body and the International Labour Conference be requested to consider the adoption of a Convention under which the governments of the home countries of multinational corporations would obligate themselves to require such corporations to adhere to existing ILO standards in all their operations, regardless of the country in which those operations were carried out. The worker experts also regretted that much of the preamble, in particular its sixth paragraph, reflected an exclusively employer viewpoint and, moreover, scarcely reflected the real problems and aspirations of the third world. However, they appreciated the difficult task that the Drafting Committee had had in

attempting to reach a consensus, and they felt that, in spite of its shortcomings, the text as a whole, as submitted by the Drafting Committee, could well serve as a basis for useful action by the ILO and offered some prospects of progress in the future.

122. Mr. Diallo associated himself with the work which had been done by the worker members of the Drafting Committee. The resulting recommendations reflected the workers' wish to see the ILO continue to study the phenomenon of multinational corporations and to act for the benefit of mankind as a whole. These recommendations would enable the Governing Body to go ahead in this field. Unfortunately, however, he was unable to approve the preamble to the Draft Conclusions: it added nothing whatever to the text and might even minimise the most important problem facing the ILO after the long and painful colonial era—namely the emergence of multinational concentrations, which must now be controlled by supranational action. It was for this reason that he, together with other worker experts, had called for the revision of the Constitution of the ILO. In doing this, he felt that he was not only defending the interests of African workers but also seeking the welfare of all the workers of the world.

123. Several experts proposed minor drafting changes with a view to improving the presentation of the text. The Meeting agreed that such minor drafting changes should be left to the discretion of the Office.

124. Several experts proposed amendments of a substantive nature.

125. Most of these proposed amendments were, however, eventually withdrawn by their authors, in the light of the discussions of the Meeting and of the explanations given by the Chairman. These included, in particular, amendments proposed by Mrs. Ljubimova in respect of paragraph 3 of the operative part of the text, by Mr. Ivey in respect of paragraphs 3, 5 and 6 of the operative part of the text, and by Mr. Preziosi in respect of paragraph 1, subparagraphs *(a)* and *(c)*, of the operative part of the text.

126. Other amendments of a substantive nature were the subject of detailed debate. These are referred to in the paragraphs below.

127. Mrs. Ljubimova proposed that the sixth preambular paragraph be amended by the insertion of the word "international" before the words "living standards" and by the deletion of the words "throughout the world" at the end of the paragraph. However, this amendment was not accepted by the Meeting.

128. Mr. Diallo and Mr. Magniadas, supported by Mr. Esponda, proposed that the sixth and seventh paragraphs of the preambule be deleted, and that

the following new paragraph be inserted after the last paragraph of the preamble:

Considering that the report of the Meeting presents the various positions of the experts concerning the growth of multinational corporations,

This amendment was not, however, accepted by the Meeting as a whole.

129. Mr. Esponda, Mr. Diallo and Mr. Magniadas, taking cognisance of the vote mentioned in the preceding paragraph, stated that they would vote for the Draft Conclusions but made it clear that they had reservations with regard to some parts of the text. Mr. Esponda stressed that the Meeting provided the only opportunity for the workers of the world to express their views and aspirations directly to governments and to employers in an international forum. The Draft Conclusions could be viewed merely as a compromise text which but faintly reflected the legitimate views and hopes of the working class throughout the world. The worker experts had rightly called for the drawing up and application of a code of good behaviour, the provisions of which should be unequivocal and binding, so as to have positive effects on the behaviour of multinational corporations, particularly as regards the workers employed by those corporations. Mr. Diallo and Mr. Magniadas stated that, while one could hardly be enthusiastic about the preamble to the Draft Conclusions, the text as a whole did represent a compromise which provided a basis for action by the Governing Body.

130. With regard to paragraph 1 of the operative part of the text, Mrs. Ljubimova proposed that it be amended by the insertion of the word "objective" in the first sentence, so that it would read—

The experts recommend to the Governing Body that the International Labour Office be requested to undertake objective intensive and extensive studies concerning issues in the social policy field. . . .

The Chairman pointed out that there was a general assumption that all ILO studies aimed at objectivity. Morover, the eighth preambular paragraph of the text already emphasised the need for objective analysis. Accordingly the repetition of the word "objective" in paragraph 1 appeared to be superfluous. Mrs. Ljubimova accepted this explanation and thereupon withdrew her proposal.

131. In connection with paragraph 7 of the operative part of the text the worker experts submitted a list of proposed topics for study by the ILO. The employer experts submitted another such list. In addition, Mr. Allen, Mrs. Ljubimova, Mr. Okogwu and Mr. Stavenhagen—all government experts—indicated a number of subjects which called for study. All the suggestions which came to the notice of the Meeting in this manner are reproduced in Appendix I.

132. Referring to paragraph 7 of the operative part of the Draft Conclusions, Mrs. Ljubimova proposed that the words "among others" be inserted in this paragraph before the words "studies suggested", in order to make it clear that the Governing Body should feel free to take into account not only such suggestions as were put forward by the various experts attending the present Meeting but also any proposals which might emanate from other quarters.

133. Mr. Ivey pointed out that the various lists submitted were in no way to be considered as exhaustive; it would, indeed, expedite the proceedings if the text made it clear that the topics included in the lists had not been endorsed by the Meeting as a whole. In order to remove any possible uncertainty on this point, Mr. Ivey proposed that the text of paragraph 7 be amended so as to read—

The Governing Body is invited to request the Director-General of the International Labour Office to take into account, among others, the studies suggested by the various experts as enumerated in the lists appended to the report of the Meeting, when drawing up the ILO's programme of research. These suggestions for studies have been put forward by individual experts and groups of experts, but have not been endorsed by the body of experts as a whole.

134. The Chairman explained that it was his understanding that the studies suggested by the various experts in the lists which had been submitted to the Meeting had not been approved by the Meeting as a whole; the suggestions would, however, no doubt be taken into account when future ILO action in this field was being considered, as would any other suggestions that might subsequently be made. If his understanding in the matter was also the general understanding of the Meeting, this understanding would be fully recorded in the report of the Meeting and would no doubt be taken into account by the Office and the Governing Body.

135. The Meeting having confirmed this understanding, Mrs. Ljubimova and Mr. Ivey withdrew their amendments to paragraph 7.

136. On behalf of the employer experts, Mr. Smith stated that, amongst the subjects which had been proposed by the worker experts for ILO research and studies, several of the topics listed under the heading "international policies of multinational corporations"—namely research and technology; investment; financial, trading, commerce and marketing policies; sourcing and using of materials; tax concessions, import-export, subsidies and financing, access to credits, investment guarantees, and government purchasing—as well as a number of the subjects listed under the heading "studies of selected countries, regions, companies and problems"—namely relations to national economy and economic policies; cost relation of multinational corporations to technological choices; investment, profits and remittances; and exploitation

and transfer of national resources—were clearly beyond the scope of the Meeting, as laid down by the Governing Body, and were also beyond the terms of reference of the International Labour Organisation.

137. On behalf of the worker experts, Mr. Magniadas rejected the criticism which had been made on behalf of the employer experts with regard to the subjects which the worker experts had proposed for study and research by the ILO: the Declaration of Philadelphia, which was appended to the Constitution of the ILO, unequivocally affirmed the responsibility of the International Labour Organisation to examine and consider all international, economic and financial policies and measures in the light of the fundamental objective of the ILO, and made clear that, in discharging the tasks entrusted to it, the International Labour Organisation, having considered all relevant economic and financial factors, may include in its decisions and recommendations any provisions which it considers appropriate.

138. Commenting on the proposal of the worker experts that the ILO should draw up a code of good behaviour for multinational corporations, the employer experts referred to the recommendation made in paragraph 6 of the operative part of the Draft Conclusions to the effect that the Governing Body should instruct the Director-General of the ILO to undertake a study of the usefulness of international principles and guidelines in the field of social policy relating to the activities of multinational enterprises, and the elements and implications of such principles and guidelines, and that, thereafter, the Governing Body should initiate action for establishing such international principles and guidelines. No such action should, however, be taken by the Governing Body until the various fact-finding studies which were called for in paragraph 1 had been completed. It was imperative that these studies should be undertaken without any preconceived ideas as to their results. Moreover, the employer experts urged that the wording of the second sentence of paragraph 6 should not be interpreted as implying advance acceptance of the usefulness and feasibility of international principles and guidelines in this field. A further meeting of experts should be convened in due course to assess any proof which might be deemed to result from the study of the usefulness of international principles and guidelines, mentioned in the first sentence of paragraph 6, before any decision be taken to proceed with the drawing up of such international principles and guidelines. Speaking on behalf of the employer experts, Mr. Smith asked if the "code of good behaviour" suggested by the worker experts in their list of subjects for further study was meant to be one of the subjects falling under paragraph 1 of the Draft Conclusions, or did the worker experts consider that it had a relationship to the "international principles and guidelines" referred to in paragraph 6?

Mr. Weinberg, speaking on behalf of the worker experts, indicated that they intended this subject to relate to paragraph 6 of the Draft Conclusions. Mr. Smith then suggested, on behalf of the employer experts, that if the worker experts wanted their suggestion, "code of good behaviour", to be considered under paragraph 6, they should use the terminology found in paragraph 6, i.e. "international principles and guidelines".

139. The representative of the Director-General made it clear that it would be for the Governing Body to reach whatever decision it might see fit at each stage of ILO action with regard to multinational corporations.

140. The worker experts rejected the suggestion that the wording of the second sentence in paragraph 6 of the operative part of the Draft Conclusions prejudged the outcome of the proposed ILO study on the usefulness of international principles and guidelines: this suggestion was evidence of an attempt which was being made by some experts to downgrade the importance of ILO action regarding multinational corporations. The ILO should now go ahead with the study of the usefulness of international principles and guidelines, with a view to drawing up a code of good behaviour for multinational corporations, the provisions of which should be clear and binding, for the behaviour of these corporations should be brought into conformity with the requirements of the present time, as reflected in the International Labour Code. The worker experts stressed that they had deliberately refrained from making any general denunciation of multinational corporations, and they felt it therefore all the more regrettable that so much of the draft text presented by the employer experts had found its way into the Draft Conclusions. In spite of these reservations, however, the worker experts indicated that they were prepared to adopt the Draft Conclusions in the form in which they had been submitted by the Drafting Committee.

Adoption of the Conclusions

141. Subject to the reservations indicated above, the Meeting unanimously adopted its Conclusions. The text of these Conclusions is reproduced in Appendix II.

Consideration and adoption of the report of the Meeting

142. At their final sitting the experts had before them a document presenting a draft report of their proceedings up to the end of their penultimate sitting.

143. It was agreed that the Office would prepare a draft record of the proceedings of the final sitting and would mail that draft to the experts, who

would be requested to let the Office have any corrections to the record of what they had individually said. Thereafter the Office would incorporate the corrected record of the final sitting in the report of the Meeting.

144. On the understanding that the last portion of the report would take account of any corrections which might be made in accordance with the procedure indicated in the preceding paragraph, the report as a whole was unanimously adopted by the Meeting.

Closing speeches

145. The representative of the Director-General, Mr. B. Bolin, Assistant Director-General, conveyed his personal thanks, together with those of all his colleagues, to the Chairman for the excellent work which he had done in bringing a very difficult Meeting to such a successful end. Thanks were also due to all the participants for a job well done: through their discussions and through the Conclusions which they had reached, they had rendered an outstanding service to the International Labour Organisation and had laid a solid basis for further action by the Governing Body.

146. Mr. Allen stated that this had been the first ILO meeting which he had attended, and it had been a pleasurable experience. He had been impressed by the skill of the Chairman, both in plenary sittings and in the Drafting Committee. The government experts appreciated the valuable work which had been done by the Office and wished to pay tribute to the employer and worker experts for their collaboration throughout the Meeting.

147. On behalf of the employer experts, Mr. Smith thanked the Chairman for the excellent way in which he had conducted the Meeting. Tribute was due to the government and worker experts for the valuable contribution which they had made to the results of the Meeting, which, thanks to the good humour that, despite some ideological differences, had always prevailed, had been able to reach final agreement. Tribute was also due to the Office for the very useful working paper which had been the basis of the Meeting's discussions, and for its help throughout the proceedings. Participation in the Meeting had proved a most interesting experience.

148. On behalf of the worker experts, Mr. Weinberg endorsed the tributes which had been paid to the Chairman. Thanks were also due to the Office. A great debt was owed to Mr. Zaidi for the invaluable contribution which the latter had made to the work of the Drafting Committee. Speaking personally, Mr. Weinberg extended his particular thanks to the experts nominated by the Worker members of the Governing Body. Although coming from organisations with conflicting views on many matters, from industrialised

and developing countries and from different sectors of economic activity, they had shown that, dispite all such differences, solidarity could in practice be achieved. The best tribute to the work which had been accomplished by the Meeting would be effective ILO action with regard to multinational corporations.

149. The Chairman expressed his gratitude for the tributes which had been paid to him. Thanks to the co-operation of all participants, his task had been greatly facilitated. This was the first ILO meeting that he, like some of the other participants, had attended, and he would be returning home the richer for the experience. Tribute was due to the Office and to all the participants, whose joint efforts had laid the foundations for what would undoubtedly become a great achievement—namely ILO action concerning multinational corporations.

150. The Meeting ended at 1.05 p.m. on Saturday, 4 November 1972.

Geneva, 10 January 1973.   *(Signed)* N. P. DUBE
                                                  Chairman.

APPENDIX I. SUBJECTS SUGGESTED BY THE EXPERTS FOR STUDY BY THE ILO

Subjects suggested by government experts

Mr. Allen

1. Study of the impact of multinational enterprises on employment in—
   (a) host countries (developing and developed countries); and
   (b) investing countries.

2. Comparative study of wage rates and fringe benefits provided by multinational enterprises as compared to national companies in—
   (a) developed host countries; and
   (b) developing host countries.

3. Examination of the extent to which multinational enterprises provide for—
   (a) upgrading of skills through manpower training programmes in the countries of operation; and
   (b) managerial training of indigenous personnel to assume positions of greater responsibility.

4. Study of the relation of multinational enterprises to development plans in developing countries in regard to—
   (a) industrial and agricultural development;
   (b) import substitution and export promotion; and
   (c) diversification of the economy.

5. Study of the attitudes and practices of multinational enterprises and national companies in regard to trade union recognition and collective bargaining practices in—
   (a) developed host countries; and
   (b) developing host countries.

6. Study of the extent to which capital mobility is affected by changes in wage costs, trade union activity and other factors in—
   (a) developed host countries; and
   (b) developing host countries.

7. Study of the effects on the labour force of technology transfers by multinational enterprises to—

   (a) developed host countries; and

   (b) developing host countries.

8. Study of the productivity effects of the spread of multinational enterprises compared to national companies.

9. Study of the effects of multinational enterprises on education, health and living standards in developing host countries.

Mrs. Ljubimova

1. Study of the impact of multinational corporations on the labour force.

   When the operations of multinational corporations are being examined, attention should be directed mainly to the host countries, particularly the developing host countries. The ILO should draw up a code of regulations concerning not only employment security but also the utilisation of manpower. In particular, such a code should require the establishment of programmes of multi-skill vocational training and retraining, which are necessitated by the rapidly changing technology and organisation of production processes. The cost of these programmes should be borne by a special fund set up for the purpose and financed by proportionate deductions from the earnings of the multinational corporations. National governmental bodies and workers' organisations in the host countries should have control over the implementation of the programmes, so as to ensure that they are in line with the programmes of economic and social development of the countries concerned.

   Since the ILO already has programmes in the field of human resources, the study could be carried out within the present budgetary and organisational framework.

2. Study of the impact of the operations of multinational corporations on conditions of work and life in the host countries, taking into account the conditions required of the multinational corporations by the national governments and workers' organisations in the countries concerned.

   It is desirable to formulate recommendations on the harmonisation of conditions of work in the enterprises of multinational corporations in different countries, taking into consideration the need to extend social security schemes and occupational safety and health measures as widely as possible. The necessary resources should be provided by funds financed by the multinational corporations. Control of these matters by the national governments and workers' organisations in the host countries should be properly secured.

   With a view to the effective control of the operations of multinational corporations, the ILO's labour standards and social principles should take account of the corresponding national programmes and legislation in the host countries. Provision should be made for the revision of existing ILO Conventions and Recommendations in order to deal with the new conditions created by the operations of multinational corporations.

   The above-mentioned questions could be the subject of an integral part of a set of guiding principles regulating the operations of multinational corporations in the field of social policy. Such guiding principles should also deal with measures to safeguard and increase trade union rights in the enterprises of multinational corporations.

Mr. Okogwu

1. Examination of the status, extent and structure of trade unions in multinational companies and of their place in the collective bargaining machinery, where such exists.

2. Study of the scope and extent of collective bargaining subjects in multinational companies.

3. Study of conditions of work, including wages, in the subsidiaries of multinational companies as compared to those in national or domestic companies. Special attention should be given to the way in which the use of advanced capital-intensive techniques of production, with relatively small labour inputs, can lead through high labour productivity to high wage rates in those sectors of developing economies that are dominated by the subsidiaries of multinational companies, resulting in inflationary pressures where these high rates spill over, as they often do, into national or domestic companies.

Mr. Stavenhagen

1. Study of the income distribution effects of the growth of multinational corporations, particularly in developing countries.

2. Study of the relationship between the growth and spread of multinational corporations and the main elements of social and economic development strategy in developing countries, particularly as related to criteria for measuring social efficiency.

Subjects suggested by the employer experts

1. Study to identify and determine the problems in the field of social policy that may be specific to multinational enterprises as opposed to national firms.

2. Within the study of "the usefulness of international principles and guidelines in the field of social policy" referred to in the Conclusions of the Meeting, (i) obtain the views of governments concerning the desirability of enacting and implementing legislation applicable only to local undertakings of multinational enterprises, and (ii) study the legal problems involved in cases of conflict between any "international principles and guidelines" and national laws and customs.

3. Study of the industrial relations policies and practices of multinational enterprises in countries in which they operate.

4. Statistical study of the contribution of multinational enterprises to national social development, including—

   (*a*) average earnings;
   (*b*) fringe benefits;
   (*c*) pension and social security schemes;
   (*d*) vocational training programmes;
   (*e*) internal manpower development policies and practices;
   (*f*) utilisation of nationals in upper levels of management;

(g) ratio of man-days lost owing to work stoppages;

(h) generation of employment;

(i) nature and structure of employment;

(j) social service contributions;

(k) labour stability: turnover, absenteeism.

5. Study of the degree to which multinational enterprises respect national industrial relations legislation, custom and practice in the countries in which they operate.

6. Fact-finding study of the industrial relations and manpower policies and practices of Eastern European multinational enterprises.

7. Study of the contribution of the activities of multinational enterprises to the objectives of the ILO's World Employment Programme.

8. Study to obtain the views of the governments of all ILO member States on the subject of "harmonisation" in the context of social policy.

Subjects suggested by the worker experts

Note. The detailed proposals under each major subject heading are only indicative and not exhaustive.

1. Code of good behaviour.

ILO Conventions, Recommendations, conclusions, resolutions and Constitution: application, observance, non-observance and adequacy.

Elements of a code, particularly on trade union rights, guarantees of employment, racial discrimination, and availability of information for effective collective bargaining, requiring actions (use of working papers, reports, etc.).

Review of pertinent national, regional and world regulations.

Matters for referral to or co-ordination with other intergovernmental organisations.

Enforcement.

Machinery.

2. International policies of multinational corporations.

Centres of decision and power: world, regions, country.

Research and technology.

Manpower, investment, production and transfers.

Financial, trading, commerce and marketing policies.

Disclosure of information, including that needed for effective collective bargaining.

Sourcing and using of materials.

Relations to home and host national economies and to national, regional and world economic policies, including legislative and administrative practices, tax concessions, import-export, employment rebate, subsidies and financing, access to credits, investment guarantees, labour legislation and government purchasing.

Problems of workers in multinational companies, particularly: trade union rights, industrial relations practices, conditions of work and manpower planning.

3. Studies of selected countries, regions, companies and problems.

> Trade union rights for workers of all kinds.
> Legislation.
> Systems or structures of negotiations.
> Labour market policy.
> Impact on manpower.
> Role of multinational corporations in specific sectors.
> Relations to national economy and economic policies.
> Cost relation of multinational corporations to technological choices.
> Investment, profits and remittances.
> Exploitation and transfer of national resources.
> Industrial relations practices.
> Conditions of work: salaries and wages; income security; sickness and injury; age; racial and other forms of discrimination; equal remuneration for women; health and welfare; hours of work; housing; safety; workers' role.
> Manpower planning: employment security; advanced training, training and retraining; redundancy, separation, indemnification benefits; structure of employment; use of contract labour; levels of employment; advancement and promotion; impact of technology.

APPENDIX II. CONCLUSIONS OF THE MEETING [1]

The experts participating in the Meeting on the Relationship between Multi-national Corporations and Social Policy,

Having been convened by the Governing Body of the International Labour Office,

Having met from 26 October to 4 November 1972,

Having examined the working paper prepared by the International Labour Office, which served as an excellent basis for discussion at the Meeting,

Being aware that the International Labour Organisation has been concerned for many years with the growing need for expanded productive employment with social justice and that it is essential to increase rapidly the number of worth-while jobs in view of the fact that over 25 million people join the world labour force each year and that in less than three decades there will be an estimated additional 3,000 million more human beings to feed, clothe, house, educate and employ,

Recognising that multinational enterprises can make available employment and appropriate vital goods and services necessary to improve living standards throughout the world,

Recognising, moreover, that the growth and spread of such enterprises across national borders has created serious concern in various national and international bodies regarding new problems of national and international scope in the social policy field,

Recognising that the time has come to try and dispel the uncertainties that have grown up around the multinational enterprise and that more factual information is needed for rational and objective analysis, and recognising also that there is controversy concerning much of the available evidence,

Finding it therefore desirable to encourage the governments of ILO member States to promote social progress through economic development, and the growth and expansion of industrial output through appropriate institutions, subject to compliance with national policy and customs and with relevant ILO standards,

1. The experts recommend to the Governing Body that the International Labour Office be requested to undertake intensive and extensive studies concerning issues in the social policy field to provide the comprehensive information needed to identify and determine the problems that may be specific to multinational enterprises as opposed to national firms. The objectives of such studies will be to provide guidance

---

[1] Adopted unanimously.

for social policy formulation pertaining to the growth and spread of multinational enterprises. In order that such studies can be properly carried out—

(a) governments should be invited to improve their statistics in relation to these studies in consultation with workers and employers. To facilitate such studies, in countries where such statistics may not be adequate the International Labour Office, upon request, should assist them in developing statistics and data-collecting machinery;

(b) employers and workers and their respective organisations should be invited and encouraged to provide the data necessary for such statistics and studies;

(c) the studies should be based on appropriate methodology and research techniques, to be developed by the International Labour Office in terms of their objectives, in consultation with other relevant institutions.

2. The Governing Body is invited to provide for adequate staff and budgetary provision for the conduct and prompt completion of the proposed studies.

3. In considering the future ILO work on multinational enterprise studies, the present group of experts agrees that at any stage in their preparation and review the International Labour Office, at its discretion, may call upon them for advice and consultation. The Governing Body is requested to consider the possibility of making provision for the convening of an expert group to review the results of the studies and to facilitate their formulation into policy recommendations.

4. The question of whether matters relating to social policy in respect of multi-national enterprises be considered at future meetings convened under ILO auspices is a matter for decision by the Governing Body, with the understanding that such discussions—if any—should be without prejudice to the in-depth studies of multi-national enterprises being entrusted to the International Labour Office.

5. The Governing Body and the International Labour Conference are invited, when reviewing the programmes and standards of the Organisation, to take into full account the discussions of the Meeting on the Relationship between Multinational Corporations and Social Policy and the results of the in-depth studies to be under-taken as recommended by that Meeting in the light of the continuing growth of multinational enterprises.

6. The experts recommend that the Governing Body instruct the Director-General of the International Labour Office to undertake a study of the usefulness of interna-tional principles and guidelines in the field of social policy relating to the activities of multinational enterprises, and the elements and implications of such principles and guidelines. If such a study were to prove that such principles and guidelines are useful and feasible, the experts recommend that the Governing Body initiate action for establishing such principles and guidelines, taking into account the informa-tion gathered by the International Labour Office in connection with the studies referred to above.

7. The Governing Body is invited to request the Director-General of the Interna-tional Labour Office to take into account the studies suggested by the various experts, as enumerated in the lists appended to the report of the Meeting, when drawing up the ILO's programme of research.

APPENDIX III. LIST OF PARTICIPANTS

Government experts

Mr. Edward L. ALLEN, Deputy Assistant Secretary of Commerce for Economic Research and Analysis, US Department of Commerce, Washington, DC.

Accompanied by:

Mr. Daniel ARRILL, Director, Investment Policy Division, Office of International Investment, Bureau of International Commerce, US Department of Commerce, Washington, DC.

Mr. Allen DE LONG, Industrial Relations Division, Bureau of Domestic Commerce, US Department of Commerce, Washington, DC.

Mr. Leo ERCK, Director, Industrial Relations Division, Bureau of Domestic Commerce, US Department of Commerce, Washington, DC.

Mr. Daniel GOOTT, Special Assistant for International Labor and United Nations Affairs to the Assistant Secretary for European Affairs, US Department of State, Washington, DC.

Mr. Paul HEISE, Special Adviser to the Deputy Under Secretary, US Department of Labor, Washington, DC.

Mr. Roger SCHRADER, Labor Attaché, United States Mission, Geneva.

Mr. N. P. DUBE, Additional Secretary to the Government of India, Ministry of Labour and Rehabilitation, New Delhi.

Mr. Harry J. IVEY, Principal, Department of Trade and Industry, London.

Accompanied by:

Mr. H. Vivian B. BROWN, Assistant Principal, Department of Trade and Industry, London.

Mrs. Valentina LJUBIMOVA, Chief of Department, Institute for International Economics and International Relations, USSR Academy of Sciences, Moscow.

Accompanied by:

Mr. Victor ARKHIPOV, Attaché, Permanent Mission of the USSR in Geneva, Geneva.

Mr. Dmitry SOKOLOV, First Secretary, Ministry of Foreign Affairs of the USSR, Moscow.

Mr. Chigeru NAKATANI, Head of the Investigation Division, Public Corporation and National Enterprise Labour Relations Commission, Tokyo.

Accompanied by:

Mr. Tatsuro MATSUI, First Secretary, Permanent Delegation of Japan, Geneva.

Mr. Gabriel C. OKOGWU, Director of Labour, Federal Ministry of Labour, Lagos.

Mr. Laurent PREZIOSI, Administrateur civil, Chef de bureau à la Direction générale du travail et de l'emploi au ministère d'Etat des Affaires sociales, Paris.

Mr. Rodolfo STAVENHAGEN, Director, Centro de Estudios Sociológicos, El Colegio de México, Mexico City.

Employer experts

Mr. Erhard BOUILLON, Member of the Board of Directors of Farbwerke Hoechst AG, Frankfurt am Main.

Mr. Ijjigu DEMMISSIE, Assistant General Manager, Administration, Ethiopian Airlines, Addis Ababa.

Mr. D. J. FLUNDER, MC, Director, Dunlop Ltd., London.

Accompanied by:

Mr. J. A. G. COATES, Central Personnel Department, Imperial Chemical Industries Ltd., London.

Mr. W. A. DAVISON, Head of Personnel Services (UK), Unilever Limited, London.

Mr. Lindsay S. DIXON, Director, Organisation of Employers' Federations and Employers in Developing Countries (OEF), London.

Mr. T. P. A. HEALY, OBE, Head of International Labour Department, Confederation of British Industry, London.

Mr. B. W. R. MOORING, Industrial Relations Adviser, British Petroleum Co., Ltd., London.

Mr. Freddie A. MEHTA, Director, Tata Industries (P), Ltd., Bombay.

Mr. David RICHMOND, Executive Director, Federation of Kenya Employers, Nairobi.

Mr. Charles H. SMITH, Chairman, SIFCO Industries Inc., Cleveland, Ohio.

Accompanied by:

Mr. Robert COPP, Overseas Liaison Manager, Labor Relations Staff, Ford Motor Company, Dearborn, Michigan.

Mr. Virgil B. DAY, Vice-President, General Electric Company, New York.

Mr. Francis J. O'CONNELL, Attorney, Bill, Fleck, Fleck and O'Connell, Garden City, New York.

Mr. John OLIVER, Director, Employee Relations Department, E. I. du Pont de Nemours and Company, Wilmington, Delaware.

Mr. Vernon O'ROURKE, Manager, Labor Relations, Standard Oil Company (New Jersey), New York.

Mr. Paul F. SHAW, Vice-President, Employee Relations, Chase-Manhattan Bank, New York.

Mr. B. SUPERVIELLE, Ex-President, Cámara de Comercio del Uruguay, Montevideo.

Mr. Georges YELNIK, Directeur des relations avec le personnel, Société Aluminium-Péchiney, Paris.

Accompanied by:

Mr. Jean-Jacques OECHSLIN, Chef du service des relations avec l'OIT, Conseil national du patronat français, Paris.

Mr. Jacques POIRIER, Directeur des relations du travail, Shell Française, Paris.

Worker experts

Mr. Dan BENEDICT, Assistant General Secretary, International Metalworkers' Federation, Geneva.

Mr. Jean DIALLO, Training Officer, Union panafricaine des travailleurs croyants, Bathurst.

Mr. Gonzalo ESPONDA, Legal Adviser, Comité Nacional de la Confederación de Trabajadores de México, Mexico City.

Mr. Peter JACQUES, Secretary, Social Insurance Department, Trades Union Congress, London.

Mr. Jean MAGNIADAS, Director, Centre de recherches économiques et sociales, Confédération générale du travail, Paris.

Mr. Heribert MAIER, Assistant General Secretary, International Confederation of Free Trade Unions, Brussels.

Mr. Nat WEINBERG, Director, Special Projects and Economic Analysis, International Union of United Automobile, Aerospace and Agricultural Implement Workers (UAW), Detroit, Michigan.

Mr. S. J. H. ZAIDI, Secretary-General, Malaysian Trades Union Congress, Petaling Jaya, Selangor.

Employer substitutes and advisers

Mr. Marcel BIART, Deputy Director, Solvay et Cie., Brussels.

Mr. Roger DECOSTERD, Chief, Personnel Department, Nestlé Alimentana SA, Vevey.

Mr. René KORN, Chief of Section, Nestlé Alimentana, SA, Vevey.

Mr. Hans-Goran MYRDAL, Assistant Director, Svenska Arbetsgivareföreningen, Stockholm.

Mr. Jules PAULY, Assistant Director, ARBED, Luxembourg.

Mr. Nils SVENSSON, Vice-President, Personnel and Industrial Relations, Tel. ab. L. M. Ericsson, Stockholm.

Worker substitutes

Mr. Burton BENDINER, Co-ordinator of IMF World Auto Councils, International Metalworkers' Federation, Geneva.

Mr. Charles FORD, General Secretary, International Textile, Garment and Leather Workers' Federation, London.

Mr. Dan GALLIN, General Secretary, International Union of Food and Allied Workers' Associations (IUF), Geneva.

Accompanied by:

Mr. Laurent ENCKELL, Assistant to the General Secretary, International Union of Food and Allied Workers' Associations (IUF), Geneva.

Mr. Sven JONASSON, Head of Research Department, Union of Administrative, Clerical and Technical Employees in Industry, Swedish Confederation of Non-Manual Workers, Stockholm.

Mr. André SOULAT, Confederation Secretary, Confédération française démocratique du travail, Paris.

Observer

Ireland

Mr. Maurice CASHELL, First Secretary, Permanent Mission of Ireland to the United Nations Office at Geneva, Geneva.

Representatives of governmental international organisations

United Nations

Mr. A. ABAKOUMOFF, Economic Affairs Officer, Export Policies Section, UNCTAD, Geneva.

Mr. C. R. GREENHILL, Acting Chief, Section on Restrictive Business Practices, Manufactures Division, UNCTAD, Geneva.

Mr. V. KOLLONTAI, Research Division, UNCTAD, Geneva.

Food and Agriculture Organisation (FAO)

Mr. Pierre TERVER, Special Assistant, Industry Co-operative Programme, FAO, Rome.

Commission of the European Communities

Mr. Herman OLLENHAUER, Chef de division à la Direction générale des affaires sociales, Commission des communautés européennes, Brussels.

Mr. Charles STRUXIANO, Administrateur principal, Commission des communautés européennes, Brussels.

Organisation for Economic Co-operation and Development (OECD)

Mr. Oliver CLARKE, Principal Administrator, Division of Industrial Relations, OECD, Paris.

Mr. Morris WEISZ, Head, Division of Industrial Relations, OECD, Paris.

Representatives of non-governmental international organisations

International Confederation of Executive Staffs (ICES)

Mr. André FERRERO, Permanent Delegate of the ICES to the ILO, Geneva.

International Confederation of Free Trade Unions (ICFTU)

Mr. Albert HEYER, Director, Geneva Office of the ICFTU.

Mr. John LÖFBLAD, General Secretary, International Federation of Building and Woodworkers, Geneva.

Mrs. Britt-Marie SÖDERBECK, Economist, Landsorganisationen i Sverige (LO), Stockholm.

Mr. Jean VANDERVEKEN, Geneva Office of the ICFTU.

World Confederation of Labour (WCL)

Mr. Michel DE GRAVE, Research Service, Confederation of Christian Trade Unions, Brussels.

Mr. Georges EGGERMANN, Permanent Representative of the WCL in Geneva.

Mr. Jacques VITTORI, Permanent Representative of the WCL in Geneva.

World Federation of Trade Unions (WFTU)

Mr. C. DE ANGELI, Permanent Representative of the WFTU to the United Nations and the ILO, Geneva.

International Federation of Commercial, Clerical and Technical Employees (IFCCTE)

Mr. Erich KISSEL, General Secretary, IFCCTE, Geneva.

Mr. Edward LEWIS, Secretary, IFCCTE, Geneva.

International Federation of Petroleum and Chemical Workers

Mr. Franz LORIAUX, Director, European Regional Office, International Federation of Petroleum and Chemical Workers, Geneva.

International Organisation of Employers (IOE)

Mr. Gullmar BERGENSTRÖM, Chairman, Executive Committee, IOE, Geneva.

Mr. N. BATTENDIERI, Legal Adviser, National Confederation of Brazilian Industry, Rio de Janeiro.

Mrs. Paulette BONNY, Senior Secretary, IOE, Geneva.

Mr. A. M. BOON, General Director, General Employers' Association of the Netherlands, Haarlem.

Mr. W. J. DE VRIES, Deputy Group Personnel Co-ordinator, Shell International Petroleum Maatschappij NV, The Hague.

Mr. Brian GODFREY, General Manager, Personnel, British Petroleum Ltd., London.

Mr. Raphaël LAGASSE, Secretary-General, IOE, Geneva.

Mr. Jacques L'HUILLIER, Permanent Consultant of the International Chamber of Commerce to the European Office of the United Nations, Geneva.

Mrs. Lucia MAZZUFFERI, Official, General Confederation of Italian Industry, Rome.

Mr. Roger McCORMICK, Manager, Staff Relations, British Petroleum Ltd., London.

Mr. E. W. MEIER, Adviser, Economic Affairs, AKZO, Arnhem.

Mr. D. NAYLOR, Head of Employee Relations, Shell International Petroleum Co., London.

Miss Doris OBERHOFF, Chairman of the Liaison Committee of the West European Metal Trades Employers' Federations, Cologne.

Mr. Alfred PANKERT, Executive Secretary, IOE, Geneva.